ARROWS
AGAINST STEEL:
The History of the Bow

OTHER BOOKS BY VIC HURLEY

Southeast of Zamboanga
Men in Sun Helmets
Swish of the Kris
Jungle Patrol
The Parthian

ARROWS AGAINST STEEL:

The History of the Bow

by Vic Hurley

MASON/CHARTER

NEW YORK 1975

PRINTED IN THE UNITED STATES OF AMERICA

Library of Congress Cataloging in Publication Data

Hurley, Victor.
 Arrows against steel: the history of the bow.

 Includes bibliographical references.
 1. Bow and arrow--History. 2. Military art and
science--History. 3. Military history, Medieval.
I. Title.
U877.H87   355.8'2   75-2002
ISBN 0-88405-094-7

Contents

Preface vii
Introduction 3

Part One
INTRODUCTION TO A WEAPON 11

    1. Origins of the Bow 13
    2. The Bow: Types and Modifications 17
    3. The Arrow As a Precision Missile 21

Part Two
THE THEORIES OF WAR 27

    4. The Principles of War 29
    5. The Schools of War 31

Part Three
THE PRELIMINARIES TO MOUNTED WAR 51

    6. First Appearances of the Bow in War 53
    7. The Persians: A Study in Retrogression 60
    8. Macedonia: Birth of the Dragoons 71
    9. The Problem of Mounted War 77

Part Four

THE TESTING OF THE THEORIES OF WAR 83

10. The Carthaginian Application of Cavalry 85
11. The Parthians versus Rome 94
12. The Sunset of the Roman Legion 113
13. The Huns: Fatal Experiment 120
14. The Byzantine Abandonment of the Bow 127
15. The Bow in the Crusades 135
16. The Feudal Knight: End of an Era 144
17. The Mongol Horse-Archers 148
18. The English Longbowmen 168
19. The Plains Indians 184

Part Five

THE IMPACT OF THE BOW ON MILITARY TACTICS 193

20. Evaluation: The Crossbow, Longbow,
    and Composite Bow 195
21. The Infantry-Archer: The Tactical Problem 205
22. The Military Tactics of Modern War 211
    Notes 216
    Addendum 221
    Index 229

Preface

It was not until 1945, when I was retired from the Navy after service in World War II, that I became fully aware of a serious omission on the part of military historians. No one had ever made a proper evaluation of the bow as a weapon of war and its enormous impact on history. The bow literally remade history for it opened up the world. This weapon completely altered all concepts of tactical war, and in the conquering of the world by bowmen on horses, the bow became a unique destroyer of men and, at the same time, a great conserver and distributor of men's knowledge.

This fact of history has been strangely ignored by the military historians.

The bow, with a few exceptions, was the exclusive property of Asiatic peoples in development and in practical use in the hunt and in war. Among Caucasians, only the English longbowmen and a few French and Italian experimenters with the crossbow were not simply borrowers of an Asiatic weapon. Only peoples of Asiatic or Negroid origin used the bow to its full capacity as the major weapon of war. Only the Asiatics perfected the perfect amalgamation of man, horse, and bow as the prime instrument of warfare. Only the Asiatics made cavalry the decisive battle commitment of war with the bow the major weapon.

Arrows Against Steel is not a history of the peoples of Asia; this can be found in standard histories and encyclopedias. The theme of this book is a highly specialized view and evaluation of the impact of the bow on history. It is an examination of the Schools of War by the nations of the West, which faced the bow either with foot soldiers who were fatally slow in deployment or with a limited usage of unwieldy armored horsemen who were unable to carry out the true mission of cavalry. There was never any proper application of the horse or of missiles in European military calculations and planning. They were exponents of massed men armed with cut and thrust weapons.

Only the Asiatics possessed the logistics, stamina, speed, and ability to live off the country that is required in the waging of war across degrees of longitude. *Arrows Against Steel* is an explanation of what these Asiatic cavalrymen did and how they did it during that period of history when men from Asia rode halfway around the world, armed, equipped, properly mounted, and trained to inflict missile death upon the enemy. The Parthians gave a preview of the tactics of true cavalry in confrontation with Rome around 50 B.C., when they launched the first all-cavalry army, which was armed with the bow as the decisive weapon.

The complete application of the bow to warfare was to come twelve centuries later, when the Mongol horsemen of Genghis Khan applied the full impact of evasive tactics of maneuver that had been enunciated in the greatest of all treatises on war by Sun Tzu in 500 B.C. The men of the East venerated the horse but saw the tarpan realistically as a vehicle of transportation and a tool of war. They appreciated the horse as a hardy domesticated wild animal capable of surviving in the fierce Gobi Desert.

In contrast, in the West, the horse became more a social asset than an active implement of war. The privilege of riding was a prerequisite of the upper classes. The horse became a ceremonial draft animal, carrying weighty hardware to such an extent that in some periods of European history the rider was placed in the saddle by a form of derrick.

No Western horse soldier carried the bow, a weapon that was available to them in the three-century period when the bow dominated the tactics of war. In Europe, the bow was a weapon for commoners —the gentleman rider carried spear and sword. The horse they rode was a blueblood social animal, bearing a blueblood aristocrat who died as a gentleman should, with a sword in his hand. The vulgar arrow that found the seams of a gentleman's armor was propelled by a composite bow wielded by an android on horseback, employing all of the principles of evasive war and maneuver.

War was a senseless brawl in the West during these centuries. War was a science to the Asiatic horseman with a composite bow.

It was no contest. The result was foreordained and inevitable.

The Huns, Magyars, and other Asiatic horsemen who overran Europe were never more than raiders and looters with a ragged and inept application of limited use of the horse and the bow. Attila the Hun is greatly overestimated as a practitioner of missile war of motion. Only in his earlier years did he use the horse properly in war. He became infatuated with the heavier formations of the West that were greatly inferior to the native tactics of the Gobi Desert men.

During the two or three centuries before A.D. 1200 Asiatic horsemen perfected mounted missile warfare in savage conflict with each other. The true era of the archer on horseback lasted from about 1200 until about 1500, when the Asiatic horsemen with the bow made their last effective appearances in the Western world.

The era of the horse archer thus began with the Mongols and ended with the Mongols, when they abandoned their felt yurts and the stern mandates of true cavalry operations for the soft luxury of Chinese civilization.

To establish historical accuracy for this short period of history, I have relied upon original sources that were compiled by contemporary writers of that period. These original writings are the source material for virtually all books written about this three-century period of military history. Fifty years ago, as a student of the great Dr. H. H. Gowen, founder of the Far Eastern School at the University of Washington, I was fortunate to have opened to my view many important books written in the thirteenth to sixteenth centuries. In succeeding years I acquired similar material during a long residence in Asia and later, during World War II, as an Intelligence and War Planning Officer on the staffs of Admirals Halsey and Nimitz. As an Asia specialist I had access to many service and government publications on the schools of war and the principles and tactics of war.

I published five books on Asia during the period 1935–1960. In 1945 my interest focused on conclusions I had formed concerning the important impact of the bow on history. This personal view is expressed here in *Arrows Against Steel* as a record of three centuries in the history of the world when the bow made mandatory the great voyages of the seamen of Prince Henry the Navigator and of Columbus—when Europe frantically sought a water route to Asia because the land caravan routes were controlled by fierce bowmen on horses who had opened up the rest of the world and sealed off their own.

The only records of this period of conflict between two schools of war are the books and manuscripts of ancient Chinese, Greek, Roman, and Russian observers who saw the bow in action. These original materials, translated into many languages, remain the original and sole source of information about this period of military science. They form the basis for all the hundreds of other books written on the general subjects of the culture and history of Asian peoples.

Arrows Against Steel describes only one facet of this period of history—the use that these Asiatic horsemen made of the bow as the decisive weapon of war. For the curious who wish to explore more fully these facets of history, a short list of these original source materials is appended.

There still remains to be written a further examination of this specialized subject that would include the war use of the horse and the bow by Asiatic Indians in North America. The limited use of the bow in the American Indian wars deserves attention, for here again, in the nineteenth century, Western military men showed no understanding of the proper use of the horse and the bow in war.

The following original sources were examined during the course of the writing of *Arrows Against Steel.*

Yuen Chao Pi-Shi, *Secret History of the Mongols,* 1240. Translated into German by the Saxon Academy of Sciences, 1931.

Juveini, *History of the World Conqueror.* 13th-century mss., translated by Von Edmann; Leipsig, 1862.

Patkanoff, *History of the Mongols.* Translation into Russian of the 13th-century mss.

Travels of Marco Polo. Many translations. First published 1299 in manuscript form.

Ruy Gonzales de Clavijo, *Embassy to Tamerlane.* 1403. Early 15th-century mss. in Madrid National Library. Translated into many languages.

Carpini, Giovanni de Piano, Franciscan friar who in 1245 was sent as Legate of Pope Innocent IV to the Court of the Khan of Tartary. Translated into many languages.

History of Herodotus. 440 B.C. mss. Many translations; in 1584, 1709, 1791, and others.

Thucydides, *History of the Peloponnesian War.* Circa 430 B.C. Many translations.

Plutarch's Lives. 46?–120. Many translations.

Xenophon, *Education of Cyrus.* Many translations.

Publius Cornelius Tacitus, *Annals.* Circa 100.

Titus Livius, *The History of Rome.* The loss of most of the 142 books he is believed to have written is a tragedy of historical erosion. He is believed to have begun this work about 30 B.C.

Ch'ang Ch'uns, *Journey to Jenghis Khan.* Published in English in Medieval Researches London, 1888.

Villehardouin, *Chronicle.* Early 13th-century chronicle.

Joinville, *Chronicle.* Early work published 1309.

Froissart, Jean, *Chronicle.* Late 14th-century book. A mirror of medieval chivalry.

Flavius Vegetius Renatus, *De Re Militari.* Manuscript copies from the 10th to 14th centuries exist. Translated into English and French before the invention of printing. First printed in Germany, 1473.

Polybius, circa 130 B.C. Many translations of these historical manuscripts.

Procopius, one of the greatest of the ancient historians. Died 562. He was the secretary of Belisarius and certainly one of the finest sources of Byzantine military history.

Sun Tzu, *The Art of War.* The greatest military writing of all time. Written about 500 B.C., this is the father of the school of evasive war of maneuver and deception practiced by the 13th-century armies of Genghis Khan in their sweep across half the world. The work has had translations into English, French, German and into many obscure Asian dialects and languages. *The Art of War* came to the attention of the German General Staff during World War II and became the guiding principle behind the formation of the idea of Blitzkrieg. (The author was fortunate during the early years of his residence in Asia in the 1920's to have access to a condensed translation of this work from the Chinese. Thirty years later the author saw a better and more complete version through the good offices of a British army officer who had obtained it in China shortly prior to World War II.)

Vic Hurley

Lacey, Washington
November 1974

"Men and horses they wound and slay with arrows, and when men and mounts are shattered in this fashion, they then close in upon them."

—*Giavanno de Piano Carpini*
A.D. *1245*

INTRODUCTION

Introduction

In considering the historical impact of the bow, we are reminded, with considerable emphasis, that this weapon was the major implementing force in the impressment of Eastern civilization upon the lagging nations of the Western world. The bow was the war instrument of superior civilizations that had been established in Asia during a period when the minds of the credulous men of western Europe were dulled by the proscriptions and dogmas of the early Church.

Strangely, these products of civilization—the accumulated knowledge and lore and the advanced understanding of the principles of mathematics, astronomy, and geography—although common property of the peoples of the East, had been originated by the peoples of the Western world. These principles had been learned—and then forgotten—by the nations along the Mediterranean. The Asiatics had translated and preserved the considerable knowledge of the ancient Greeks. To this was added the enormous early knowledge of geography possessed by the Arabic peoples. The Asiatic nations reacquainted the West with this knowledge during the great population movements that accompanied the rise of the power of Islam.

In considering the historical background of the bow, three periods stand out as pivotal points.

The first of these dates is the period that centers about 200 B.C., when the science of geography, later lost to the West, was developed by Greek philosophers and mathematicians. The remarkable Eratosthenes produced an incredibly accurate measurement of the circum-

3

ference of the earth, apparently overestimating a mere 170 miles. Knowledge that the earth was a sphere was an early acquisition of Asiatic peoples. Although that knowledge lay dormant for many centuries, it was to have a profound effect upon history.

The Asiatics learned very early to think in terms of degrees of longitude. They were a restless people, eyeing far horizons, and developed, early in their history, the capacity for extended and prolonged movements of armed, mounted men. The horse and the bow were always closely identified with the peoples of Asia for they best understood the application of these ingredients of war. In that understanding lies the theme of this book, for it is concerned with the impact of the bow on the history of the world.

In contrast, Europe came of age in a far different manner. In the West the Church taught that the earth was a flat plate with Jerusalem the center of the universe. There was no room in the European mind for geographic speculation during these Dark Ages. Men settled comfortably in their small valleys and lived out their lives in vast ignorance of what lay beyond the horizon. As they held together in their valleys, so they held together in their brief excursions into war. They developed the principle of relatively immobile men en masse, with no capacity for evasive maneuver. Nor did war of that period in Europe call for it; the tactic was direct and brawling assault. These Europeans were ignorant of the great expanding of the mind that was developing in Asia.

During all this period of darkness in Europe, the seeds of scientific curiosity were firm in the Asiatic mind; this knowledge was to be the heritage that Asia extended to Europe. Translations of the Greek mental processes were treasured in Asiatic courts and, in time, the physical movements of Asiatic peoples began to keep pace with their intellectual endeavors.

For eight hundred years after Eratosthenes, the men who were to carry the bow were distilling and refining the knowledge that was to breed conquest. The bow had not been sheathed during these centuries: There had been savage conflict in Asia. The ancient civilization of China had encountered the problem of Tartar horse-archers when restless hordes moved from their Gobi Desert home. The conquest of Alexander had been recorded in history. Parthia had enforced a brief respect for the bow, and the Roman legions were moving blindly to extinction. But these had been mere flexings of the bow in the pre-bids to the real impact upon world history that was to be made by this fearsome weapon.

As the centuries rolled along, the Muhammadan conquest appeared to mark the second great date in the history of the bow. Civilization acknowledges a great debt to the Muhammadans, for the dramatic interchange of ideas that began about A.D. 600 was implemented by a conquest that was far greater than that of Alexander. Muhammad, by instinct a mere religious crusader, became, in effect, the great benefactor of the West. The Muhammadans were, and are, curiosities of history, for they combine the conflicting qualities of fanaticism and tolerance.

These warriors of Islam disseminated priceless geographic and scientific knowledge, and they were ever ready to accept the best features of the civilizations they conquered. Although the Muhammadans generally have been credited with offering the Word or the Sword to conquered peoples, we sometimes fail to remember the third alternative that they presented: tribute. The Muhammadans were content to live with other religions—in fact, they were not always eager to offer the benefits of Islam to their conquered vassals. If tribute was paid, the Muhammadans were highly receptive to new ideas that did not conflict with the Word of the Prophet.

The Muhammadans imparted a global psychology to the world as they mastered an empire that stretched over western and central Asia, northern Africa, and half of the Mediterranean. Their military successes brought on the Crusades—far more important for cultural aspects and implications than as a military study. The Arabs made great contributions to cartography and geography and had added to the physical knowledge of the world by great voyages of discovery centuries before the first explorations of the Portuguese under the auspices of Prince Henry the Navigator.

The flight of the Arabs and the Turks before the armies of Genghis Khan signaled the third great period in the story of the bow. As Genghis Khan progressively destroyed the civilizations of central Asia in campaigns against the Khwarzian shah and others, the tribesmen of High Tartary fled before his horsemen, carrying along their accumulated knowledge. The movement of the Turks was not rapid, for it was not until 1453 that they were able to consolidate their position sufficiently to destroy the Roman Empire with the capture of Constantinople from the Byzantines. The Mongol bowmen had long held the East, and now, in 1453, the trade routes between Europe and the East were sealed by Turkish bowmen. Europe stirred from a great lethargy to seek new routes to Asia and to begin the great sea voyages of the fifteenth and sixteenth centuries.

The bow had aroused peoples of the world into flight, into exploration, and into a dramatic exchange of ideas.

Not the least dramatic impact of the bow was the advanced development of the science of war that had been achieved in Asia. Until a period well beyond the sixteenth century—extending, in fact, into the seventeenth century—the highly professional armies of Asia were far superior to the military effort that had developed in Europe. The great horsemen of Asia, weaponed with the composite bow, had modified or refused entirely all concepts of position war, or the massing of men into offensive or defensive formations. The Asiatics had developed cavalry that hinged on no base, and the army occupied itself with campaigns that traversed degrees of latitude and longitude.

These great movements of population, fleeing before the bow, established newer and greater empires. Increased contact among the various peoples served to integrate and expand knowledge.

With this setting in mind, let us examine the bow.

Twenty-five centuries ago, men began to fight under new concepts when the principle of economical war—mobile offensive war with missiles—was enunciated by Sun Tzu in the most remarkable military study of all time. This principle was successfully explored by Parthia with an all-cavalry army that rewrote military history at the expense of the legions of Rome. These offensive tactics were brought to frightening fruition by the dreadful armies of Genghis Khan.

This Asiatic school of war was built to serve the composite bow, the beautiful and deadly weapon that has influenced the tactics of war more than any other weapon ever carried by men in battle. The tactics of mounted firepower, as expressed by the initial union of horse, bow, and man, remain as valid today as they were when they were first reduced to a science by Sun Tzu, circa 500 B.C.

The Asiatic theory of distant war, as first enforced by the precision bow—and as can be expressed today by newer and better missile weapons—is based upon quick and decisive field action. It envisions the movement of armies as possessing virtually no flanks and does not accept long drawn-out campaigns of attrition or frightful hand-to-hand slaughter.

For many centuries, the armies of the Western world did not subscribe to these theories of war. In the West, Caesar had laid down the principles and the precepts of shock infantry. His magnificent lance- and sword-bearing legion had been only a small improvement upon the phalanx of a Greek city-state. But Caesar had been a great soldier, and his school of heavy infantry established the military thinking and dominated the military systems of the Western world for many centuries. Rome was the preeminent nation. Contrary theories of war, as practiced in the East, had been the development of Asiatics who were barely known to the peoples of western Europe in the Middle Ages. Only recently have the advanced tactics of the Asiatic horse-archers been studied and evaluated.

The most important omission in the body of Western military literature has been the lack of appraisal of the influence of the bow in war. No rounded exposition of the bow in battle exists. This weapon, launching the first precision missile, gave meaning to the principles of economical war. Great missiles, combined with great mobility, have always produced spectacular military results with a minimum of casualties. Aggressive and highly productive military campaigns of the past have established this premise as sound.

The military minds of the last seven hundred years and the military chroniclers of that period have been singularly resistant to accepting as valid any school of war that offered small mobile armies that were dependent upon firepower and speed at the expense of shock power and mass. The stubborn adherence of the Western world to army compositions that were committed to mass and shock and position war persisted in the face of evidence that such tactics were too costly in human life. The Western military systems were so organized that all generals of this area were inclined to overvalue position as an objective of war. This was the common weakness of the greatest of the Roman generals. It was a weakness that was perpetuated in the minds of all the later European generals.

The theory of missile war with the bow mandated that the objective be the field armies of the enemy. The mere occupation of territory or the physical possession of cities was only an aftermath of the campaigns. The ability and the will to resist was first destroyed by relentless field action. In contrast, the Western armies fought for a city wall, a valley, or a plain, and they tried to hold these positions at all cost. The West offered battle freely and military contact was a brawling collision.

In maintaining this stubborn adherence to shock infantry, the West was ignoring the lessons of history, for the Asiatic school of war had stalemated the best shock army of the ancient world as early as 53 B.C., when the Parthian horse-archers, in minor strength, had engaged the Roman legions. More than a thousand years later, in the thirteenth century, the Mongols of Genghis Khan had contrived the greatest military conquest of history. But the exponents of this type of warfare had lived in a corner of the world that was virtually unknown; their great field commanders had not been endowed with glitter by history. It was not until proper studies were conducted in the interval between World Wars I and II that these great Mongol tacticians received our proper attention and respect; yet, the principles under which they had conducted war had been known to many peoples and for many centuries.

The theory of mounted missile war of motion with the bow has been the greatest military system for almost twenty-five hundred years, and through all of those years, the bow has remained the basic war weapon. The rifle, the field gun, and the mortar are but sons of the bow. The bullet, shell, and bomb are projectiles that were sired by the arrow. The tank, armored troop carrier, and the airplane are but transportation improvements of the horse that carried the archer of Genghis Khan.

For thousands of years the bow was man's finest implement for solving the problems of war. The school of tactics established around the bow reduced lesser schools to impotence. When the bow was in proper hands, it maintained control of the military situation.

The bow brought increased complications to war. As we shall see, it required advanced military tactical and stragetic planning to bring out the full capabilities of this remarkable weapon, for the element of precision had entered into missile war. The tactics of infantry rushing at each other for hand-to-hand battle after the casting of ineffectual volleys of stones or propelled darts became subject to great revision. Maneuver, as opposed to mere movement, attained new importance in all military calculations. The problem of defense against missiles occupied the military minds. The casting of aimed accurate projectiles—typified by the arrow—necessitated the reevaluation of all previous concepts of war. Heavy infantry lost much of its importance as the implications of this new type of war became apparent.

When the bow appeared on the battlefields of the world, the science of logistics was born. Supply became of increasing importance as the new weapon brought new problems. These problems were never solved by some of the peoples who made war use of the bow. In many periods of history, the bow suffered from lack of proper organization of supply and from deficiencies in tactical operation.

That the ancients developed a good bow is evinced by the fact that the few of these ancient composite bows—mostly of Turkish manufacture—that have survived, are the subjects of fascinated appraisal today. Possibly the most expertly constructed bow of all time was the great sinew, horn, and wood bow that was used by the Janissaries of the Ottoman Empire. This bow, manufactured by a great guild of craftsmen and by subsidiary guilds of fletchers, gluemakers, stringmakers, and processors of sinew, was years in the making and long-lived in effective operation. The average pull was about a hundred pounds, and the bowyers who made this great weapon were a distinguished class of craftsmen who were set apart and awarded great honors.

Some of these magnificent weapons still survive and, although more than a century old, can still be strung. It was this enormously powerful bow that established all of the records for distance casting of the arrow. The Turks approached archery in the same manner that we view baseball and football. It was the national sport, and accurate records of performance were maintained as standards for future competition.

Modern archers, able as they are, are still humiliated by some of these records of the past. Some of the distance marks still remain unchallenged. Turkish archers are credited with propelling an arrow more than half a mile.[1]

As the bow made war more efficient, it made the waging of war immensely more complicated and calculated. The raising and equipping of levies for national defense or offensive aggression was no longer a simple matter of arming spearmen. The preparations for war grew much more deliberate and the training period of soldiers was greatly extended. The training of a military archer required at least two years. Science and proficiency with arms began to replace mass and muscle. Armies took on a professional polish and the demands upon leadership were greatly increased.

The spearman, the halberdier, the pikeman, and the swordsman had all carried weapons of recurrent use in their hands. The hand weapon could kill a dozen men without leaving the possession of the wielder. Replacement of hand weapons was of infrequent occurrence. The arming and supplying of a hand-weapons soldier had been a matter of issuing a sword, a spear, or a pike.

The bow changed all of this, for the archer in war was insatiable in his demand for arrows. To supply that demand, a great manufactory came into being, with skilled bowyers, arrowmakers, and fletchers to service the weapon. With them came the forerunner of the ammunition train.

As the bow made war more complex, it completely negated the principle that superiority in numbers was the decisive factor; it developed the killing of enemies into a routine of expert maneuver. The bow brought quick decisions in battle and fewer casualties to the soldiers who relied upon it. The bow made it possible, in many periods of history, for numerically weak peoples to defend themselves and their rights against strong aggressors who depended upon mere mass and numbers.

The school of tactics developed by the use of the bow in war survives on modern fields. Tanks, armored troop carriers, and airplanes have combined the elements of shock, mobility, and firepower into a great, new, modern school of offensive warfare with missiles.

Sun Tzu fathered that school and Genghis Khan first perfected its principles in the field. It has always been the most economical and decisive form of war.

Part One

INTRODUCTION TO A WEAPON

1

Origins of the Bow

Before we examine the bow in the field, let us locate it in history and delve as far as we can into its prehistoric origins. The bow was invented to solve a great need. Man's desire since Paleolithic times has been centered on the possibilities of propelling a missile a great distance to inflict harm upon another man, or an animal, with a minimum of danger to himself. The development began when Og, the prehistoric man, made use of a natural missile when he picked up a round stone from a riverbank. The Middle Stone Age produced the miracle of the *atlatl*, or spearthrower. This contrivance, a casting stick upon which a spear or dart was supported, was a mere extension of a man's arm to impart greater range and velocity to a cast missile. For its age, the *atlatl* was a notable achievement; for some thousands of years, it remained the most efficient weapon of distant attack. The sling entered history to contribute to long-range hunting and to war as did the boomerang of the aborigine. It was the bow, however, that was first capable of launching an aimed *precision* missile that could be expected to reach out and destroy a target with reasonable certainty.

The invention of the bow is lost in the fog of prehistory, but the records and monuments of the earliest peoples and the stone rubbings of men of the Mesolithic Age tell us that for a period of at least eight thousand years the bow has been man's greatest basic offensive weapon. As a mechanism for storing energy, the bow in its various forms has remained the partner of man. It was an effective weapon long after the invention of gunpowder, and remains so today.

No firearm approached the bow in range, rapidity of fire, accuracy, or reliability for more than five hundred years after the practical use of gunpowder in war. Firearms appeared in Europe as early as the fourteenth century, and there is some evidence that gunpowder was used in war somewhat earlier in Asia. Interesting, if obscure, references point to an extremely early use of gunpowder in China and India, and there are intimations of the use of some detonating agent by the armies of Alexander. There is also a baffling hint of some form of detonation at the Battle of the Trasimeno in the war between Carthage and Rome. Ample historical evidence exists to support the use of gunpowder by the armies of Genghis Khan.

These early experiments with gunpowder had no adverse effect upon the popularity of the bow, for it was not until the development of the first practical breech-loading rifle, just prior to the Civil War, that a rifleman could have met the composite bow on even terms. The so-called Kentucky rifle, a Pennsylvania product of the eighteenth century and a weapon of great reputation, would have been hard-pressed against the horse-archers of Asia. These early riflemen would have been overwhelmed by the speed of fire of the composite bow and by the elusive mobility of the archers. The earlier musketeers of the American Revolution, encumbered with clumsy, large-caliber muskets, would have died in their tracks if they had been forced to pit their slow-firing and inaccurate smoothbores against the composite bow that was fatal at 200 to 300 yards. It is fortunate that our pioneers did not meet with the Asiatic expert, composite bow archery. The Brown Bess musket of revolutionary times had an effective range of scarcely more than 50 yards. It is a matter of historical record that Benjamin Franklin seriously advocated a return to the very primitive Indian bow as a superior weapon for use against British grenadiers.[1]

It was the inventor of the first successful breech-loading rifle the Big Fifty Sharps, Christian Sharps, who would have given the rifleman his first chance of survival against the composite bow. The Big Fifty could reach out and kill at a mile.[2] As we shall see, the bow was still a weapon of account as late as 1876. Indeed, the bow has never been discarded as an active weapon of war.

It was the stored energy inherent in a strung bow that first placed beasts and men at the mercy of a distant antagonist. The weapon must be ranked as one of the outstanding inventions of man. With the bow in his hands, man's relationship to himself and to the world underwent drastic change. Through its various developments, from primitive arched stick to wooden self bow, to composite bow and crossbow, or arbalest, the weapon has maintained itself in the affections of men for thousands of years.

The bow can still do many things that the most modern firearm cannot accomplish. It has the virtue of quietness of operation. The British used this quality in the jungle fights against the Mau-Mau. Archers were included in the personnel of British patrols. They were able to kill single Mau-Maus silently to prevent the flight of other natives into the deeper jungle. It has been mentioned that the bow proved its worth during the commando raids into Norway during World War II, where it was sometimes effective against lone German sentries.[3]

The bow is an effective long-range weapon that can be operated from concealment. Men in a fixed defensive position on terrain providing enemy cover can be overwhelmed by arrow flights, launched without the archers exposing themselves to reprisal fire. The bow has mastered firearms on many fields because of this advantage of being able to present effective indirect fire. This indirect application of arrows was effective against emplacements or walls. The Normans used the tactic successfully at Hastings where arching arrow flights killed Harold at a desperate and decisive stage of the battle and brought to William the crown of England.

In company with the *atlatl*, the bow made its appearance as an invention of the Middle Stone Age. We think loosely of the bow as the weapon that succeeded the *atlatl*. It is more probable that the bow, although of later development, survived the *atlatl* after a parallel use of both weapons for many centuries. The earliest pictographs of the bow are those rubbed on the rocks of eastern Spain. There, Middle Stone Age archers are depicted in the attitude of the chase, holding in their left hands spare arrows as they draw their bows. The bow is quite probably an African invention, dating from as early as 7000 B.C.

By the Late Stone Age the bow had developed into a deadly and efficient weapon. The skeleton of a wild bull has been found in Denmark that bears the scars of the flint arrowheads that killed him; one of the heads remained in the skeleton. Many of the skeletons of Late Stone Age men carry the flint arrowheads that brought them down. There is always the possibility, however, that these early flint arrowheads, so-called, are, in reality, darts or spearheads that had been projected from an *atlatl*. No definite date, or even an approximation, can be assigned to the introduction of the bow as a weapon of man.

These early self bows were merely straight staves of wood, possibly reinforced with crude lashings of leather or animal intestines. The refinements were very slow, but it is known that prior to the dawn of recorded history, possibly as early as 4000 B.C., the people of Lower Egypt used a long recurving bow of the type that apparently developed in Africa. The reed arrows had chisel-shaped stone heads. With this weapon, the earliest peoples of the Nile conducted lion hunts on the edge of the desert, and we know that the weapon was used in war.

The recurving shape of early Egyptian bows indicates that the people understood the principle of reflexing the bow. If these prehistoric bows did reflex (that is, bend backward in the opposite direction when unstrung), they were probably true composite bows in which various materials were bonded together to form such recurving.

This composite bow, one of the principal subjects of this book, called for a high order of workmanship and, in this respect, the Egyptians were eminently qualified. Everything that these people made showed great refinement in design and construction. If the compound reflexed bow did exist in Lower Egypt as early as the year 4000 B.C. (as seems probable), the development of the weapon, in all of its intermediate stages to its final perfect form, was accomplished in three or four millennia. Certain it is that this earliest Egyptian bow, if not a composite bow, was at least a high development of reinforced bow and that it was brought into the Nile valley by the first people who occupied that territory.

Let it be said then, that for a period of at least eight thousand years and possibly longer, the bow has been associated with man as a partner to his development and group security.

3

The Arrow As a Precision Missile

The arrow is among the most dangerous of all missiles. Long after the introduction of gunpowder had substituted the bullet for the arrow, the feathered shaft remained the more formidable missile. The arrow wings with great authority even today; our era of modern arms has not relegated it to the position of a toy.

In range, the arrow is still respected. When used as a weapon of war, the extreme range of the cloth-yard (i.e., 37 inches) arrows of the longbow was close to 300 yards. In the reign of Henry VIII, the usual military target practice was conducted at 200 meters, 1/8 of a mile. The great composite bows of the Mongols and other tribes of horse-archers could propel a 26-inch arrow for more than 800 yards maximum range, and to an effective range of more than 300 yards. No firearm for many centuries could approach the effective ranges established by the bow.

The penetration achieved by ancient bowmen was remarkable. The Egyptian bows could send an arrow with a reed shaft through 4 inches of brass. Chinese arrows could penetrate as many as seven thicknesses of the boiled hide armor of the period. The Mongols are credited with piercing European armor at 200 yards. The relatively weak American Plains Indian missiles could pierce the body of a buffalo, the arrowhead protruding a span's breadth on the opposite side.

It is interesting to note that the obsidian arrowheads of some of the western American tribes penetrated deeper than modern steel points. The light reed arrows of the Florida Indians, tipped with flint, went through Spanish armor, continuing on to embed themselves in tree trunks.

When plate mail came into use, the English developed a bodkin point to achieve maximum penetration. It was the English practice to place a bit of wax on the bodkin. A bodkin so treated was less liable to glance from the metal surface; full energy was thus concentrated at the point of impact. Experiments have shown that a 75-pound bow, using bodkin arrows, will penetrate steel plate to a depth of 1/4 of an inch. In tests made on ancient armor, sparks flew when the bodkin made contact. The armor was pierced; the arrow continued on to penetrate 8 inches of wood.

Against horses, the damage inflicted by a cloth-yard arrow was greater than that inflicted by a bullet. The English bow would kill horses at ranges approaching 250 yards.

The desperate efforts of the mailed knights to protect themselves from arrow fire were lessons in futility. Armor heavy enough to resist arrow penetration was not practicable in battle. James I of England, speaking wryly of the defensive efforts of the knights and of the increasing weight of the armor worn in the field, said, "Armor was an admirable invention, for while it protected the wearer from being hurt, it effectually prevented, by its weight, the wearer causing injury to others."

The frightful fatality of arrow wounds caused the French to protest bitterly (and without foundation) that the English poisoned the arrowpoints. There seems to be no record of the use of poisoned arrows in battle by the English although they did, occasionally, poison the points with hellebore for hunting.

The earliest chain mail, when supported by a layer of felt, would keep out the light Saracen arrows but not the shafts of the longbow or the bolts of the crossbow. It was the arrow, and not the later firearms, that destroyed the effectiveness of the armored knight in battle.

The velocity of an arrow in flight depended, of course, upon the strength of the bow. Estimates of the speed of an arrow have varied from 100 to 200 miles per hour. A strong composite bow could produce a velocity of about 300 feet per second. This would be the equivalent of about one-third the velocity of the present Colt .45 semiautomatic pistol used by our armed forces.

The tissue destruction resulting from an arrow wound was very great. It was in fact much more severe than that accomplished by any small-caliber, high-velocity, metal-jacketed bullet of any type permitted by the restrictions of the Geneva Convention. The laceration and internal hemorrhage caused by an arrow was frightful.

At maximum effective range, the arrow was probably as deadly, or more so, as at point-blank range. Given sufficient remaining velocity and energy to achieve partial penetration, the arrow delivered enormous shock. At the end of its flight, an arrow still traveling with sufficient rapidity to ensure deep penetration tended to waver slightly in flight preparatory to its fall. Under such conditions, the arrowhead was subjected to vertical and lateral pressures. The resulting wound was enlarged and irregular in its course through tissue.

In cases where the arrow did not achieve complete penetration but remained in the body, the victim faced the additional ordeal and shock of surgical extraction. In many cases where the arrowhead was bound to the shaft with sinew, the body heat melted the fastening, leaving the detached arrowhead in the wound. This was often the case in the American wars in the West against Plains Indians.

Not the least horrifying effect of an arrow wound was the strong possibility of infection. An arrow offers a very large germ-bearing surface in head, shaft, and feathers. The dragging of this long projectile through a badly lacerated wound offered enormous possibilities for fatal infection.

The fact that an arrow could be seen in flight but not avoided often forced troops into unreasoning panic. In this respect, the arrow had a psychological effect superior to that inflicted upon men under rifle fire. A man with an arrow in him, even though the wound was not fatal or even dangerous, was out of action until the arrow could be extracted. He was seemingly unable, psychologically, to continue in action with an arrow protruding from any part of his anatomy. Here again, a minor arrow wound, not normally dangerous, inflicted severe shock when the missile was surgically removed.

The arrow cannot be compared with any high-velocity bullet, but it was inevitable that it be compared with the round balls of the earlier firearms. Sir John Smith made such a comparison of the bow and the musket in 1590. His conclusions indicted the musket as follows:

1. Extreme nicety was required in taking aim with the musket.
2. Even at short range, the bullet was uncertain in flight.
3. Firearms were hot and dangerous after seven or eight rounds.

4. Powder was very deficient in quality.
5. When the musket was lowered, the bullet was prone to fall from the barrel.
6. The musket was subject to erosive rust and to dangerous over-charging.
7. Weather conditions ruined powder and blew powder from the pan.
8. A large body of musketeers was unable to resist a lesser body of cavalry.
9. Few were killed by musket fire after hours of battle.

Almost two centuries after Sir John Smith had made his estimate, the controversy was still raging in England. In a match at Cumberland in 1792, between the musket and the bow at 100 yards, 16 arrows pierced the target while the musket scored only 12 hits. During the same year, in London, an exhibition on a 4-foot target at 100 yards produced a score of 15 hits in 21 shots from the bow and 12 hits in 21 shots from the musket.

In 1792, Lieutenant Colonel Lee, of the Forty-fourth Regiment, advocated a return to the longbow, in preference to the flintlock musket. He based his conclusions on the following points:

1. The bow was more accurate.
2. Four arrows could be cast while the musketeer was discharging one bullet.
3. The bow produced no smoke to spoil the aim.
4. The flight of an arrow inspired terror.
5. A man wounded by an arrow had to be attended at once.
6. The bow was much easier and cheaper to produce.

The early muskets had not one point of equality with the bow save the effect created by flash and smoke of the explosion. When firearms first appeared in battle, it was reckoned that eight thousand bowmen could handle twenty thousand musketeers. The dependable range of the first muskets was hardly more than 20 yards, and the earliest firearms were able to fire no more than 7 rounds in eight hours without great danger to the operator. There was always the threat of a misfire, and it was necessary to change flints after 8 or 10 rounds.

The Revolutionary War arm of the British, the famous Brown Bess musket, was far inferior to the longbow at any range of more than 50 yards. It required a skilled musketeer to drop his man at 50 yards, and the musket was not a particularly dangerous weapon as late as the eighteenth century.

In the middle 1700s, Saxe, the greatest military mind of his day, was exceedingly critical of the effects of musketry fire. He mentions that, quite often, salvos at close range killed only four or five men. One incident at Belgrade, in 1717, is particularly illuminating. An attacking regiment of Turks was fired into at a range of thirty paces by a triple line of musketeers in two-battalion strength. The volley fire killed thirty-two of the Turkish force, which forthwith closed with the bayonet and annihilated the musketeers before they could reload.

Body Protection against Arrows

Defense against the arrow sets up a peculiar problem. It took the trial and error of many centuries to produce effective protection—with methods that in many ways are simple and obvious.

The first armor, flexible chain mail with *gambesons* (a quilted garment worn under the mail), was far more effective than the later plate mail. To be effective against arrows, plate mail had to be so heavy as to render its use impracticable. Reinforced chain mail, including banded mail, was developed, circa 1250, for protection against arrows and it was relatively effective. The arrow had to penetrate two flattened rings, reinforced by the heavy leather. Under this, the gambeson greatly resisted penetration and reduced shock of arrow impact. The wearer of chain mail, however, was subject to multiple wounds caused by splinters from the arrow shaft seeking interstices of the mail. It was a very heavy outfit and excessively warm, but it blunted the efficiency of the Saracen arrows during the Crusades.

Plate mail was one of the worst possible protections against arrows unless it was made strong enough to completely deny entry. Sheets of metal set up an inflexible and unyielding surface. A steel arrowhead, traveling in excess of a hundred miles per hour and helped by the driving force of a following shaft, was capable of holing all but the very best plate armor. The relatively thin metal plates offered just sufficient resistance to create a localized and highly concentrated shock center. Usually, the arrow was slowed sufficiently by the plate to ensure retention of the missile in the body after deep penetration was accomplished, resulting in dangerous wounds.

The field experience against the Saracens taught the Crusaders that a better defense than any type of armor was a thick quilting of padded cotton that absorbed much of the original shock and strongly resisted penetration. The quilted surcoats of the crossbowmen stopped arrows even when not reinforced with armor.

The Spanish *conquistadores* used the same principle in the adoption of felt, 4 inches thick, to protect the forequarters of the horse. The Spaniards also accepted the quilted cotton armor of the Aztecs.

Probably the best defense of all was the method devised by the Mongols, who accepted the possibility of casualties with great realism. They minimized the effect by going into battle relatively unprotected, but wearing thick inner clothing of silk. In no sense a substitute for armor, as it had no resistance to penetration, the raw silk is remarkable in one respect—an arrowhead would not usually cut through the fabric. As a result, the silk was carried into the wound, permitting relatively easy extraction of the arrowhead. By gently pulling on the enclosing silk, the head was gradually withdrawn from the wound. The casualty was thus spared enlargement of the wound by surgery and was given considerable protection against infection.

Whatever protective device was utilized, the arrow could be depended upon to deliver a very dangerous wound. The design of the head and shaft of an arrow, which makes for a missile with great sectional depth, is effectively used in the manufacture of modern bullets, where great penetration is required. The 6.5 millimeter *Mannlicher* bullet, small in caliber and long in form, is a modern derivative of the excellent design that is inherent in the shape of an arrow.

Part Two

THE THEORIES OF WAR

4

The Principles of War

A volume detailing the tactics of war with the bow must necessarily use certain professional military phrases that may not be within the understanding of a layman reader. For that reason, it seems in order, before beginning the discussion of the bow in war, to detail briefly the principles of war and the various schools of war under which men have gone into battle.

The principles of war have been so formalized by the battle experience of so many people for so many centuries that every army in the world has accepted them as mandatory rules for the conduct of war. These principles are deceptively simple.

1. THE OBJECTIVE. The mission for which the army took to the field. Every army has a main mission, and the activities of an army in the field are subordinated to the accomplishment of that mission. The mission may be a defense against aggression, an offensive invasion of a victim country, or the occupation of strategic territory prior to an active shooting war. Sometimes faulty generalship can result in losing sight of the mission and strategic planning fails to establish the correct mission.

2. THE OFFENSE. Obtained only by offensive action. This rule of war may seem inconclusive or carelessly stated on first examination, but the immutable fact remains that any defensive situation is only an avoidance of defeat. Field battles are won by offensive action and by offensive action only. Defensive actions result in stalemate or defeat.

3. MASS. Not necessarily to be construed as meaning the massing

of men into a formation such as the phalanx—although under some conditions, the military meaning of mass might be accomplished by such a formation. To the military mind, mass means assembling combat power at a decisive place at a decisive time. Military mass is not necessarily numerical strength in men. The purpose of mass is to gain a temporary local numerical superiority or to achieve a temporary or permanent superior tactical deployment of available troops. This principle is tied closely with the fourth principle of war.

4. ECONOMY OF FORCE. The systematic weakening of one section of a line to obtain temporary local superiority in numbers at some other point of the line. This is the most important principle of war as pitting strength against weakness is the aim of all generals. It can be accomplished only by expert maneuver and the possession of superior speed to that of the enemy.

5. SURPRISE. In time, place, direction, or weapons. Surprise is also tied closely with economy of force as it usually refers to unexpected movements of troops. Rarely can a nation be surprised with a new weapon in these modern days, although the use of the atom bomb against Japan was a notable exception.

6. SECURITY. Denying the enemy the element of surprise or the benefits of hampering operations. Here again, army speed is often the decisive factor. Equally important is the security of messages. The failure of Japan in World War II to provide adequate message security resulted in the breaking of their secret code.

7. TEAMWORK. The coordination of all arms of the service into a unified supporting whole. This is a major preoccupation in military circles today as global alliances have produced many problems in weapons, tactics, and strategy that must be coordinated. The United States, at the moment, is attempting to tighten the bonds that unite the various arms of its military service. Unification of the services is a familiar phrase in the present organization.

5

The Schools of War

As this volume will attempt an evaluation of the performance of the bow, operating within its own school, against conflicting theories or schools of war, it is necessary that the nonprofessional reader have a clear understanding of the formalized schools of war as they existed in ancient times. These schools of war were three in number, and they still exist to a degree today as the modern philosophy of war has combined the best elements of each into a modern offensive theory of battle.

During its centuries of battle service, the bow, in its various forms, engaged each rival school of war. We propose to show the battle results of these encounters, not so much by a description of the battle action but rather with an analysis of the performance of the weapon. The great triumphs of the bow as well as its historic failures will be illustrated as the bow was not a weapon beyond reproach.

In following the bow through history we will be equally interested in the defenses that were set up against the weapon. Both imperfect and proper applications of the bow as a mounted weapon of offense will be examined. The tactics of the bow will be considered in its use as an infantry weapon; in the hands of chariot-archers; as light flanking auxiliary cavalry; and in the hands of horse-archers, where the bow was the decisive weapon and cavalry the decisive service.

Throughout its history the bow had its resurgencies and its declines. It was a highly specialized weapon, requiring inspired leadership and sound tactics to bring out its destructive capabilities. In many of its battle appearances, even when used as the major weapon, the bowmen were victims of such bad tactical disposition that the offensive worth of their weapons could not be realized. As we shall indicate, the bow was much too versatile a weapon for its capabilities to be explored by any school of tactics that relied upon infantry as the decisive arm.

This book will not be greatly concerned with mere descriptions of famous battles in which the bow was a factor. These accounts may be read in any standard history. We propose to examine the reasons for the great victories and the stunning defeats and our interest will be in the military thinking (or the absence of that thinking) on those famous fields. We will be concerned with the lethal efficiency of the arrow when it was opposed to all other hand and projectile weapons of its era. This will be the story of a weapon and of the men bearing that weapon. We will see that the bow, although displaced by greater weapons that succeeded it in history, has never lost its vitality. As a weapon, and particularly for the tactical school that was built around it, the bow is still viewed with respect by modern military minds. The bow has not yet been relegated to the walls of museums beside its contemporaries —the spear, the halberd, the battle-ax, and the pike.

It is still mandatory that we remember the war lessons that were taught by the bow.

In order to understand the performance of the bow in battle, we should be familiar with the various troop compositions, tactical conceptions, and orders of battle that the weapon encountered in the field. As mentioned, these schools were three in number and their conflicting theories were expressed by the hand-to-hand shock of heavy infantry, by the limited maneuverability of armored cavalry, and by the fluid, mobile war of horse-archers.

The School of Shock Infantry

The peoples along the Mediterranean had concentrated their school of tactics about the foot soldier. Greece and Rome had committed themselves to a doctrine of position war, with its attendant bloody battle. Here in the Mediterranean area was the hand-weapons school of cut and thrust. The armies were deficient in mobility and firepower and dependent upon the willingness of an opponent to fight upon a chosen field. War had bogged down to become deadly in execution and frightening in slaughter. Superiority in numbers became the criterion for judging an army. A synomosy of slaughter was established. It became correct to present straight, close-order lines to enemy attack and it was usual to ignore innovations or departures or improvements. An acre of ground was taken by frontal assault and that ground held at all costs. Possession of the field was the measure of battle success.

The ancient peoples along the Mediterranean were never able to develop effective distant war with missiles. The Greek and Roman theory of war had always centered about the phalanx, or a form thereof, in which a tightly massed force, using hand weapons, was brought to a high development. The Greek city-states soon concentrated upon the premise that the elemental military issue could best be settled, hand to hand, with the sword and spear. It was a premise accepted by the later Romans whose legion became synonymous with any concept of disciplined close-order battle.

Although missiles were used to some degree in the Mediterranean theater, the missile troopers were never valued as anything more than auxiliary backing for the swordsmen. No missile weapon attained major stature as the decisive weapon. The bow was used sparingly; the sling became the preferred weapon of distant war. While the sling was a weapon that could sometimes be very effective, it had neither the precision nor the range to be able to seriously inflict damage at long range. The catapult and the ballista were used against city walls and in the defense of field defensive perimeters, but the field soldier, standing with sword or spear, placed no real reliance upon the projectile arms. The Mediterranean soldier adhered to the principle of cut and thrust—man to man.

A mass of men operating in close formation is difficult to maneuver and is subject to rapid disentegration if breached. The efficiency of the phalanx depended upon the ability to maintain a close and orderly alignment. War in the Mediterranean soon became a matter of waiting out the opponent. The massed formations preferred to stand on the defensive, on ground open and level, behind formidable hedges of spears. When offensive movements were undertaken, the advance was slow and deliberate to ensure holding formation. As we shall see later in a discussion of the Battle of Marathon, the Greeks sometimes violated this principle by sending spearmen forward on the run, but it was not the usual practice in the era of the heavy phalanx.

As the tactics of heavy infantry slowly improved the fundamental principle of "an army in being in the field" developed. An army in being implied disciplined mass and group solidarity that could be broken only by serious assault. In the Mediterranean, the phalanx was greatly refined and improved until it became a hard core of dangerous, armed men who could be approached only at great peril—and then only by a similarly armed and disciplined formation. It may be seen that there was no reliance upon missiles. The armies simply moved into a battle situation and collided.

The phalanx was sufficient to handle any undisciplined, barbaric opponent who could be decoyed or infuriated into a positive hand-to-hand action. These simple phalangial tactics were sound when applied against other hand-weapons troops, and the disciplined soldiers of the Greek city-states were able to impose mass shock upon opponents on many fields. Against an enemy lacking in organization or military experience or against opponents who had no effective presentation of missiles, the phalanx worked very well indeed. When opposed to other armed masses of equally disciplined men, the result was often an inconclusive and costly stalemate.

As all of the contestants for power in this area used the same weapons and the same tactics, the weakness of the phalanx against missiles did not become apparent for many years. An overestimation of the virtues of heavy infantry was the result and it inflicted itself upon the world for centuries. The lesson was rarely apparent because of the few contacts the phalanx ever had against missiles. There had been a few such contacts, impressive for the moment and then forgotten. A Spartan phalanx had been cut off by Demosthenes in 424 B.C. and four hundred of the surviving Spartans had surrendered to light missile troops. Although a great blow to Spartan prestige, the lesson was not learned.

The chief Mediterranean missile weapon, the sling, had undergone certain refinements; on isolated fields, sometimes it had been effective. The sling had the merit of great simplicity. There was nothing that could not be repaired on the field in a few moments. Nature provided the ammunition, stones 3 or 4 inches in diameter, weighing a good, solid pound. The weapon itself, weighing a few ounces, could be wrapped about the waist when not in use. The sling was the field mortar of the ancients. It could deliver effective, indirect fire. It was no toy. A well-directed stone, delivered at high velocity, had the crushing impact of an ax or a mace. A grim little weapon, it could stun a horse or drop a rider from the saddle. A stone from a Roman sling had killed Pacorus of Parthia in one of the few successes of the legion against these horse-archers.

The Mediterranean armies made certain improvements in the sling. In the Third Macedonian War came the cestrosphendens, a wicked battle missile. It consisted of a pointed iron head, two palms in length, affixed to a shaft of pine about 9 inches long and as thick as a man's finger. It was feathered to ensure steadiness in flight, and when cast from a sling, it was vastly superior to a stone in range and velocity. This missile placed the Roman legions in great peril at the Battle of Phalanna, for it was the cestrosphendens that accounted for the majority of the casualties.

Another innovation in the use of the sling was the casting of *caltrops*, iron balls with projecting sharp points to disable horses and impede cavalry charges.

But the sling, or any other missile weapon, did not influence Mediterranean military thinking to any great degree. The minor reverses and casualties occasionally inflicted by the stone, the cestrosphendens, or the arrow in no way diminished the glamour or the reputation of shock infantry along the shores of the Mediterranean.

During this cycle of military history, the phalanx tried only for temporary local superiority. Not much attention was paid to maneuver, deception, or the possibilities of surprise attack. The armies moved slowly into precise positions that had been predetermined by experience and past successes. It was not strictly a principle of maneuver that was involved. It was, rather, a matter of unimpeded and leisurely placement of troops on a chosen field.

Let us examine briefly the typical Greek phalanx. The smallest command unit was the *taxis* of one hundred men, four junior officers, and a captain, in a formation eight or more files deep. Ten taxes constituted a chiliarchy, commanded by a *stragetos*, or colonel. The chiliarchy could be detached for independent action as a small phalanx but maneuverability under any condition was severely strictured. Four chiliarchy made up a phalanx. The Greek phalanx at full strength was, therefore, forty-two hundred men and officers.

This massed unit was the basic formation of the armies of Athens, Sparta, Thebes, Corinth, Syracuse, and others of the Greek city-states. The men were very heavily armed and armored; the equipment of a Spartan soldier weighed more than 70 pounds.

The weakness of the phalanx was resident in its rigidity and relative inability to maneuver. The phalanx was very vulnerable on the flanks; once penetrated, it fell apart rapidly.

It remained for Epaminondas of Thebes to bring about the first great tactical improvement in the maneuver and disposition of the phalanx, in 371 B.C., at the Battle of Leuctra. This early tactician had been aware of the drift to the right that inevitably occurred when swordsmen and spearmen came to close quarters. The hand-weapons man naturally sought the protection of the shield held by the man on his right and he moved in that direction to expose his neighbor's shield to the enemy. To counteract this drift, Epaminondas regrouped the phalanx into an oblique line of battle, with one wing advanced and the other refused. He was one of the first men in history to apply economy of force by the numerical superiority of a reinforced wing. Theban tactics involved a heavy concentration on the left where a depth of fifty ranks was massed to crush the right of the enemy. This innovation in troop deployment crushed Sparta and established the Theban phalanx as the best military formation of the period.

The next development of the phalanx and the last, true tortoise formation of men packed into a mass was the tremendously powerful Macedonian phalanx as conceived by Philip. The Macedonian phalanx was organized into files of 16 men, sixteen of such files making up a syntagma. Equivalent to a modern company, this syntagma had a strength of 256 men. Four syntagmas constituted a chiliarchy of 1,024 men; four chiliarchy made up a simple phalanx of 4,096 men. Two simple phalanxes formed a division of 8,192 men and two divisions formed a Grand Phalanx of 16,384 men. A simple phalanx was commanded by a brigadier general, and a division by a major general.

The Macedonian phalanx was capable of setting up sound defensive positions. It could form a hollow square with a center of archers and slingers when in a desperate defensive situation. On the offense, it could shift into a wedge and with equal facility form a pincer with extended wings to receive an enemy wedge. The phalanx could also operate independently by syntagmas or with a chiliarchy, although this capacity for small-unit operations was much inferior to the later developments of the Roman legion.

Independent action of units of the phalanx of Macedonia was not a usual tactic except, possibly, in the late stages of a mopping-up exercise conducted against a beaten enemy. The phalanx was primarily a center of raw and bristling power to secure a safe pivot for the far-ranging maneuvers of Alexander's powerful armored cavalry.

The principal arm of the phalanx was the sarissa. This was a spear that some authorities consider to have been 24 feet long, although the actual length has been subject to several estimates. One classical scholar (who prefers to remain anonymous) states flatly that the sarissa was 12 feet in length. This does not seem a reasonable estimate as all of the ancient sources state that the fifth rank spear projected beyond the first rank, impossible with a spear 12 feet long.

Probably a better source than our anonymous scholar would be Tarn's published statement in *Hellenistic Military and Naval Developments,* where a length of 17 feet is established, and it is suggested that various ranks may have used different length spears. *The Saga of the Sword* states on one page that the length of the sarissa was 21 feet and at the bottom of the same page the length is given at 24 feet. Mitchell's *World's Military History* says that the sarissa was 24 feet in length. This is the figure usually quoted by military historians. As no sarissa seems to be available for measurement, after twenty-two hundred years, the discussion is futile.

The phalanx formations of Greece and Macedonia survived for many years, long after their usefulness on the field had been disproved. Northern and western European use of the phalanx is mentioned briefly in a footnote.[1] The Roman modification of the phalanx, as expressed by the legion, is detailed in the chapter devoted to the Parthian wars.

From the above discussion of the phalanx order of battle, it will be seen that war in the Mediterranean placed great emphasis on position as the objective. The importance of the destruction of a field army was often obscured by the mandate that a city or hill be taken at all cost. There was much aimless marching in search of battle sites and little of tactical maneuver.

Having described the disposition of heavy infantry, let us consider, at this point, what this school of pure shock can and cannot do. Heavy infantry forces were able to penetrate deep into hostile territory and to present unit force and action against any irregular force that could be organized against them. They could set up and maintain a formidable holding force under most conditions of battle. The inherent strong organization permitted them to continue an inexorable and relentless advance into a victim country; such advance could not be checked or contained, short of disruption of the formation.

Relatively small detachments of heavy infantry, possessing the essentials of cohesion and discipline, were able to maintain themselves in the face of huge barbarian concentrations. This fact was well demonstrated by the horse-supported heavy infantry of Cortez in Mexico, Pizarro in Peru, and by the earlier campaigns of Caesar against the Gauls.

In theory, heavy infantry was sound; it was orderly and precise, thus appealing to the military mind. In practice, its relative efficiency depended upon many factors. Heavy infantry was fatally slow in deployment against determined and organized opposition. Shock was not sufficient to obtain a decision, for heavy infantry was subject to grave and insoluble weaknesses.

Loss of the Initiative

Heavy infantry was not capable of sustained offense. The privilege of battle could be denied such infantry by any enemy possessing greater mobility. Heavy infantry could be decoyed by evasive action into a battle situation that favored a mobile enemy and subjected to long campaigns of attrition by an inferior force of active and determined soldiers. Shock infantry could be denied favorable conditions of battle by the mere refusal of the enemy to give battle on such terrain. If the enemy was willing to forgo the defense of strong points, heavy infantry could degenerate into a holding force surrounded by a devastated countryside that was filled with dangerous and elusive guerrillas. This was the situation that had confronted Marcus Antonius in the Parthian campaign.

Any mobile enemy could obtain a local superiority at a selected point of a heavy infantry line. By such tactics, the movement of heavy infantry could be seriously impeded or stopped completely. Heavy infantry could be subjected to disastrous surprise attacks from enemies who could not be denied that privilege and constant preparation against such attack was wearing on morale and the physical condition of an infantry group in hostile country.

Denial of Supplies

A determined enemy could apply a scorched-earth policy before the advance of heavy infantry and stop it completely without battle, thus subjecting the massed troops to aimless and frantic marches through a denuded countryside. Because of its slow rate of progress, heavy infantry could literally be starved by the systematic destruction of all food supplies along the line of march.

Vulnerability to Missiles

The greatest weakness of heavy infantry was its fatal vulnerability to the arrow and other effective missiles. Infantry-archers, agile and lightly equipped, could evade and erode heavy infantry. Foot-archers, properly handled, could annihilate the best heavy infantry of any period when in open country. In dense forest or mountain areas, a stalemate could be effected by foot-archers as the shock power of heavy infantry rapidly lessened under such conditions. Caesar discovered this fact in the forests of Germany, an area he left severely alone after initial reverses. The Roman legion in all periods of its history suffered terrible casualties in such country areas.

The School of Armored Cavalry

The horse had been domesticated and trained for war for more than seventeen centuries before the possibilities of mounted shock were fully assessed. All of the earlier peoples making use of the horse —the Persians, Egyptians, Mitanni, Kharri, Kassites, Medes, Chinese, Assyrians, and others—had relied on the chariot or rudimentary cavalry in their applications of the horse to war. These first empires built in war had encountered great difficulty in solving the many problems inherent in armored cavalry.

The technical problems involved in the use of the sword and the lance by mounted men were not so severe as those confronting the horse-archer. Therefore, as early as 350 b.c. a second great school of tactical warfare came into being. This was the first successful attempt to place a heavy infantryman on a horse.

Let us consider this school of heavy armored cavalry and infer what such an army composition can accomplish and what it cannot be expected to do. Theoretically, at least, this school united the elements of shock and mobility. With the ability to carry hand weapons, the sword, and the lance, plus the shock of a plunging horse, such cavalry was able to overwhelm heavy infantry that did not possess adequate missile support. In placing a heavily armed infantryman on horseback, the horse became, in effect, a projectile supporting an armed man.

The fact that these early cavalrymen were armored does not necessarily imply sluggishness. Armor of the period had not yet reached the ridiculous and almost unsupportable weight it later attained. The cavalrymen of Alexander should not be compared with the medieval knights; they were much more lightly armored and much more agile in massed maneuver.

Armored cavalry were able to apply, with considerable speed, the principle of economy of force against infantry of any class. As a flanking agent and as an instrument for surprise attack on an enemy's rear, armored cavalry broke heavy infantry on many fields with a minimum of offensive casualties.

On the debit side, armored cavalry had two fatal weaknesses. One of these was tactical; the other was psychological or social. The two weaknesses displayed equal virulence in hastening the decay and the disappearance of armored cavalry as the decisive arm.

The Tactical Weakness of Armored Cavalry

Heavy cavalry, although relatively mobile and able to inflict great damage upon infantry, did not possess sufficient agility to cope with missiles delivered by light horse-archers or by determined infantry-archers. Armored cavalry required two supporting arms to be successful. The first of these was an infantry pivot to exploit the cavalry breakthrough and the confusion attendant upon imposing battle on two fronts, resulting from cavalry attacks on an enemy's rear. Second, and more important, armored cavalry required the protection of light cavalry-archers against the missile attack of the enemy. Enemy light cavalry, employing the evasive tactics of distant war, could not be ridden down and destroyed by heavy armored horsemen whose armor could not withstand the arrows of such light horsemen. Evasion of the arrow was a problem that could be solved only by speed and mobility. As a consequence, although heavy armored cavalry could, and did, operate on a few occasions as the decisive arm, it was never able to continue sustained independent action. The horse was a vulnerable target for arrows and a dismounted heavy cavalryman was, to all practical purposes, out of the action.

The centuries-old problem has always been, as Bedford Forrest has paraphrased it, a question of "getting there firstest with the mostest." It is the immutable law of economy of force which can be applied only by the army possessing the greater speed.

The Social Weakness of Armored Cavalry

Since earliest times possession and use of the horse has been a preemption of a social class considering itself superior to common men. In many countries—Egypt, China, Assyria, and the early Persian Empire—the use of the horse by commoners was proscribed or severely limited. The *hetaerae*, the Companions of Alexander, were favored men, as were the Imperial Horse Guards of the Byzantines, the *yurt* sentries of Genghis Khan, the Imperial Household Cavalry establishments of Europe, and, to some lesser extent, by the romantic cavalry of Jeb Stuart in our own Civil War. The Khmer of Indochina seldom saw the horse except in the rare appearances of the animal in state parades as allowed by the emperor. In many periods of history, the horse has been a mere show animal of war. The mounted men were always the elite corps, hedged in by tradition and ritual. It has always been so, for man has preserved a unique relationship with the horse.

In Europe, the cult of the horse reached a ridiculous climax in the development of the knight-errant, a noble gentleman on horseback who was dedicated to the defense of womanhood and to the tournament joust. It became increasingly distasteful to these gentlemen to die under the missile fire of an ignorant yeoman or a wild Tartar from the desert of Mongolia. To shut out the singing arrows, body protection became heavier and heavier until the use of dray horses became necessary to support the intolerable weight. It took many centuries to do so, but in time, the armored horseman equipped and armored himself out of existence.

It began with the chain mail period, which lasted from the tenth to the fourteenth centuries. Chain mail was succeeded by the plate mail era, beginning circa A.D. 1200 and lasting until the seventeenth century. The complete plate mail was a staggering load. In the final days of the armored horsemen, the rider was unable to swerve to right or left in the charge and was helpless when dismounted. He was hoisted into his saddle by a system of derricks.

Not the least contribution to the decline of armored cavalry was its excessive cost. Provision of the arms, armor, horse, and horse equipment was a severe drain upon the economies of the early nations of history. It is amazing that the small country of Macedonia in the time of Philip and Alexander was able to field such tremendous wings of this expensive arm. This volume will discuss the performance of heavy armored cavalry as presented by Macedonia and the Byzantines and will witness its final collapse at Crecy, Agincourt, and Poitiers. It will be noted that, in actions where this arm had conspicuous battle success, it was strongly supported by efficient missiles.

The School of Missile War of Motion

The true theory of mounted war with the bow called not for the occupation of cities but for a widespread control of the land, food, and labor resources. With a country demoralized and the rural population at work for the invaders, the cities could be taken at leisure. This was true offensive war of motion, and when properly executed, it did not call for the siege of cities or for close-order battle at all.

The very size of the great cities of the ancient world was a defensive weakness. The population was walled within the city; their subsistence lay outside the walls. The larger the city and the more powerful the defensive works, the larger the garrison and the resident population. Denied food from the countryside, these great cities could not long stand a passive siege.

Although its greatest practitioner, Genghis Khan did not originate the mobile missile school of war. The field practice of this theory may be best understood by an examination of his campaigns later in this volume.

The principles of this school that sent horse-bowmen out to battle were laid down as early as 500 B.C. in a remarkable military treatise. *The Art of War,* by the Chinese general Sun Tzu, was, in many translations, the standard textbook on the prosecution of war for warlike generations of Asiatic peoples and had a wide distribution throughout Asia. These military precepts of Sun Tzu are as clear and as valid today as they were twenty-five centuries ago when this greatest of all military minds formulated them.

The remarkable Cathayan scholar Yeliu Chutsai may have been responsible for bringing *The Art of War* to the attention of Genghis Khan. He had come to the court of Genghis Khan in A.D. 1215 and had survived to become the prime minister of Ogodai, son of Genghis Khan and second khan of the Mongols. Yeliu Chutsai brought much accumulated Chinese lore to the court of Genghis Khan. He introduced the Chinese specialists who constructed the siege and investment equipment that proved necessary to bring down the walls of the great Chinese fortified cities. The scholar successfully controlled and softened the savage instincts of Genghis Khan and Ogodai and taught them that ruined vassal countries were of no value to the conqueror.

From whatever source Genghis Khan obtained the manuscript, it is certain that he used *The Art of War* as his guide in laying down the thirteen principles for the conduct of war. Many of those *principles* had been well understood by the Scythians, Kassites, Kharri, Mitanni, Avars, and Huns. The more disciplined Parthians had used these principles to build a military system that envisioned the essentials of maneuver, deception, training, expert horsemanship, and military supply.

It remained for Genghis Khan to distill the essence from the writings of Sun Tzu and produce the most awesome army in the history of the world. The thirteen principles are as good reading today as they were to the German General Staff in 1939. Founded upon the bow, they are equally adaptable to the highly specialized missile weapons of today.

These are the principles of mounted war with the bow, as practiced in the field by the armies of Genghis Khan:

1. DECEPTION. An army, when unable or unwilling to attack, must seem able and willing. An army, planning immediate retaliatory or strategic moves, must appear passive and inactive. When thought to be far away from an enemy, the army should be nearer than it seems and able, by sudden marches, to confound the enemy by an unexpected appearance. When too far away for effective action, an army should make the enemy believe it to be capable of such action. Bait should be held out to entice an enemy and *his* bait refused. Disorder should be feigned in order that an enemy will pursue rashly and be crushed. An enemy should be kept on the march, then with selected men in good positions, attack unexpectedly. With the enemy on the move, arrows expended that do not reach the target should be recovered. Pretend to be weak in order that the enemy may grow arrogant. Remember that simulated disorder requires great discipline and that simulated fear requires great courage. Simulated weakness requires great strength.

2. SITUATION. It should be remembered that the armies of Genghis Khan considered ground only in its relationship to the possibilities of positive and successful battle. His armies drew no formal lines in a struggle for mere possession of a field or valley. Position was usually refused. It was accepted only when field conditions were such that the advantages of holding the ground were obvious or when field conditions made it impossible to avoid battle. The tactical school of Genghis Khan recognized nine situations and enunciated an acceptable tactical maneuver under each situation. *Contiguous Ground.* This was the boundary area of the horde as

represented by the frontiers of the khan's empire. Whenever possible, battle was refused or avoided in these areas. The khan believed in inflicting destruction upon enemy territory, and his generals endeavored, by maneuver or deception, to lead threatening forces away from the homeland.

Tentative Ground. Such ground was represented by minor penetrations into hostile country. Under these conditions, the Mongol armies maintained close communication and kept on the move. Battle was not sought but was given if offered.

Contendable Ground. This was ground not completely favorable for battle under Mongol conditions although important in that its possession was advantageous. The army was compacted under such situations, but battle was neither provoked nor sought.

Favorable Ground. Such ground was open for extended maneuvering and, thus, favorable for action. It was not the policy of Mongol armies to block enemy movement on such ground but rather to counteract such movement by offensive maneuver in an attempt to gain mass through economy of force.

Strategic Ground. This controlled the entrances to passes, gorges, mountain trails, and main arteries of communication along national boundaries. The Mongols tried to control these areas with field garrisons detached from the main force until such time as their possession was no longer an advantage. A Mongol army was always ready to give battle to an enemy concentration at such points.

Hostile Ground. The area represented by deep penetrations into enemy country in the course of which the Mongol columns had left strongly fortified cities or points in their rear. In such circumstances, great efforts were made to strip the country of supplies to deny the shut-in garrisons subsistence. Battle was eagerly sought with any field force of the enemy encountered.

Difficult Ground. When the Mongol armies encountered forests, marshes, bogs, and difficult rivers on their line of march, the columns were closed up and movement was continued as rapidly as possible. After crossing a river, the Mongols made haste to get away from the region in order not to have a barrier in the way of maneuvers to the rear. If difficult ground was strongly held, the Mongols detoured or camped in a favorable area and invited attack. No Mongol offensive was launched in such country.

Enclosed Ground. Ground that could be reached only through narrow passes or difficult trails was avoided. If such ground was strongly held, feints and deception were the usual tactics. A typical feint would be a simulated attack upon the nearest enemy point that it was considered the enemy would hasten to defend; then, a quick return to the entrance to the enclosed ground. "Draw the enemy away from enclosed ground by feigning attack on that he holds dear."

Desperate Ground. It was a rare situation where the Mongols found themselves trapped with no escape ground available or no practical route thereto in the face of overwhelming force. In such a situation, the Mongols exercised their sole choice and fought to the last man.

3. ECONOMY OF FORCE. The end result of the maneuverability of the Mongol armies was the unusual ability to exert the influence of economy of force upon the enemy. If battle situations were favorable, the Mongols were contemptuous of enemy superiority in numbers. By means of confusing and puzzling maneuver and a seeming disorder in their ranks, they were able to conceal the spot where they intended to fight and to force an extended enemy to prepare for attack at several possible points. With such a situation set up, the Mongols were able, by great speed in maneuvering, to inflict crushing local superiority upon any point of an enemy formation.

The basic Mongol tactic was always an attempt to pit the whole against several parts. They operated on the sound basis that enemy numerical weakness resulted from the necessity for preparing against *possible* Mongol attacks. Mongol numerical superiority, locally, would then result from this necessity for the enemy to make useless preparations for prospective attacks. Never has the principle of economy of force been practiced so successfully as in the maneuvers of the Mongol horse-archers.

4. MANEUVER. The prelude to battle was more important to the Mongols than the actual shock of collision. An enemy army in the field was usually led to the slaughter (and to the place that had been designated for the slaughter) by the efficient Mongols. They were masters in the art of holding out apparent advantages to the enemy to cause him to approach; they had equal facility in the exercise of maneuvers that would make it *impossible* for the enemy

to approach. The fundamental precepts of the Mongols stipulated that their armies could march great distances without distress *if they marched in country that contained no enemy.* To gain a preliminary advantage, the Mongols would travel great distances by circuitous routes. A Mongol army moved only when there was a real advantage to be gained. "You may advance and be irresistible if you rapidly approach the enemy's weak points; you may retire and be safe from pursuit if your movements are more rapid than the enemy."

The Mongols believed that the purpose of maneuver was to turn the devious into the direct and the unsatisfactory into the satisfactory. After enticing an enemy out of the way, they would take a longer route and manage, although starting later, to arrive first at the predetermined destination. The excellence of the Mongol discipline is reflected in the ease with which the armies of Genghis Khan handled this most difficult problem of war. Movement with an army can be decisive. Movement with an undisciplined mob is dangerous. "Let your plans be dark as the night, and when you move, fall like a thunderbolt."

5. MODERATION. The Mongol generals were great practicing psychologists. They were aware that soldiers in desperate straits lose all sense of fear. Their policy was not to press a desperate foe too hard. A simulated flight on the part of the enemy did not decoy the Mongols into a pursuit. When the Mongols had a beaten enemy surrounded, they left, with seeming carelessness, an escape route; they were well aware that an enemy could be easier killed when in panic or rout than when standing in a defensive circle of hopeless resistance.

Any prolonged field operation was looked upon with disfavor by the khan as such operations exhausted the resources of the state and nullified the effects of a successful campaign. The khan warned that although there can be no stupid haste in war, cleverness was never associated with long delays. As a result, Mongol generals controlled their irritation when under great field pressure and did not rush their armies into ill-advised situations.

6. EVASION. The Mongols fought only on their own terms. When an enemy was of superior strength and in a favorable position, the Mongols always resorted to perfected evasive tactics. When con-

fronted by an enemy in great strength and imposing array, they evaded action by seeking other ground that it was necessary for the enemy to defend. Once an enemy was on the move, he could be subjected at will to the application of economy of force. "Make the enemy wonder where you are, and seeking you, find you not."

7. COMMUNICATIONS. The Mongol communications were so efficient as to be almost beyond belief. Until the advent of modern equipment no army was ever held so firmly in complete communication as were these formations of speedy horse-archers from the Gobi Desert. Battlefield communications were maintained by drums, gongs, flags, and battle lanterns. There was also communication by means of whistling arrows. Intercolumn and interarmy communications were maintained by courier detachments manned by great horsemen. The couriers of Genghis Khan had precedent over all other ranks. They could commandeer any horse if additional speed was required and even generals were required to dismount if their horses were needed. Couriers rode incredible distances in all weather. A thousand miles from a field army, Genghis Khan retained complete control and received full information.

8. FIELD CONTROL. The khan's field army commanders enjoyed unusual freedom of action. They mastered their own field problems and contrived their field successes without interference from the head of state.

9. PATIENCE. Genghis Khan exhorted his generals not to let patience delay their movements but to sublimate enthusiasm and be willing to wait for the appearance of disorder or confusion in the enemy ranks. The khan did not wish impatient or irritated armies to destroy assets of value. An attempt was usually made to keep an enemy country intact if possible, a development in Genghis Khan's later years. In the earlier campaigns, the Mongols used much less moderation, often destroying cities and killing all inhabitants if the enemy had waged a prolonged resistance. Genghis Khan learned in time that this was not profitable although the philosophy of fear was used occasionally to intimidate enemies into surrendering without fighting. The later Mongols were much more temperate in their relationships with captured populations.

History has preserved one incident of the growing Mongol tolerance toward captured people. After a year-long siege of Kai-feng-
fu, the Mongol general Subotai reported to Ogodai Khan, son of
Genghis, that when the city of two million fell, the inhabitants
would be put to the sword. Yeliu Chutsai intervened: "When the
city falls, the inhabitants will become your subjects. Among them
are able craftsmen, the best artists in the country. Will you despoil
yourself of the best of your possessions?" Under such persuasion,
Ogodai spared the people of Kai-feng-fu. Bayan, the great general
of Genghis's grandson, Kublai Khan, was noted for his humanity.

10. SPEED. The precept was that no campaign should be prolonged or indecisive, for inaction dulled weapons and dampened
ardor for battle. It was required that sharp field actions force a
decision.

Knowing that siege operations sapped the strength of an
army, Genghis Khan preferred to avoid such operations unless
there was severe military necessity that a city be taken. The sole
military weakness of Genghis Khan had been his awed respect for
walls. He could not, in his lifetime, complete the conquest of
China because of his exaggerated respect for fortifications. Ogodai, his son, was better equipped with siege materials.

11. THE ESSENTIALS OF VICTORY. He will win who knows when to
fight and when not to fight. He will win who knows how to handle
both superior and inferior forces. He will win whose army is ani-
mated with spirit in all ranks. He will win who prepared himself,
waits until the enemy is unprepared. He will win who has military
capacity and is not interfered with by the sovereign.

12. ENERGY. Genghis Khan saw energy in terms of control of a
large force to gain impact when the collision with the enemy
occurred on the field. "Energy may be likened to the bending of
a crossbow; decision to the releasing of the trigger." Energy was
momentum gained as the result of intelligent maneuver, followed
by sustained attack.

13. ESPIONAGE. The Mongols believed in foreknowledge, and they
were most efficient in gaining information about the enemy. They
classified their spies and rewarded them liberally. Enemy spies

6

First Appearances of the Bow in War

The wars of prehistory were casual and informal conflicts of individuals or small, disorganized groups of men. The first military maneuver was defensive—the act of concentrating men into a mass for mutual protection. After many centuries of loose, irregular field operations, the earliest example of welding men into a tight formation seems to have been the development of the Sumerian phalanx. This was sometime prior to 3000 B.C.

With this nascent massing of spearmen into a square, the Sumerians obtained a limited control of portions of the valley of the Euphrates to become the first military power of the Near East. They laid the foundations for civilization—language, law, and the concentration of men in cities. They developed pictographs and cuneiform characters, established the bases of astronomical observation, and were the first librarians. This civilization does not appear to have had the bow, but the Sumerians were soon to meet the weapon in the hands of the Akkadians, Semitic desert nomads who moved down the Euphrates into the territory of Sumer.

The Akkadians had no discipline in war and no apparent order of battle, but they had a weapon and they were in process of learning its effective use. The first conflicts against Sumeria were indecisive actions in which the Akkadians depended solely upon their individual skills as archers. They were simply a mob of bowmen evading the Sumerian spears with an irregular line of battle. The arrow fire of the Akkadians hurt the Sumerians massed in their phalanx but the archers were unable to destroy the massed spearmen. For a century or two, the phalanx withstood the arrow attack.

About 2500 B.C. one of the great tactical experimenters appeared
in Sumeria. This was Sargon, the first great warlord of western Asia.
Under his direction, the Akkadians developed the tactical use of the
bow and became the first great infantry-archers. Sargon introduced
elusion by maneuver and the principle of economy of force. The
Sumerians were unable to stand in formation against this application
of distant war and they fell before the Akkadian arrows. With the bow
as his major weapon, Sargon then built up the first united and powerful
nation of western Asia, and the Akkadians developed a new way of life.
They moved from their tents into cities and began to develop arts and
crafts. They have the distinction of being the first people to make use
of metal helmets in war.

Although Sargon used his bowmen as the decisive arm, he was in
many ways the father of multiple weapon war as he was the first to
develop the principles of shock and firepower into a coordinated service. He conscripted the conquered Sumerians and built them into
compact wings of spearmen to support his center of infantry-archers.
He was one of the first field commanders to become preoccupied with
the problems of vulnerable flanks and maneuver for position. This
Akkadian line of fluid offensive bowmen, operating between strong
defensive islands of spears, was the best military formation of its age
and, with it, Sargon and his successors controlled the Euphrates valley
for two centuries.

The Akkadians were probably the first people in history to place
reliance upon infantry-archers as the decisive arm.[1] They won their
country with the bow, and they continued to rely upon the bow as their
major weapon. The type of bow they used is not known. It was undoubtedly a self bow, possibly reinforced with strips of leather. As the
Akkadians understood the use of metal, the arrowheads were probably
bronze.

As a military study, the Akkadians must be credited with being the
first people to use the bow properly and effectively in an army dedicated to the offense. They waged a war of movement to as great a
degree as was possible in their era. Because they were able to evaluate
the destructive possibilities of the bow, they became the first people
in history to break the massed phalanx. This was no mean achievement; it must be remembered that the phalanx, in its various forms,
was the chief tactical problem of all of the armies of the world until its
final elimination by the fast-moving Roman legion. And the legion
itself, to be technical, was a connected series of small phalanxes, moving in coordinated unison.

In their initial defeats of the phalanx, the Akkadians showed a high degree of ability in applying the principle of economy of force by maneuver. Only by strong flanking movements and a concentration of arrow fire could these light bowmen have conquered the massed spears. Had they possessed the horse, the Akkadians might have been able to produce a truly great offensive army. Certainly, they understood the application of missiles to massed force. Their armies represented the first historical collision of firepower and infantry shock. It was many years before the equal of the Akkadians as infantry-archers appeared on the battlefields of the world.

The first people of western Asia who can be classed as great soldiers were the Assyrians, who were the terror of the Near East for centuries. Theirs was a truly great military state producing magnificent soldiers. They are sometimes credited with the introduction of the horse to warfare, but this may be an honor due the Kassites who had mastered Babylonia.[2] Certainly the Assyrians developed the military possibilities of the horse with an efficient corps of charioteers.

These people had lived in the region north of Babylonia for many centuries before they came into historical prominence. They spoke a Semitic tongue and probably were related to the Akkadians. A strange and ferocious people, hardened by unceasing war, they became the strongest military force the world had yet seen. They built up first a militia and then a standing army. In the end the demands of the military organization they created became so great that it destroyed the national economy, and the Assyrians fell.

In the beginning of their career, they fought many peoples of the Near East including the dreaded chariot warriors of the Mitanni and the roving Phoenician traders. The year 1000 B.C. found the Assyrians a great military power. They were making the transition from the Bronze Age to the Iron Age; in doing so, they became the first nation completely equipped with iron weapons.

By 700 B.C. the Assyrians were supreme in the Near East, with their capital at Nineveh. The army that had won that superiority was composed principally of archers, supported by wings of heavily armed spearmen and by far-ranging charioteers and horsemen. They had well-developed siege equipment; they also had the earliest form of tank. This dual-purpose machine, the Assyrian battering ram, was mounted on wheels and had an armored tower to house archers.

The Assyrian war tactics were similar to the *tulughma,* or surround, a hunting device used later by Genghis Khan. The charioteers and mounted archers drove the enemy inward against the massed archers and spearmen where they could be destroyed. As their tactics developed, it was seldom that an enemy tried to stand in the field against the Assyrians.

The ferocious Assyrians were centuries ahead of the military efforts of their enemies and were the first truly mobile army of antiquity. Possessing the great mobility that had been denied the Akkadians, the Assyrians were able to continue the tradition of the infantry-archer and to greatly expand the usefulness of such archers by supporting them with chariots, spearmen, slingers, and rudimentary cavalry. The horse was used in its most important military role as they experimented in the techniques and tactics of mounting an armed man.

The Assyrians were never able to develop the horsemanship necessary to exploit cavalry as a dangerous offensive arm as they were unable to adapt the bow to mounted men. Assyrian tactics were based principally upon the chariot. The upper classes rode to war in the chariot as this form of war was considered the most honorable. The chariots were usually drawn by two horses, with a third horse in reserve, attached behind by a leather thong.

None of these early adaptations of the horse to the chariot was efficient because there was no proper harness to permit the horse to properly draw the load. The development of traces and the horse collar was unbelievably slow, such items not appearing until about A.D. 900 in France.

When in pursuit of a scattered and demoralized enemy, the Assyrian archer used his bow while the horse was in full gallop. In normal offensive practice, it was preferred to halt the chariot—the horses were trained to stand—and advance a few paces on foot before discharging the arrows. The archer was protected by a shield held by his charioteer, who was armed with a spear for possible close-order combat.

The Assyrian chariot was greatly dreaded by opponents who faced it. The Bible comments on the Assyrians, "whose arrows were sharp and all their bows bent; their horses' hooves shall be counted like flint and their wheels like a whirlwind."

The Assyrian infantry made up the bulk of the army, with approximately one hundred infantrymen for each chariot and ten infantrymen for each horseman.[3] Although the chariot was spectacular, it was the corps of infantry-archers who contributed most to the Assyrian successes. Some of the infantry carried short javelins about 5 feet long, but the archers were the elite of the infantry corps.

The Assyrian archers were of three classes. The light armed bow-man was a fast-moving fighter. He was practically naked, with no equipment except his bow and arrows; his usual position was in the van of the attack. The medium-heavy armed infantry-archer was a shock trooper. He wore a coat of mail extending from the neck to the knees and a pointed, metal helmet. The third class was very heavily armed archers, also in armor, who carried a short sword in addition to the bow. Both of these classes of heavy armed archers had attendants. The medium-heavy armed archer had one attendant spearman who carried a shield. The very heavily armed archer had two attendants, one of whom rested a long wicker shield on the ground in front of the archer. The second attendant posted himself slightly in the rear and protected the head of the archer with a small, round shield.

It is interesting to note the protection the Assyrians gave their infantry-archers. Usually infantry-archers were on their own as highly expendable troops. This understanding of the vulnerability of foot-archers in defensive actions is remarkable for any age. As the Assyrian archer-attendants also wore mail, the trios formed solid and formidable islands of attack and defense. It was very difficult for an enemy to overrun Assyrian foot-archers.

In addition to the archers and attendants, there were detachments of Assyrian infantry armed with spear and sling, but these were considered auxiliaries, contributing principally to mass and numbers.

The development of Assyrian horsemen was a very early experiment in the use of the cavalry arm. The Assyrians visualized the horse-archer but they were unable to produce a truly efficient mounted bowman. To solve the problem of the management of the archer's horse, the Assyrians provided each mounted bowman with a mounted attendant who steered and controlled the horse. The cavalryman of this period rode bareback with his knees drawn up on a level with the horse's back. A relatively firm seat was obtained by gripping the base of the horse's neck with the bare knees.

During the latter period of their history, the Assyrians developed a rudimentary saddle—a simple flap or pad of leather that was bound to the back of the horse. This small improvement made the services of the mounted attendant unnecessary. The archer now let the reins lie across the neck of the horse and the animal was trained to halt and stand firm while the arrow was launched.

The bow used by these terrible warriors was probably a form of the Egyptian compound bow. Early Assyrians had a strong wood bow, but after their defeat of Egypt it is certain that these professional soldiers would have made use of the superior Egyptian equipment.[4] Whatever their type bow in 700 B.C., it was a powerful weapon. It is known to have been able to cast an arrow with great velocity for 300 or 400 yards.[5]

The Assyrian bows were of two designs. That of the foot archer was rounded and about 4 feet in length. Apparently it was a bow with great elasticity; the string was drawn until the arrowhead touched the left hand as it propelled an arrow 3 feet in length.

The Assyrian angular bow was somewhat shorter and was considered a reserve weapon. At either end of the bows were small carved knobs in the form of a duck's head, with grooves carrying the bowstring. The bows were seldom unstrung. Even when battle was not imminent, they seem to have been carried strung in a bowcase.

The arrows of the Assyrians had thin shafts of light wood, with heads of bronze or iron. The arrowhead was diamond-shaped and, for greater strength, had a raised rib down the center. The string notches were very wide, giving the arrows a peculiar appearance. The bowstring was almost as wide as the diameter of the arrow shaft. The Assyrians shot their arrows from the left side of the bow, as we do, and the bow was drawn, not to the eye, but to the right shoulder.

The Assyrians probably were the first people in history to provide uniforms for their army, which was carefully organized into companies and regiments. They had pioneer troops, equipped with hatchets, to clear the ground for chariots. Although they relied mainly upon the bow, these professional soldiers used every weapon available in their period. At a late point in their history they developed a type of lance cavalry that was useful in mopping-up operations.

Although they could, and did, take walled cities, the Assyrians were at their best in open-field battle. The stone carvings they have left of their spearmen and foot-archers drawn up in orderly double lines, with wings of cavalry and chariots, show them to have been poised and confident fighters under discipline.

The great empire of the Assyrians lasted from circa 1200 B.C. until circa 700 B.C. The ranks of the ever-growing standing army drew too great a percentage of the population from productive effort, and the Assyrians were finally conquered by a coalition of Medes and Chaldeans.[6] The revolt of the Medes reduced the Assyrians to a limited kingdom that survived until the destruction of Nineveh in 600 B.C.[7]

In this early period of experimentation with the bow, we find the weapon being accepted as a major weapon of offense. We have seen bowmen in irregular formation engaged against massed spears, and we have noticed the birth of conscious military tactics. We find already, at this early date, a denial of hand-to-hand fighting when it can be avoided. This fundamental lesson of warfare was learned by men of antiquity and then forgotten for many terrible years of war. The possibilities of long-range conflict were explored vaguely by the Akkadians and the Assyrians. They were no more eager to die in battle than are modern men. To soldiers, there is much that is repugnant about facing a spearhead or a blade at close quarters.

In their groping toward the principle of battle at a distance, these archers of antiquity found their weapon superior to their talent for war. This was usually the case throughout the history of the bow. In a few instances, the bow was developed to its full importance; in general, its application to war was limited and imperfect.

The strange and terrible Assyrians take a deservedly high place as the fathers of offensive war with an all-weapons army. They made effective, if limited, use of the horse with their chariot-archers. They explored the tactics of the mounted-bowman. This first professional army prepared the way for their pupils, the Persians, who failed to develop their heritage and who remain one of the most baffling contradictions in military history.

7

The Persians: A Study in Retrogression

The original people of Aryan stock have always been closely identified with the management of the horse. This branch of the Indo-European family had moved from their ancestral grounds north of the Caspian Sea onto the Iranian plateau. About 2000 B.C. they were settled in the highlands on the edge of the Mesopotamian and Chaldean plains. They are known to history by many names. As Parthians, they occupied Khorassan; as Medes, they moved south of the Caspian; as Bactrians, they occupied the northern highlands; as Persians, they looked down on the gulf that bears their name.

The Persians made their first tribal appearance in history as vassals of the Medes, a position they occupied until about 552 B.C. when Cyrus was able to unite the various tribes on the fringe of the Mede Empire into a new nation. Under the leadership of Cyrus, the Persians began aggressive warfare beyond their boundaries that resulted in the defeat of the Medes and the beginning of an extraordinary career of conquest. In fourteen years Cyrus conquered the great states of Lydia and Babylonia and destroyed completely the Semitic east. By 538 B.C., there was no real resistance to the Persians in western Asia.

Four years later Egypt was conquered and the Persian Empire was rounded out to include the whole civilized east from the Nile Delta to the Aegean Sea, and eastward almost to India. This great conquest, requiring hardly more than a quarter of a century, was completed in 525 B.C. It was two million square miles in area—four times as large as the preceding empire of Assyria. The vast territory was divided into twenty satrapies, united by a great system of post roads. The military road from Susa to Sardis was highly contributory, in later years, to the successes of Alexander whose armies traversed it at the rate of twenty miles a day.

The Persians were the first nation in history to be endowed with the twin heritages of advanced military tactics and almost unlimited manpower with which to execute those tactics. Their field successes, great as they were, were not consistent, for although they had far greater resources, they were not the equal of the Assyrians whose tactics they had adopted. The Persians suffered from strange flaws of temperament.

Supplementing the knowledge gained from Assyria was the cavalry experience acquired from the Medes, who had shown unusual adaptability in mastering the war use of the horse. This military inheritance had enabled the Persians to maintain supremacy in western Asia for seven centuries. The Persians were naturally an archer nation and, by original acceptance of the bow as their major weapon, they had created the greatest empire of ancient times; however, there is little evidence to support any supposition that the Persians understood the use of the bow, or the horse, in war. They present to an investigator the strangest chapter in the military history of the world. It is almost incredible that the Persians, with their lack of military talent, could ever have risen to the commanding position they occupied. This nation looms large in any discussion of the bow in war as it represents the most historic failure of that weapon in war.

Persian military history divides easily into two periods—the original successful period of early conquest followed by a later, and highly unsuccessful, experimentation with foreign arms and tactics. Each period will be considered in its proper relationship to its military history.

The Period of Early Conquest

The hard core of the Persian army at the beginning of its history was a center of infantry-archers who attempted to overwhelm the enemy with volume arrow fire of great intensity before an action could become hand to hand. To inflict this fire, they had one of the great bows of antiquity.

In conjunction with this body of foot-archers, the Persians employed harassing cavalry on either wing, supported by charioteers. One weakness of their tactical disposition was the notable lack of support or protection for their foot-archers.

During these early years the Persians were noted for their energy. Herodotus states that the three precepts taught the young of Persia were, "to ride, to draw the bow, and to speak the truth." The young Persian began his military training for war at the age of five with exercises in running, archery, and the use of the spear. At seven he was taught to ride and to accomplish the maneuvers and agilities necessary to war. He learned to jump on and off the back of his horse while the animal was in full gallop and to use the bow from the back of a running horse. The training of the Persian youth in this period was Spartan in character. The boys were exposed to heat and cold; were taught to cross rivers without wetting their equipment; to be content with a single meal in two days; and to sleep without protection in an open field in all seasons.

As a result, the Persians were excellently conditioned for war and were the most expert horsemen of the period. At the age of fifteen, the young Persian began his military service which ended at fifty. The most proficient of the recruits became members of the elite cavalry corps. The Persian cavalry of the period rode virtually unprotected by armor. They were weaponed with the bow, a short javelin, and a sword-dagger.

Although the bow was the primary weapon of the Persian infantry, the foot soldier also carried a short sword and sometimes a spear. The sword was little more than a long dagger although the spear was apparently about 6 feet in length. Occasionally, the infantry used a form of battle-ax and there were auxiliary detachments of slingers.

The Persian bow was one of high development. It was short, not more than 4 feet long and powerfully made. It was reflexed and, therefore, probably a composite with long ears that bent backward when the bow was strung. The arrows of reed—tipped with metal points—were about 30 inches in length and were launched with great rapidity and velocity.

The early Persians did not value the chariot highly as an instrument of war although they did use it. Their objection to the chariot was based on the fact that drawn by two horses and carrying two men, the vehicle was a large and highly vulnerable target to missiles. In this rejection of the chariot as a major arm, the Persians showed sound military judgment, for it was far too uneconomical in the relationship of space occupied to firepower presented.[1] In addition, the disabling of a horse could remove the entire unit from the action.

An examination of the tactical use of the Persian services reveals that the chariots, when used, were deployed in a long line in advance of the main body. Their sole function was a quick, morale-shattering attack to attempt to break enemy formations. With rare exceptions, the charioteers were unable to gain any decision against massed spearmen or determined archers. Too often the chariots went out of control when the horses were made unmanageable by missile wounds.

Directly behind the chariots, the infantry was drawn up in the center, massed into small squares, touching or nearly touching each other. These small squares could maneuver independently in the press of battle, giving full play to their bows on targets of opportunity. It was a not dissimilar formation to the fluid mass of infantry that made up the Roman legion and it was strikingly similar to the herse formation used by the longbowmen of England.

On the wings, the Persian cavalry massed in compact formations, withheld in attack until the enemy were scattered. In pursuit of a beaten enemy, each cavalryman operated as an individual with minor unit action. It may be seen that using cavalry only as individual combatants in mopping-up exercises was an unrealistic approach to the arm as it placed a great burden upon infantry-archers who were meeting the first impact of the enemy attack or defense. The Persians were also tactically weak in lack of reserves behind the battle line.

After the chariots had made their attack, the main mass of the center, the infantry-archers, began a slow advance upon the enemy but made no attempt to close with them. Instead, they took shelter behind shields and presented deliberate, aimed fire at the best effective range of their bows. In their rear, the slingers sent arching volleys of stones over the heads of the archers.

It was usually the enemy who brought this first phase of the battle to an end by charging into the Persian archers. It was then that the cavalry attempted charges into the enemy flanks. If the cavalry were able to break up the enemy attack, the battle would then become a rout with the foe in complete disorder. The weakness of the Persian assault tactics was the exposure of infantry-archers to direct enemy attack by hand-weapons soldiers. Persian support of infantry-archers was always too little and too late.

If the enemy was able to resolutely press home a charge, the

Persians considered the battle situation temporarily untenable. They had no stomach for hand-to-hand fighting nor the composition to successfully attempt this type of combat. In the face of a direct charge they gave ground immediately and abandoned the field. Such a retirement did not necessarily indicate final defeat; repelled once, they rallied again and again with their combined attack. They placed reliance in numbers to overwhelm an inferior enemy. It was wasteful war and costly in casualties.

Because of this delayed and insufficient protection for their foot-archers, the Persians throughout their history subjected that service to disproportionate casualties. Although this deployment of their infantry bowmen into a position of great peril in the front line was a tactical error, the Persians must be given credit for at least an understanding of the limitations of the bow. During the earlier period of their history, they were never decoyed into unfavorable defensive situations for the bow as they simply refused a defensive situation at all. Although sometimes overrun, the Persian bowmen attempted no defense. Insofar as it went, the Persian tactic was sound. It was denial of this same tactic against the Greeks that resulted in heavy Persian defeats against the Athenian phalanx at Marathon and Plataea. The tactical weakness of the Persian application of the bow lay in the fact that their archers had no freedom of evasive maneuver.

This, then, was the Persian army of 500 B.C., the high point of military organization in the Near East and the instrument upon which a tremendous empire was based.

With it, Darius sought new fields—his objective, the final defeat of Greek heavy infantry with a Persian force that was deficient in cavalry support. In September, 490 B.C., a Persian fleet transported an army that has been grossly overestimated at one hundred thousand men into the Bay of Marathon, near Athens, and effected a landing. Actually, the Persian army was probably forty thousand or less and the cavalry arm was very weak because of the transportation difficulty. Of this total force, the Persians fought the Battle of Marathon with not more than fifteen thousand men. The balance of the army remained on the ships in anticipation of proceeding by sea to Athens.

Under the command of Datis, a Mede, this force disembarked to begin the subjugation of Greece. On the hills overlooking the landing, ten thousand Greeks, well-trained, highly disciplined spearmen, waited to contest the march upon Athens. Before them was the Plain of Marathon, in a valley constricted by mountains, with the coast road winding away to the city.

The Greeks had the choice of position and the initiative. They chose not to contest the landing operation. For several days the Persians held to their beach position, waiting for a Greek attack that did not materialize. Wearied of the inaction, Datis disposed his force across the valley and began minor feints with his small cavalry force.

Miltiades, the Greek commander, made a careful examination of the Persian defensive position. He knew the Persian custom of massing strength in the center and therefore built up concentrations of his spearmen on the right and left into massive dispositions more than twelve spears deep, even though this meant that the Greek center was reduced to a depth of four spears. With this line of battle, he moved down to attack the Persian defensive site.

The Greeks crossed the open plain for more than eight hundred yards, directly into the Persian arrows. Herodotus tells us, "When the Persians saw the Greeks rushing down upon them, without horse or bowmen, they thought them a set of madmen, rushing to destruction."

The Persian archers, shooting from their customary protection of shields although the Greeks offered no missile attack, sent clouds of arrows into the Greek spearmen without apparent effect. The Greeks came on without wavering in a fine exhibition of sustained attack into missiles. It was spear against bow, with every tenet of war indicating that the spearmen were overmatched.

The Greek line penetrated the Persian center and recoiled as the four ranks of spearmen met the massed strength of the Persian center, but the strong Greek wings enfolded the Persian flanks. The helpless archers were enclosed within a ring of spears, their bows useless. At close range, the Persians were no match for the heavy weapons infantry. On every side the line of disciplined Greeks reformed into strong units of the famed phalanx. The Persians died swiftly on the long spears.

Six thousand Persian dead are said to have been left upon the field and the Battle of Marathon was ended. The Greek loss of less than two hundred reflects the impotence of the Persian archery. In this manner ended the most convincing defeat for the bow ever detailed by history. It seems almost incredible that men armed only with spears could have survived a half mile dash under heavy arrow fire. By all of the rules of warfare, the Greeks should have been shot to pieces at Marathon.

The Persian defeat can be explained by a valid assumption and a hard military fact. The assumption is that the Persian archery was mystifyingly bad. The men behind the Persian bows at Marathon could not have been proficient military archers. No spearmen in history, however well disciplined, could have completed that charge against expert determined archers armed with strong bows.

The hard military fact explanatory to the Persian defeat was the complete failure of the Persians to field a representative army. We have seen that the Persian tactics made mandatory the withdrawal of the archers whenever there was an attack by the enemy. Persian tactics had dictated that such pressure on Persian foot-archers should be relieved by chariot and cavalry support from the wings. None of these fundamental tactical concepts could be executed at Marathon. The infantry-archers were hemmed in within a narrow defensive position with the sea at their backs. There was no retreat possible and small room for evasive action. There was no chariot support at all. The small strength of Persian cavalry was completely ineffective as there is no evidence that any cavalry effort was made against the Greek phalanx. There is, in fact, no positive evidence of cavalry at Marathon. Datis may have landed only a few horsemen for patrol activity. There is no evidence that the static Persian bowmen made any effort to evade the Greek spears or attempt to keep extended the proper range for effective military archery.

The Persian archers elected to defend a position. The risk, if calculated at all, was too great; the Persians staked the entire issue of the battle on the premise that archers could break up, *within a few minutes,* the entire line of the Greek charge. The Greek attack, from its starting point about a half mile distant, could have reached the objective in a matter of six or eight minutes; they would have been within effective arrow range, 200 yards, for not more than two minutes. In this short space of time, the Persian archers, static in position and under great pressure, were expected to break the Greek attack. This they were unable to accomplish. Infantry-bowmen, in close quarters and unsupported, cannot defend a position. Marathon was the most convincing historical example of this truism.

No truly successful military application of the bow could be made by infantry-archers. The great weakness of the bow in battle has been that imperative necessity for *maintaining control at proper arrow range.* The bow is a weapon designed to kill at a distance and the enemy must be contained at that distance.

No sustained defense can be maintained by foot-archers unless they are disposed within a strongly fortified defensive situation behind walls or within a highly tenable field perimeter that will hold an enemy at bow range. A determined adversary, pressing home a resolute and sustained attack upon any hastily constructed field position, was in a situation that could destroy any formation of infantry-archers.

The foot-archer, under such pressure, had the option of giving way and conducting an offensive retreat; he could not survive if he stood his ground. At close quarters the archer was virtually an unarmed man. Therefore, under normal conditions of battle for a position, the infantry bowman was subject to weapon limitations that could be fatal; it usually *was* fatal.

This was the battle lesson taught at Marathon where Greek infantry, armed with the spear, exploited bad troop disposition and composition of the enemy, the nature of the terrain, and the weakness of the bow under certain battle conditions into a resounding victory.

The Battle of Marathon was a classic example of what not to do with the bow.

Eleven years later, at Plataea, the Persians had the lesson reinforced. Here, the Persian tactics and leadership were worse, if possible, than the exhibition at Marathon. The tactical situation was reversed. The Greeks stood in formation—on the defensive. The battle at Plataea presented a force stated to have been ninety thousand Persians confronting fifty thousand Greeks. The armies were separated by the Asopus River, small but difficult to ford under attack. Neither side offered battle. After several days of inaction, the Persians captured a supply train in a minor melee in the course of which the Greeks retreated before a small detachment of Persian cavalry. The Persian horses, then withdrew, and Mardonius, the Persian general, led his archers forward, double time, into the Greek line.

The archers advanced in waves, launching clouds of arrows. The archery at Plataea was apparently more effective than at Marathon. The Greek losses were heavy, but as men fell, they were replaced from the rear and the phalanx held firm. Although restive under the arrows, the Greeks maintained discipline, and when the Persians came incautiously near, the phalanx charged. When the battle was joined, the Persians were again spitted on the Greek spears. After the battle was lost, the Persian cavalry covered the disorderly retreat. There is no evidence that the cavalry supported the attack of the Persian archers. Apparently at Plataea, the Persian horse was again in small force.

The Persians again violated their own school of tactics at Plataea.

Rather than avoid the Greek spearmen, rather than keep their bowmen at arrow flight distance, and rather than attempt an erosion of the flanks of the phalanx with cavalry, the Persians chose to attack heavy infantry, in formation, with infantry-archers. The result could only be disaster for again the fundamental weakness of the bow at close quarters was manifested. Although the battle situation was the reverse of the Marathon situation, the principle remained the same. No sustained offense can be generated by foot-archers against any type of hand weapon. The offensive value of the bow decreases to zero when the action is closed.

At Plataea the Persians made their last appearance on Greek soil. Although the empire was not yet finished the Persians remained the lords of western Asia and they were to continue as a threat for another century and a half. But never again were the Persians disciples of the bow. The proper handling of the composite bow in war was a tactic the Persians were unable to solve. It is apparent that Darius and his successor, Xerxes, stunned by two crushing defeats, did not make a tactical study of the battles of Marathon and Plataea. Nor did they evaluate with realism their field performance with the bow. Neither was any study given to the terrain or the conditions of battle. It is apparent that the Persian leaders did not note that the army that had entered Greece was deficient in chariot and cavalry support for their infantry-archers. What was in the minds of the Persian kings we cannot know, but it is obvious that the two defeats caused a great overevaluation of Greek heavy infantry and that the Persians lost all confidence in missile troops. The result was a sweeping reorganization of the Persian army.

The Period of Later Reorganization

The Persians were a strange and inconsistent people. They were ever ready for improvisation and for ill-considered acceptances of foreign ideas. This was a trait that was endemic to the Persian temperament. It was reflected strongly in the use they made of the ideas of other nations. The original military organization had been borrowed, almost intact, from the Assyrians, even to the extent of duplicating the duck's head on the ears of the Assyrian bow. From the Medes, the Persians had taken the complete national costume, abandoning their own. Now after Marathon and Plataea, in defiance of their own national aversion to hand-to-hand battle, they plunged headlong into an unsuccessful imitation of Greek heavy infantry.

Within the next half-century the Persians made radical and fatal tactical experiments in the use of heavy weapons. The foot-archer and the light cavalry-archer were, to a great degree, supplanted by the heavy chariot and cumbersome mailed horsemen. The Persians made the further mistake of arming this new cavalry arm with instruments of cut and thrust. Possessing no missile or projectile weapon, this Persian cavalry, fully armored, was unable to carry out the mission of providing mobility.

With this new accent on power and shock, the pivotal center of the Persian army now became a form of phalanx, employing large numbers of mercenary Greek spearmen. Supporting this phalanx, missile troops, as represented by infantry-archers, were retained in greatly reduced numbers. The Persian chariots were never successful adjuncts to the offense because of their extreme vulnerability to enemy missiles.

As the result of this misarming of their services and the new reliance on power and shock, the Persian army now had virtually no distant offense. The failure of the Persians to develop missile cavalry brought them national disaster. They were never to be successful exponents of hand-to-hand warfare.

Although they had retained portions of the corps of light infantry-archers of the center, it is apparent from examination of their altered military commitment that the bow had been relegated to a position of secondary importance with little attention given to military archery. Darius saw, not the tactical misuse of the bow that had produced the defeats at Marathon and Plataea, but only the results, greatly magnified in his mind, that the Greeks had accomplished with heavy infantry. The Persians became preoccupied with the heavy weapons that they were temperamentally unable to master.[2]

The cavalry soldier of this later Persian period was now fully protected with armor: helmet, coat of mail, and greaves (plate armor for the legs). He no longer carried the bow. His offensive weapons became the spear and the short sword. He was, in effect, a Greek infantry man on horseback. The horses were now encased in mail with the heads guarded by frontlets or chamfrons, the necks and chests by breastpieces, and the forelegs by special armor casings. A breed of large and powerful horses came into favor and cavalry movements became slow and deliberate.

The chariots that now came into use were heavy and slow. The body stood 5 feet from the ground, on wheels of large diameter. The charioteers, two in number, were mailed to the eyes. All Persian emphasis was now concentrated on the development of shock, this in the face of their demonstrated inability with the sword and the spear.

With this composition, the Persians moved to destruction at the hands of the armored cavalry school of Alexander. War tactics were in the process of evaluation, but real military field proficiency had not yet appeared on the battlefields of the world. With this study of the preliminaries of formal war in hand, we find ourselves ready to consider the relationship of the bow to the great tactical schools that were to contend on future fields. The issues among these rival tactical schools became sharply joined. Each protagonist presented a decisive arm and relied upon that arm for victory. The relative values of missiles, shock, and mobility remained to be established, for the tentative trials of various weapons and maneuvers in the hands of Sumerians, Akkadians, Assyrians, Persians, and Greeks had not been conclusive. The seeds of tactical warfare had been planted. It remained for the three contending schools of war to contest for the harvest of victory.

Into this period of military history, circa 350 B.C., came the great armored cavalry school of Philip and Alexander of Macedonia, with its grim applications of shock and mobility. The Macedonians produced the first all-services and rounded attack of history. The school of mobile missiles that was developing in Asia had not yet enforced a demand for recognition as eastern Asia was *terra incognita* and the preliminary battles of the bow in that arena were unrecorded.

8

Macedonia: Birth of the Dragoons

In 360 B.C. Philip gained mastery over Macedonia and began the development of the most remarkable army of ancient times. As a hostage in Thebes, Philip had had opportunity to observe the great Theban phalanx in action. Unique in its employment of an oblique line of battle, this formation had shattered Sparta. Philip, a military perfectionist, was quick to note that the Theban phalanx was the best massed formation in the world. He was equally quick to note that the phalanx, subject to many weaknesses, was not the proper commitment for the decisive arm. Philip saw the phalanx, properly, for what it was: a secure pivot for the activities of a far-ranging army.

The armored cavalry school that began its development in Macedonia was an advanced evaluation of the limits of heavy infantry in phalanx and a primary appreciation of the shattering effect of proficient armored horsemen. Philip produced one of the few completely successful armies of history in his conception of pivoted heavy cavalry as the decisive arm. The field use that Philip made of heavy horsemen is an outstanding example of the principle of offense by means of the application of economy of force.

Inversely, the most intelligent use ever made of heavy infantry was also expressed by the tactics of Philip and Alexander. Each of these great soldiers understood and properly evaluated the limitations of foot spearmen and swordsmen. As the result, the Macedonian armies presented an all-around balance in shock, mobility, and missile strength that was not equaled by any other army of antiquity.

The organization of the Macedonian center, the Grand Phalanx, has been detailed elsewhere (see Chapter 5). This great mass of men, although important in the battle calculations of Macedonia, has often been overestimated in assessments of the armies of Philip and Alexander. The phalanx was highly attention-arresting because of its brutal power, but it was never considered to be the decisive arm by the Macedonian generals nor did it usually close to action until the final stages of a successful battle. The Grand Phalanx was no more than a pivot upon which Philip and Alexander hinged their decisive cavalry sweeps.

The fact that the center of the Macedonian army was composed of infantry spearmen did not limit in any manner the operations of the heavy cavalry wings. Alexander's lance horsemen were free to range widely and were not required to furnish any protection for the brutish and bristling center. Not only was the phalanx exceedingly powerful in defense in its own right, it was the most completely protected infantry in all history. In order to sustain itself under any condition of battle, the phalanx was additionally guarded by hypaspists, shield-bearing heavy infantry organized into small mobile units and able to move quickly to any threatened flank of the tortoise formation of spears. A Mecedonian army at full strength carried some three thousand of these troubleshooting swordsmen.

In the rear, a massed reserve force of spearmen stood ready to replace any losses incurred in the phalanx and thus ensure that the formation remain intact. Behind this reserve, a corps of about eight thousand foot-archers and slingers, the pelasts, were a guard against intrusive attacks on the rear by enemy horsemen or missilemen.

The decisive arm of the Macedonian army was the gigantic wings of heavy lance cavalry, the famous *hetaerae,* the Companions of Alexander. They wore helmets of brass and iron scale armor with greaves for the legs. The forepart of the horse was armored. This striking force, with its auxiliary missile light horsemen, contained an average strength of about six thousand.

Ceaselessly, on the extreme flanks, rode the hipparchies, the light cavalry bowmen who were charged with the protection of the *hetaerae* and the phalanx from missile attack. No casual strength of enemy horses or foot-archers could penetrate this shield of about seven thousand hipparchies.

This awesome display of power, speed, and missiles made up the first all-services army of history. It was a perfectly conceived offensive and defensive order of battle, with every combat contingency cal-

culated. It must still be regarded as one of the great battle compositions of history, whatever the period. This wide and deep formation
moved into battle in the oblique line that had originated at Thebes.
Philip and Alexander opened their battles with the terrible plunging
attack of massed cavalry of the advanced right wing, charging four
abreast at the gallop. This concentrated assault on the enemy left was
assisted by a broader sweep of light horse-archers in strength who
rained arrows into the enemy left rear. Under cover of this confusion,
the phalanx moved in slowly, in formation, to add its weight to the
attack.

The Macedonian left of armored cavalry in lesser strength refused
battle until the enemy had been assaulted in their center, their left
flank, and their left rear. The actions of the phalanx and the cavalry
of the left were usually mere mopping-up exercises.

The importance of missiles and cavalry in the Macedonian calculations is best illustrated by a review of the comparative strengths of the
various arms. The phalanx of the center represented about one-third
of the total strength. Heavy lance cavalry made up about one-sixth of
the total strength. Aside from the force of hypaspists, the remainder
of the composition were missile troops, afoot and mounted in about
equal proportions. The great offensive power generated by this coordinated attack was equaled by a tremendous defense in depth that the
battle order set up against enemy missiles.

Philip of Macedonia was one of the greatest military organizers
and tacticians of all time. He was not a great captain of the bow as he
considered all missiles to be minor weapons, but he must be reckoned
with in any discussion of the bow in war. Philip represented the bridge
between the loose and mobile formations of Asiatic horse-archers and
the highly formalized heavy infantry tactics of the Mediterranean peoples. Although he placed his greatest reliance upon massive wings of
armored cavalry and in the raw power of a bristling center, he was
keenly aware of the value of the bow. Philip used his light horse-
archers effectively and properly as evasive harassing agents on the
flanks and rear of the enemy.

The defensive value of Philip's archers was very great. He imposed arrow for arrow on the flanks. The phalanx was seldom, if ever,
exposed to eroding missile fire, and it was able, therefore, to perform
its function without harassment.

Not the least of Philip's talents was his ability to protect his infantry from arrows. It was a lesson that the Romans, who succeeded him,

were never to learn. Philip took full advantage of the one weakness of the bow on offense: the inability of archers to withstand any close contact with the enemy. The advancing Macedonian battle line, very wide and very deep, was an impossible target for archers. The main target, the phalanx, was buried in this great defense in depth. This broad, many-weaponed formation of battle as devised by Philip was the most effective field defense ever set up against the bow.

Although the Companions of Alexander were the elite corps and favored by the conqueror, Alexander showed an unusual respect and affection for his infantry mass. They shared prestige with the cavalry; indeed, Alexander seems not to have regarded any of his troops as expendables. The mutual respect between the various arms of his service would have been unusual in any period of history. Much of the esprit de corps can probably be traced to Philip, the organizer. Philip was a rough and practical man, approachable and with little regal dignity. He was too much a realist to have tolerated petty jealousies within the arms of his service.

This volume is not greatly concerned with Alexander. His accomplishments are familiar to all. With the inherited military organization of his father, Alexander took the Macedonians into a series of gigantic battles against Persia. A floundering giant in the last stages of military decay, Persia was formidable only because of its population of forty million, but the mere size of the adversary taxed the genius of Alexander to its limits.

In the first battle against Alexander (Granicus, 334 b.c.), the impotent Persians were unable to penetrate the Macedonian wings, and the heavy armored infantry, composed of Greek mercenary spearmen, fell victim in thousands to the Macedonian heavy cavalry assault.

At Issus, a year later, Alexander met the main Persian army under the direct command of Darius III. The Persians were in a strong position behind a stream and Alexander took a grave calculated risk in launching his attack. The horsemen of the right wing broke the Persian left, and the exposed Persian center, under attack from three sides, folded in disorder.

Alexander completed the destruction of Persia in the great Battle of Arbela in 331 b.c. The Persians, hopelessly deficient in tactics, called upon an outworn and outmoded instrument of war when they launched a chariot attack. Against a Persian force, the number unknown but probably not more than one hundred thousand, Alexander led a force of forty-seven thousand, supported by slingers and archers.

A tremendous battle developed on the Macedonian right wing; the issue was in doubt in the early stages when it seemed that the mere mass of the Persians might prevail. But the archers of Darius were unable to penetrate the Macedonian defense in depth. The phalanx, undisturbed by missile fire, moved in to crush the Persian center.

As the phalanx advanced, Darius launched his scythe-wheeled chariots but Alexander's light archers destroyed the drivers of the unwieldy vehicles; the few that reached the phalanx passed harmlessly through intervals opened in the formation. When the Macedonian center struck the main Persian concentration, the last great power of western Asia fell.

This Macedonian line of battle, as conceived by Philip, was centuries superior to its period of history. Philip was the first and probably the greatest exponent of the school of mounted shock. He presented a proportioned and coordinated all-arms, all-services attack as well as a complete defense against every weapon available in his period.

Philip stopped the bow.

The Macedonian army, wide in front and exceedingly mobile on the wings, had the power to gain and to hold the initiative. An enemy could not evade battle. Philip shares with Genghis Khan the distinction of having created an invincible army. Each proved that the only defense against missiles was mobility and countermissiles. Each defeated enormous opposing armies with small and active forces and with negligible casualties. The Macedonians might be considered the first people to have used the horse with complete effect in war.

The greatness of the Macedonian army is sometimes obscured by the fact that Macedon was later conquered by Rome. After the death of Alexander, the country was torn by internal revolutions and a scramble for power that resulted in the ultimate division of Alexander's empire into three segments. The small segment that opposed the Roman legion had been erected upon the ruins of Philip's original territory and it was able to place hardly more than thirty thousand troops in the field. Of the formidable military establishment that had been created by Philip, only the phalanx of the center remained to oppose Rome. Macedonia was no longer able to bear the expense of the great armored cavalry wings that had been decisive in the days of Alexander.

In these later battles of heavy infantry against heavy infantry, the rigid phalanx had been unable to withstand the fluid attack of the great

Roman swordsmen of the legion. Rome had destroyed the vestigal resistance of Macedonia with victories at Pydnia and Cynoscephalae.

A comparison of the Macedonian phalanx and the Roman legion should not be made. A comparison of the Macedonian and the Roman military systems is another matter. To evaluate the military proficiency of the two schools, the decisive arm of Rome, the legion, should be compared with the decisive arm of Macedon, the heavy armored cavalry.

The two systems never met in battle.

This Macedonian development of heavy cavalry was to have a permanent effect upon all future horse soldier experiments in Europe. The Companions of Alexander became the pattern upon which the European dragoon system and tradition was founded. Six centuries after Alexander, prototypes of his horsemen, the lance-bearing cavalry of the Goths, destroyed the Roman legion at Adrianople. Two centuries after Adrianople, the Byzantines were bolstering a faltering and beset empire with heavy cavalry supported by Hun missiles.

The Byzantines, in turn, were to fall before the European armored knights. This dragoon school of Philip and Alexander persisted in Europe for more than seventeen centuries until the mailed knight had his usefulness destroyed forever in the fourteenth century by English arrows during the Hundred Years' War.

Even the disappearance of the knight in plate mail did not destroy the dragoon tradition, for dragoons were the cavalry commitment of Europe and the United States until the twentieth century, when the horse soldier exited forever. The traditions of Alexander endured for twenty-four centuries.

The armored cavalryman had a long and glorious history until his military efficiency was blunted and his useful career ended by the arrows of the English longbow and the brine-tempered missiles that were propelled by the composite bows of the archers of Genghis Khan. Unfortunately, when no longer a military threat, these slow horsemen remained as a ritual and show force of war.

Alexander's Companions had many successors in the eighteenth and nineteenth centuries, and they were much less successful. . . .

9

The Problem of Mounted War

We know little about the earliest battles between the mounted men of earliest history and prehistory as practiced by the Medes, the Kharri, the Mitanni, and others of the people of Asia Minor who first conquered the horse. The early battles between the Chinese and the Tartars are equally obscure. It is certain, however, that many, if not all, of these earliest peoples who fought on horseback were merely armed, mounted men and not cavalry at all. They were capable of great movement, but they had small understanding of the principle of maneuver. The early formations of horsemen were merely armed bands.

The term "cavalry" requires more definition than military writers have indicated. In the strict sense, cavalry is a highly disciplined armed force, operating from horseback in calculated maneuver. Furthermore, cavalry is in no sense a glamour arm; the demands that are made upon true cavalry are the most severe of any service. Few nations have been willing to pay the price that is demanded from a successful cavalry campaign. The nations of the world that have possessed a true cavalry arm can be numbered, almost, on the fingers of one hand. The Huns at one period of their history had cavalry. The Parthians developed true concepts of cavalry. The Saracens of Saladin were a tenacious cavalry. The early Byzantine experiments produced cavalry but the tactics were applied by Asiatic Huns in the Byzantine service. The Mongols and the kindred Tartars and Turks produced a cavalry arm. There the list seems to end.

It is noticeable that all of these people were Asiatics—all realistic and battle-hardened peoples who were willing to pay the price. It is noticeable also that many of the Asiatic tribes of horsemen cannot be classified as cavalry. The Magyars were mere armed, mounted bands with no discipline and little tenacity. The mysterious Scythians were a borderline experiment in horse warfare. Too little is known of the Cimmerians, Kharri, Kassites, Avars, Phrygians, and others to rate them as more than armed bands.

The most noticeable omission in any consideration of nations producing authentic cavalry is the lack of mention by historians of the fact that no Western nation ever possessed such an arm. No nation of the Western world ever produced cavalry as the decisive arm. Cavalry of the European and American areas were show arms in minor force. The horses were selected for conformation and not for the essential stamina necessary to cavalry war. The riders were too often selected on a basis of their genteel breeding, for cavalry in Europe was the branch of favored men; its prime use was as escort for generals and for a gaudy appearance in parades. An English cavalry officer of the Napoleonic Era summed up the European attitude toward cavalry very completely when he said, "The purpose of cavalry in warfare is to give tone to what otherwise would be a vulgar brawl."

In no European army was cavalry numerous, decisive, or even important. Horses and riders were pampered—neither had the stamina or the fiber to meet the stern demands of the service. As a matter of record, European cavalry was never called upon at any time to meet these stern demands. European cavalry had operated from supply bases that were under the protection of infantry armies. Fighting their minor skirmishes on the fringes of these infantry armies they were in the field for only a few hours. Their wounded were retrieved by infantry stretcher-bearers under elaborate flags of truce and well-accepted conventions of war; they fought enemies who observed truces and did not slaughter wounded. Seldom had they carried rations or burdensome supplies of ammunition. They had never been exposed to the chill problems of logistics, for they had conducted no prolonged or extended mounted operations. As the result, European cavalry had had no capacity for serious extended action. In battle, they had been committed to heroic and showy charges into cannon fire— sabers swinging and lances leveled.

In contrast to these casual dragoon tactics of the Western world, the Asiatic peoples had approached the problems of mounted war with great realism. Their horses were animals of stamina and speed and were not subject to pampering. The animal was capable of carrying a rider for incredible distances, and the riders were required to perform superb exhibitions of horsemanship and endurance in the saddle. Asiatic cavalry could take the field on campaigns that reached over degrees of latitude and longitude and were months or years in duration. They needed no supply base nor supply train. Wounded were strapped to their saddles and the advance continued. The riders were androids in the saddle—with a chill ferocity and an inhuman endurance. They were willing to pay the price. If necessary, they rode eighty miles in a day—and arrived at their destination able and willing to give battle. They welded horse, man, and bow into a dreadful composite picture of savagery, iron endurance, discipline, and tenacity.

The greatest contrast between Eastern cavalry and Western dragoons was the dictum in Asia that a mounted man stayed on his horse whatever the battle situation. It was recognized that the principles of cavalry could not be applied by dismounted men. The mobility and evasiveness that made cavalrymen with bows effective and deadly in offense could be as well applied to provide a safe withdrawal from an overmatched situation. As long as the horseman was mounted, he was dangerous; dismounted, he was subject to grave weaknesses. There was no situation in the Asiatic concept of cavalry that called for the establishment of a defensive perimeter to be held by dismounted cavalrymen. Whenever an advance was contained, causing a deterioration of the situation that indicated defensive action, the situation was solved by evasive maneuver or orderly mounted retreat. There was no loss of readiness for effective battle.

The Asiatics made punishing demands upon horse and rider. It was recognized that cavalry, to complete its mission properly, had to push through to a decision without regard to the punishment inflicted upon the rider and his mount. It was mandatory that cavalry have the stamina to push through a relentless and sustained pursuit—across degrees of longitude and for a duration of months, if necessary.

The greatest weakness of mounted war with missiles was in the lack of cohesion that was always an inherent possibility in any formation of restless horsemen. The constant invitation and availability for free movement tended to destroy their effectiveness. The leadership demands of light missile cavalry were very severe and a continual evaluation had to be made of the principle of maneuver as opposed to mere movement. Lacking in shock power, these Asiatic mounted bowmen could enclose a column under attack but had little ability to anchor such a column.

A man with a horse under him is by nature restless, reckless, and, to an extent, suspended in a private world of free motion. Such a force of mounted men requires strong leadership and stern discipline. It was for that reason alone that many of the tribes of Asiatic horsemen degenerated into mobs of armed, mounted men without the ability to inflict the true principles of cavalry war upon an enemy. The problem had been to hold them as a force in being, subject to orders, without curtailing their great value as far-ranging skirmishers and foragers. It was always possible that mounted troops, flushed with a field success, would get out of hand and out of control during the process of mopping-up and looting operations.

Light missile cavalry was a tenuous force, lacking the stability of infantry or the power of armored cavalry. The horse-archers were not a perfect solution as a force for inflicting war. They could be, and sometimes were, defeated when terrain and other conditions of battle were not favorable. Light missile horsemen without tenacity were useless for they could sting only from a distance.

The adaptation of the horse to archer-riders was a severe problem.

Whatever his weapon, the horseman needed a firm seat and this was provided by the stirrup. The invention of the stirrup was one of the most important gifts to man, and it was one of the last articles of horse equipment to be provided.[1] As early as 850 B.C. the Assyrians had constructed a crude wooden platform to support the foot, an improvement that did not accomplish much in gaining a firm seat. Macedonian cavalry rode with no form of the stirrup except a modification of the Assyrian platform. As late as 53 B.C. the Parthians, the greatest horse soldiers of the era, were still riding by gripping the necks of the horses with the bare knees.

The first real support for the foot seems to have been a leather sling employed by the Scythians as early as 300 B.C. For all practical purposes, this was a true stirrup, and it contributed greatly to the military successes of the Scythians. The Scythian improvement did not greatly influence other early riders—the leather sling does not seem to have been adapted by other horsemen. This was most unusual as the Scythians were a nomadic people and it is remarkable that this improvement in horse furniture went so unnoticed.

The true stirrup is believed to have been invented by the nomads of Inner Mongolia and appears to have been carried from that country

10

The Carthaginian Application of Cavalry

The first severe test of the Roman school of heavy shock infantry, as expressed by the legion, was offered by the remarkable armies of Carthage. The term "Carthaginian army" is actually a misnomer as the armed force of this city-state of traders and navigators was a heterogeneous collection of mercenaries who were bound by no ties of patriotism to the city of Carthage. The military effort of Hannibal is therefore all the more remarkable, for never in the entire history of war has a general accomplished so much with so little. Hannibal must be rated as one of the great military geniuses of all time; his conduct of the Second Punic War with Rome expressed that greatness.

The Situation

Carthage, although a formidable threat to Rome, was no more than an isolated city-state with little contributing territory other than widely scattered trading posts. The total city population of 900,000 was virtually contained within the walls. The Carthaginians endlessly sailed the seas to support that population. By contrast, the Punics were traders and merchants, with little time for war. They are one of the rare cases in history where a population was almost completely urban.

The Carthaginian senate trusted their field armies so little that they employed senate deputies with each army in the manner of the

Russian commissars who accompanied Stalin's armies in World War II. In the midst of a serious war, the Punic oligarchs, jealous of Hannibal, refused to send aid to support the campaign in Italy. We can find no other case in history where a state so consistently refused to support its army in the field. Hannibal's minor reinforcements, from time to time, came from Spain.

The contention with Rome was based upon the fact that Carthage controlled northwest Africa, the islands of the Mediterranean Sea, and the commerce of the West. As in the case of Parthia later in Roman history, this African city of traders was too large to sit comfortably on the Roman frontier. Three severe wars were necessary to resolve the situation to the benefit of Roman aspirations in the Mediterranean.

The Roman Military System—260 B.C.

The school of Mediterranean tactical employment of heavy shock infantry reached its highest development in the Roman legion. All future proponents of the infantry arm were to be heavily influenced by the composition, equipment, and tactical attack of the legion. The Romans were latecomers to the historical scene, but their development was rapid. As late as 400 B.C. Rome was a small, unwalled city subject to barbarian raids. A century and a half later, only Carthage was a rival to Rome in the western Mediterranean.

The aggressive military expansion of Rome was expressed in the field by their famous legion. For a century following the founding of the Roman Republic, circa 509 B.C., the military establishment followed the pattern of simple mass that had been developed by the Greeks. Little is known of the Roman army of this period other than the fact that a type of phalanx was the field commitment.

The nascent legion of this early period was a mass composed of sixty centuries of heavy infantry, supported by twenty-five centuries of light auxiliaries. This formation proved adequate while Rome was establishing her supremacy on the Italian peninsula and against the Greeks, but mountain warfare against the Samnites exposed the inflexibility of the phalanx legion when it maneuvered in rough country. During this period Rome was also exposed to severe and recurrent raids from other barbarian tribes and the phalanx legion was unable to trap and contain these invaders at the frontiers. Rome was sacked and burned by Gallic tribes in 387 B.C.

The *manipular* legion was the first solution accepted in the solving of this military problem. This legion formation was a jointed modification of the phalanx, coupling mass and power with greater mobility and maneuverability. The first line consisted of ten *maniples*, closely spaced. Each maniple was a formation six men deep and twenty men wide. This front line, called the *hastati*, was manned by strong young recruits newly transferred from the corps of slingers. They were the expendables of the legion, meeting the first shock of the enemy. The second line, the *principes*, was formed in the same manner into ten maniples, spaced according to battle conditions, from 6 feet to 250 feet behind the first line. The third line, with the same space interval, was made up of ten maniples called *triarii*—the elite of the legion. The maniples of the triarii were only half the strength of the first two lines, being six men deep and ten men wide. The triarri were the veterans of many campaigns and were held out of action until the moment of decision.

Each man in the first and second lines carried three light casting spears, the hasta, and a heavier hurling spear, the pilum. All troops carried the gladius, the bronze thrusting sword of the legion. The third line of battle carried a heavy pike, 10 to 14 feet long, and a supply of darts or small javelins. The long pike was not hurled but retained until close action necessitated the use of the sword.

As may be seen from the above description, the manipular legion was composed of twenty maniples of 120 men each and ten maniples of 60 men each, for a total force of 3,000 men. The auxiliary support varied greatly. The usual auxiliary strength was about 1,200 slingers and 300 cavalry for a total striking force of about 4,500 men.

No more than an approximation of the tactics of the manipular legion may be attempted. There is no satisfactory description of this legion in battle but the drill regulations, as detailed by Livy, indicate that the formation was capable of precision maneuver. The training of recruits was very severe and the discipline was stern.

It is believed that normally the auxiliary troops opened the battle with a javelin and dart or sling attack that persisted until the missiles were expended or the interval between the legion and the enemy had been lessened. The auxiliaries then retired through the ranks of the legion to a post in the rear. At a distance of ten to twenty paces from the enemy, the hastati then cast their javelins and pilums and secured momentum by closing on the run with the sword. If the battle conditions were favorable, the two front lines, the hastati and the principes, passed and repassed each other in waves in a leap-frog maneuver, casting and recovering their missiles until the sword rush was made.

Tactically, the manipular legion had developed a flexible phalanx, divided crosswise and lengthwise into thirty mutually supported maniples, each able to apply swift and concentrated pressure upon an enemy line. In the earlier stages of the development of the manipular legion, the maniples do not seem, however, to have engaged in much independent action.

By 200 B.C., though, the manipular legion had opened up and the individual maniples became exceedingly adaptable to varying conditions of battle. They were able to change front with ease or to shift rapidly to another part of the field to fight unsupported. It was this factor that gave the legion its great edge over the Greek phalanx.

When engaged against *less maneuverable and less disciplined troops,* the manipular legion was able to apply crushing local superiority at any focal point of attack, even when outnumbered. From their basic three-line position, the legion could develop single wings, double wings, and heavy pressure points in a variety of attack formations and special patterns. They could wedge; they could encircle; and they could rapidly extend their flanks. The Roman battle line could be extended at will by springing the second-line maniples to the right and the third-line maniples to the left. They could, with equal facility, regroup into a compact column of march or a dense mass for defensive purposes.

The Carthaginian Military System

The battle strength of Carthage rested upon superior field leadership and a highly developed conception of missile cavalry in support of infantry mass. The Carthaginians were able to apply a decisive missile cavalry arm against Rome and, with it, they quickly exploited the fundamental weaknesses of the manipular legion.

As Hannibal operated in an era when shock was held to be supreme, the essentials of his army composition are sometimes obscured by an assumption that he was a proponent of heavy infantry. Actually, Hannibal followed the precepts of Alexander as faithfully as his resources would permit. The main striking force of Hannibal was heavy cavalry equipped with the lance and the bow, and this force was supported by light and active horse-archers. The heavy infantry of Carthage was employed as a pivot for the operations of the mounted troops. The shock this heavy infantry generated was applied after the legion had been overrun, or, at least, greatly eroded by cavalry, or badly cut up by arrow infliction.

Hannibal's heavy infantry was only relatively strong. A point that should be remembered is that a considerable portion of the infantry strength of Hannibal was not shock infantry. His African foot soldiers, sometimes as much as 30 percent of his total strength, carried the lance and the bow and did not engage at close quarters until the battle had reached the point of decision.

The Field Actions

The First Punic War, in 260 B.C., quickly established the pattern of the conflicts. Xanthippus cut the legions of Regulus to pieces with an elephant corps and wings of efficient cavalry-lancers and -archers. One interesting sidelight of these campaigns concerns the possibility that the Carthaginians had tamed the African elephant, a feat that many believe to be impossible today. After severe reverses, Rome raised new legions and persisted in the field until a Roman fleet destroyed the Carthaginian navy in a great battle at the Aegusa Islands in 241 B.C. Carthage, deprived of food and trading opportunities, signed a disadvantageous peace with the armies in the field intact and victorious.

The Second Punic War began in 218 B.C. with Hannibal's incursion into Italy. In that year the great Punic general departed from Carthage with a force of eighty-two thousand infantry, light and heavy, and twelve thousand cavalry to attempt the perilous crossing of the Alps. Mountain defensive actions and exposure of the army to the elements cost Hannibal severe casualties and he arrived in Italy with a force that has been estimated at sixty thousand.

Almost immediately he collided with an army led by Scipio. Hannibal decoyed this Roman force into a pass near Ticinus and destroyed it with a vigorous cavalry attack. A circling assault struck the legion and turned its flanks. All but ten thousand of a Roman consular army of thirty thousand were killed.

A few months later, Hannibal ambushed and trapped the legions of Flaminius at Lake Trasimino and annihilated them with a powerful cavalry and missile attack. All the Romans were killed except six thousand who were captured on the following day.

In December, 218 B.C., Hannibal's army had been reduced to forty thousand by the previous battles and minor skirmishes when he met a Roman army of four legions with auxiliaries at the Trebia. In this engagement, the opposing forces were of equal strength. Hannibal was inferior in infantry but his strong and well-disciplined cavalry enveloped the Roman wings after dispersing the inferior Roman horse. The legion was compressed on its vulnerable flanks, and only ten thousand of the Romans escaped.

The pattern was consistent and deadly. The legions huddled like herded cattle under the broad offensive sweeps of Hannibal's horsemen. His mounted archers and foot bowmen, supported by the Carthaginian infantry pivot of shock soldiers, shot the legions to shreds before the infantry and lance cavalry closed in for the kill. The days of Alexander were relived on the fields of Italy where heavy horsemen and mounted- and foot-bowmen demonstrated and pointed up the inadequacy of Roman shock infantry in an open field. The great swordsmen of Rome, a century or more behind the current military developments, died by the thousands with no opportunity to come to grips with the enemy except in the mopping-up stages of a lost battle. Hannibal toyed with the Roman principle of virtually unsupported shock infantry, enforcing the premise that the horse and the bow were decisive and dreadful implements of war.

For two years Hannibal raged back and forth across the Italian peninsula, looting and destroying at will while the Romans were renewing their capacity for war with the frenzied enlistment of new legions. Roman mothers threatened disobedient children with the dread word "Hannibal." Not until 216 B.C. were the Romans able to offer another effective field force to horrendous slaughter.

At Cannae, in 216 B.C., Rome suffered one of the greatest disasters in its history. Hannibal's tactics at Cannae have been a textbook study for centuries. The battle is too well known and too well documented to warrant more than a mention in this volume. A book of this broad scope must content itself with a sampling of the military campaigns of many peoples. It will be sufficient to state the situation and the result at Cannae.

A Roman army composed of fifty-five thousand heavy infantry, eight thousand light infantry, and six thousand cavalry was at Cannae. It was supported by two fortified camps, each containing thirteen hundred heavy infantry and thirty-seven hundred light infantry, for a total Roman strength of seventy-nine thousand men. Against this force, Hannibal offered thirty-two thousand heavy infantry, eight thousand light infantry (mostly archers), and ten thousand cavalry—totaling about fifty thousand men.

The action began when the Carthaginians deployed in a single arched line with the wings refused. When the armies collided, the Carthaginian center was badly pressed by the legions. The highly effective Carthaginian cavalry then drove in against the flanks of the legions in the rear while the light missile troops showered arrows into the Roman position. All discipline was lost in the legion as the maniples tried to repel attacks from three fronts. The manipular legion proved to be lacking in the maneuverability necessary to re-form and change fronts under the combination of shock applied against them and the heavy arrow fire. All but three thousand of the Roman infantry were killed. The performance of the legion was so feeble that the soldiers who escaped became objects of national scorn in Rome. Hannibal suffered casualties of six thousand, the majority of these incurred in the early stages of the battle when the thin line of Carthaginian heavy infantry engaged the legion hand to hand.

The war was to go on for twelve more years after Cannae, in the course of which Rome prevented the union of Hannibal with Hasdrubal with a victory at the Metaurus. Caius Claudius Nero, the most capable Roman general of the war, had marched his legions 250 miles in seven days to cut off Hasdrubal at the Metaurus. Hasdrubal was bringing infantry replacements to Hannibal from Spain and he had no cavalry. Because the deficiencies of the manipular legion had been under investigation in Rome, Nero was supplied with strong cavalry wings. As usual, the Roman cavalry was inferior in quality, but having no Carthaginian cavalry in opposition at the Metaurus, they were able to collaborate successfully with the legion and win a great victory. It is astounding that this positive demonstration of the virtues of cavalry against heavy infantry made so little impression on the Roman commanders. The Romans did make use of cavalry in the final battle of the war, but they were never able to develop a serious cavalry strength that could decide the issue under normal battle conditions. Their success at the Metaurus had been based upon the lack of Carthaginian cavalry. Nero lost eight thousand killed, but the Carthaginian infantry was completely destroyed. This was the sole Roman victory of the Second Punic war until the final battle when Hannibal, all resources gone and abandoned by his own country, was defeated.

At Zama, in 202 B.C., much the same condition existed as at the

Metaurus, and Hannibal closed his military career with a defeat that lost the war. His military potential had been so weakened by unreplaced losses in his cavalry corps that he was unable to field a representative Carthaginian army. The Romans threw cavalry attacks against the Carthaginian rear as maniples of the legion operated independently against the weak Carthaginian center of heavy infantry. The result was the second Roman victory of the war and the end of the conflict.

The Third Punic War saw no field action. Carthage surrendered after a savage three-year siege. The site of the city was plowed under by the Romans and Carthage was not occupied again until a desperate Rome invited the Vandals to set up an African empire in A.D. 475.

The field operations of this Carthaginian army of the Second Punic War were probably the most remarkable exhibitions of sustained occupation of armed enemy country in the history of war. With very little support from Carthage and with no reinforcement save occasional levies of Gauls, Hannibal conserved an army in Italy for fourteen years. He destroyed four Roman armies and kept 200,000 Romans in the field while the republic desperately avoided battle and sought to quiet the alarm of the populace. The Carthaginian army moved at will, sometimes within sight of the walls of Rome. It is notable that Hannibal made no attempt to storm the city. He adhered to the sound military principle that the mission of an army is to destroy the field forces of the enemy.

The Roman legions earned no plaudits for their field performances against Hannibal. Of seven major battles detailed in history in the three wars, Rome was defeated in five. The maneuvers of Hannibal left southern and central Italy a shambles from which they never fully recovered during the life of the Roman Empire. The losses in manpower and resources were too severe to have made profitable the elimination of Carthage as a commercial rival.

It had been an expensive war by a military organization that had shown fatal flaws. Only the tremendous economic strength of Rome had made possible survival from the continuous disasters of the Second Punic war. The Carthaginian force opposing Rome on Italian territory, including the lost army of Hasdrubal and the reinforcements from Gaul, had not exceeded a grand total of 150,000 troops. In the principal actions of the Second Punic War and in incidental small engagements, Hannibal killed 250,000 Romans. To oppose this small, virtually unsupported, army, Rome placed an additional 200,000 troops in the field during the fourteen years Hannibal was raging across the peninsula. The services of almost 500,000 Romans were required to quell the Carthaginian. The weakness of the legion was never more completely exposed than in these campaigns of the Second Punic War.

Today, we have as the sources of information of these wars only the biased Latin accounts. No Punic records survive save one. That was the field efficiency record of Hannibal's armies that could not be minimized by even the most biased Latin chronicler.

11

The Parthians versus Rome

This was an important war, and it has not received proper attention from the military historians. The Parthian series of wars with Rome were probably the most significant conflicts in the whole period of military history between 3000 B.C. and the beginning of the Christian Era. They were significant and history-altering for many reasons:

1. These wars marked the first full-scale meeting of heavy infantry and determined and efficient horse-archers. For the first time in history, the relative merits of the two schools could be objectively assessed.

2. These wars marked the first appearance in history of an all-cavalry army. The Parthians were committed entirely to the principle of distant war with mounted missiles.

3. These wars stopped the eastward expansion of Rome in its tracks. The Roman consuls of this period were desirous of emulating Alexander with an extension of Roman influence to India.

The Parthian experiment represented the first check to expansion ambitions and the first Roman loss of a major war. That Rome lost this war is not seriously questioned. However, from the military point of view, it might be adjudged a stalemate. Politically and prestigiously, it was humiliating defeat, for Rome purchased a peace. Their eastern trade routes were sealed. Rome never recovered from the Parthian wars. The magic was gone; it was never recovered. Rome won many little wars against minor resistance after the Parthian wars but always the legions suffered severely before the issue was gained.

The Situation

In 55 B.C. Crassus obtained the consulship of Rome and began immediate preparations for taking the legions across the Euphrates in an all-out assault on Parthia. It was his announced intention to eliminate Parthia, whose territory had expanded to reach the Pamirs on one side and the Euphrates on the other—to include Persia, a part of Afghanistan, much of Turkey in Asia, and a part of what is now Russia. Parthia, expanded to an area of eight hundred thousand square miles, had become too large to rest comfortably on the eastern frontier of Rome. This projected conquest of Parthia was considered to be only a minor part of the great Roman ambition. It was intended to take the legions into India in a great conquest of the East.

It was recognized in Rome that the attempt on Parthia would be a full-scale war of possible serious proportions and not a mere border dispute.

The Roman Military System—55 B.C.

As this was the first major historical test of the unsupported bow as a decisive weapon against heavy infantry shock, it seems necessary to devote a few paragraphs to the conflicting military systems that met on the plains of Parthia. In the preceding chapter, we noted the adaptation to war that the Romans made of the manipular legion. We are now ready to consider the modifications that were expressed in the *cohort* legion. This was the creation of Marius and the instrument of Julius Caesar; it represented the highest development of men in mass that the heavy infantry of antiquity achieved, coming into existence as the result of the severe reverses that had been sustained by the manipular legion in the wars with Carthage.

The reorganization of the legion divided it into ten cohorts, each retaining its maniples and each capable of more severe independent action. Now each cohort was to control its own wing of cavalry in pursuance of the lesson learned at the Metaurus.

The cohort legion formed up with the specially distinguished *Millarian Cohort* on the right, with a strength of 1,105 infantry soldiers. The other four first-line cohorts had each a strength of 555 men. The five cohorts of the second line also had strengths of 555 men. The fifth or first-line left flank cohort had carefully selected men as did the third, in the center of the first line; the sixth, on the rear right flank; the eighth, in the rear center; and the tenth, on the left rear flank. The sixth cohort had preference over all others except the first, as it occupied a position directly behind the Eagle and the Images of the Emperor that were carried by the Millarian Cohort in the days of the empire.

Official auxiliaries of this legion were 132 heavy cavalry for the first cohort and 66 heavy cavalry for each of the other nine cohorts. In addition, the legion had light missile troops in varying strengths. The cohort legion thus had a field strength of 6,100 foot soldiers and 726 cavalry, plus missile troops.

Tactically, the cohort legion operated in much the same manner as the earlier manipular legion. Greater independent action was possible but the assault tactics seem to have been essentially the same. Each cohort soldier carried five small throwing jevelins in the concavity of his shield. Two other javelins of heavier weight—the verriculum and the pilum—were retained until the range shortened to 10 or 15 yards. They were then cast and the action was closed as usual—with the sword. The attack was supported by overhead casts of missiles from the auxiliaries in the rear.

The battle order was greatly extended and loosened. The hastati of the first line occupied a normal front of 400 yards. The second line, the principes, formed 250 feet behind the hastati, and they were, in turn, supported by the triarii an additional 250 feet to the rear. In action, the triarii rested upon one knee as they waited to reinforce the front line.

The triarii now carried two missile javelins in addition to the long pike. All troops carried the sword for the final melee. In the time of Caesar, the sword had been greatly improved by imports of fine steel blades from Spain. At a very early date these blades from the region near Toledo were approaching the reputation they later enjoyed. The limitations of bronze had dictated the length of the old Roman gladius as bronze is unreliable in a sword more than 20 inches in length. With the introduction of the newer steel blades, the length of the sword remained the same as the method of its use was unchanged. The Romans used the sword solely as a thrusting weapon with an upward stroke beneath the shield of the enemy. For that type of stroke, the 20-inch blade was a desirable length.

A legion was commanded by a *legatus legionis*, assisted by as many as six young *tribunes* and by the *ordinarii*, the division officers. Responsibility for the execution of the field orders and for troop discipline rested largely with the sixty *centurions,* who were remarkable combinations of first sergeants, company commanders, and platoon leaders.

The insignia of the legion, the Roman Eagle, bore the inscription, *Senatus Populusque Romanus,* "The Senate and the People of Rome." Each cohort carried its own dragon insignia, and there was an ensign for each centurion. Battle communications were maintained by use of the cornu and the tuba and by battle drums and signal flags.

The individual legionary was heavily laden with arms, cooking equipment, armor, and food supplies. The romantic picture of precise lines of swordsmen on the march would be marred could we have an actual view of the legion in column. The variety of equipment carried by these soldiers was amazing. The weight of the arms of the Roman soldier has been estimated at 60 pounds. In addition to his arms, the soldier carried stakes for palisading the camps, shovels, axes, and other utility equipment.

The marching records of these laden infantrymen are among the greatest in history. On several occasions, Caesar marched his legions fifty miles in a day. The average daily march was eleven miles although the legion was trained for, and capable of, a march of twenty-four miles, quickstep, in five hours, or twenty miles ordinary step in the same time interval. As a matter of comparison, the average European army in the sixteenth and seventeenth centuries marched an average of six or seven miles a day and did not prepare nightly secure camps as was the custom of the Romans.

The soldier of Caesar's time was a well-paid professional fighting man. His pay scale in actual currency was not exceeded by any modern army until very recent times. The private soldier earned 225 *denarii* a year, pay possibly equivalent to $25 per month in our money, perhaps more. The denarius of Caesar's time would have a buying power of possibly as much as fifty cents today. Caesar's soldiers may have been the highest-paid warriors of history. In addition to his cash emolument, the Roman soldier received victory bonuses, special grants from generals, and plundering and slave-gathering privileges. He was allowed four measures of wheat a month—equivalent to four pecks. He was able to purchase additional food supplies from the private markets at a special discount of 10 to 25 per cent of the market price. Caesar's soldiers were also awarded land grants when they completed their military service. It was theoretically possible to retire in some opulence, and private soldiers sometimes rose to high positions—even that of emperor. If the legion soldier could survive the thrust of a

Goth's sword in the forests of Germany and the other fields where Rome fought, he could look forward to a fairly secure future.

In battle, the *impeditus,* the foot soldier, was well protected by a cuirass of metal scales sewn on a heavy leather jacket that was equipped with metal shoulder pieces. He wore a bronze helmet and sometimes a greave on the right leg, the left leg being protected by his shield. In cold weather, the Roman soldier added heavy leather breeches and a woolen cape. Another type of cuirass, the *lorica segmentata,* was an articulated breastplate, not as efficient as chain mail but easier to manufacture. All of the infantry wore sandals with heavy hobnailed soles. Their shields were of bronze, oblong in shape; they were 4 feet in length and convex to provide a glancing surface for missiles.

Missile Organization and Cavalry

The auxiliary organization of the legion was its weakest link. The light missile troops, the *velites,* were usually distributed 120 to the maniple. Their principal missiles, the light javelin and the stone cast from a sling, were not capable of great range or precision. The sling had a range of about 50 paces at maximum effectiveness; the javelin was effective at 20 to 25 paces. The bow was seldom used by the Romans until late in the days of the empire when the Huns, fighting as allies of the city, saved many battles against the Goths.

Roman youth did not take kindly to the horse. Roman cavalry was usually ineffective and always deficient in strength. A cohort legion, as we have noted, had only 726 cavalrymen—and they remained indifferent in performance, often retiring hastily at the first shock of battle.

Siege Arms and Fording Equipment

The legion carried fifty-five ballistas, for propelling darts, and ten onagri, or catapults, for hurling huge stones against the walls of cities. Light boats were carried by special detachments to facilitate the construction of pontoon bridges.

The Roman Camp

The Roman camps were prepared in accordance with the military situation. They may be divided into classifications that depended upon the stay and the condition of the country. The process of camping for the night was highly organized and formalized.

1. ONE NIGHT CAMP—COUNTRY QUIET. A square was surrounded by a trench 5 feet wide and 3 feet deep. The dirt from the trench was piled on the inner side to provide a parapet that was surmounted by a palisade of stakes.

2. COUNTRY HOSTILE—DANGER NOT IMMINENT. The surrounding trench was widened to 9 feet and deepened to 7 feet. The inner wall was palisaded as usual with stakes.

3. COUNTRY IN SERIOUS DISORDER—DANGER IMMINENT. The ditch was 12 feet in width and 9 feet in depth. This amount of excavation gave a wall 4 feet high, surmounted by stakes.

4. PERMANENT CAMP—INDEFINITE STAY. The ditch was 18 feet in width and 10 feet in depth, permitting an inner parapet 8 feet in height and some 10 feet in width. This high mound was also palisaded with stakes for additional security.

Whatever the condition of the country, the Roman camp was constructed at the end of each day's march. This remarkable system of security played no small part in the Roman successes in the field. Roman soldiers were always well rested, well fed, and in a state of readiness for battle. No night alarms or disorganized night fighting were possible. In this respect, the Roman army was unique. The exactitude with which these camps were constructed reflects the order and discipline of the Roman military system. The camp remains may be seen today, exact day marches apart, in many sections of Western Europe.

The Parthian Military System

The very name of these people is associated with cavalry—Parthian is a Chaldean word meaning horsemen. The Parthians, presumed to have originated in the country to the southeast of the Caspian, built their empire upon the fragments of Alexander's domain. They first appear in history as vassals of the Persians—the Parthva mentioned by Darius. Ethnologically, they may have been a branch of the Scythians, those obscure people who appear so often in the pages of Eastern history.

Apparently, the Parthians broke away from the Persians about 250

B.C. to set up a small empire in the province of Khorassan. In the beginning it was no more than thirty thousand square miles in area. Their dim and confused history shows a pattern of wars against the Medes and other northern nomads—waged with mixed success. Their war tactics during these years were experimental and were largely borrowed from Persian and Mede sources. A campaign against Syria was fought wholly with infantry. Although successful, it was not decisive. Later, in 125 B.C., unidentified nomad tribes of horsemen defeated Parthia, thereby calling the attention of the Parthians to the virtues of horse-archery, which they were quick to emulate.

Using these cavalry tactics, the Parthians defeated Armenia and made their first contact with Rome, circa 120 B.C. This contact, on Rome's eastern frontier, rapidly diminished the neutral buffer ground that had existed and, by 70 B.C., there was a general distrust of Rome throughout Parthia.

For about ten years, hostilities were averted, although war was imminent in 60 B.C. when Pompey compromised a border dispute. Five years later, it became obvious that Rome and Parthia would do battle.

Parthian cavalry was of two types. The main body of horse was the lightest of light cavalry. The horse equipment consisted solely of a head stall and a single rein; the horses were selected for speed and agility. The riders wore only tunics and trousers. The sole weapon was the bow—with a large carry of arrows.

The Parthian light horse-bowman gripped the neck of the horse with his knees. He was a great, natural horseman, the product of training that began when a small boy. He could use the bow when the horse was at full gallop, and he could fire to the front, rear, or to either side with accuracy and speed.

The second class of horsemen, the Parthian heavy cavalry, rode sturdy mailed horses. The riders were protected in the Persian fashion with coats of mail that reached to the knees. The armor was of rawhide covered with scales of iron; the horsemen wore a burnished helmet of iron with a peculiar chain-mail ruff to protect the neck. The weapons they carried were the long spear, a short sword, and the bow.

The Parthian bow was similar to, or identical with, the great composite bow of the Persians. It may have been slightly larger than the Persian bow as all the early references to the Parthian army comment upon the unusual size of their bow. This strong bow, probably reinforced with sinew and horn, was of wood; it may have had the additional reinforcement of thin bands of iron. It was heavily reflexed, of great power, and it could propel steel-tipped arrows with high velocity and great range. The Parthian arrows could penetrate the best Roman armor.

The arrow supply of the Parthian archers was maintained to permit extended operations. At Carrhae, the Parthians operated with a camel supply train of one thousand animals loaded with spare arrows. In common with the majority of the horse-archers, the Parthians carried as many as sixty or eighty arrows. When this supply was exhausted, the Parthian bowman had only to seek the camel train.

The tactical unit of the Parthian army was the *dragon* of one thousand men.

The Field Actions.

The Parthian wars with Rome began with small reconnaissance operations in Mesopotamia where minor detachments of Parthians were defeated in 54 B.C. In the spring of 53 B.C., Crassus made a full-scale attack. In May, he crossed the Euphrates at 37° Lat. with seven legions, four thousand cavalry, and four thousand slingers and foot-archers. The legions were apparently not in full strength for the total strength of the Roman army is given at forty-three thousand men.

The force which Orodes, the Parthian king, assigned to his *surenas*, or general (who must be referred to by his title as history has not preserved his name), was composed entirely of cavalry. The usual composition of the Parthian order of battle provided one cavalryman to three infantrymen. At this particular period of history, all of the Parthian infantry was needed for a rough mountain campaign in progress in Armenia. Thus, by an accident of history the surenas led out an all-cavalry army for the first time in documented history.

It was on the third or fourth day after crossing the Euphrates that the Roman army, after a hot and dusty march, reached the Balikh River below Carrhae, the site of modern Harran. Crassus made contact with an advanced force of the Parthians near the banks of the Balikh River. He deployed his cavalry on the wings on a broad front but with little depth. Crassus had high expectations regarding the performance of this cavalry force of four thousand horsemen. They were Gallic cavalry, sent by Caesar who, at the time, was in Gaul.

The Parthian surenas had taken up a position on high wooded ground. At first contact, the Romans moved to form a hollow square, with the light armed troops in the center and the cavalry wings on either flank. In this position they waited confidently for the Parthian attack that would bring the armies to close quarters. Instead of attacking, the whole line of Parthian archers halted when within effective arrow range and began to subject the legions to a ceaseless heavy fire.

The Romans could not withstand this destructive hail of arrows and immediately threw forward the light missile troops and the highly regarded Gallic cavalry. The Parthians gave way in feigned retreat as the Roman attack was launched. When drawn some distance from the legions, the Roman pursuit detachment found themselves under arrow attack from antagonists who suddenly turned upon them. The Roman light troops disentegrated and the Gallic cavalry was overmatched. The survivors retired with difficulty to the protection of the legions.

The Parthians returned to effective arrow range and began a concentration upon the main target—the massed formation of the legion. The Romans soon stood within a ring of fast-riding horsemen.[1] A continuous flight of arrows poured in upon them. Spearmen began to fall as the casualties mounted. No opportunity for close-order action was offered; the Parthians maintained the proper range for maximum execution with the bow. The Romans stood their ground—there was nothing else for them to do. When Crassus saw the Parthian archers replenishing arrow supply from the camel train, he realized that offensive movement must be undertaken.

He sent his son Publius with one thousand Gallic cavalry, five hundred other horsemen, five hundred foot-archers and slingers, and eight cohorts of infantry (four thousand men) to attack.

In the face of this attack, the Parthians again retreated, leading the assaulting force away from the Roman defense perimeter. Publius, pressing home the attack, found himself cut off and surrounded by the Parthian heavy cavalry and the terrible mounted-archers. The four thousand swordsmen took refuge behind their shields on a small hill, but the Parthians closed to point-blank range and destroyed them to a man. Of the entire attacking force of the Romans, hardly a soldier escaped. Publius and his chief officers threw themselves upon their swords when the Parthian heavy cavalry moved in with lances.

With the head of the consul's son on a pikestaff, the Parthians renewed the main attack. Their heavy cavalry closed in to thrust at the Romans with their long lances as the light horse-archers concentrated upon the destruction of all of the Roman auxiliaries.

At nightfall, the Parthians withdrew a considerable distance to encamp (as was their custom), leaving the Romans in possession of a

field that was littered with dead. Crassus began a slow retreat toward
Carrhae, leaving six thousand killed and four thousand wounded on
the field. He might have had temporary safety behind the walls of
Carrhae, which he reached at midnight, but he chose to attempt a
retreat to Sinnaca in the Armenian hills. In deciding to retire, he was
influenced by the lack of provisions and the low morale of his troops.

Shortly after dawn the Parthians were again on the flanks of the
column, riding in and out of the dust clouds, slaughtering the Romans
who could establish no defense. In the disorder that followed, Crassus
was killed—or committed suicide. Of the Roman army of forty-three
thousand men, less than ten thousand escaped the Parthian arrows. An
additional ten thousand were captured during the battle. The remainder, more than twenty-three thousand soldiers, went down before the
Parthian bow. The Roman captives were settled at Merv where they
married Parthian wives and became loyal subjects.

The Parthians at Carrhae showed the Romans the devastating
power of the bow as a completely unsupported weapon in the hands
of horsemen. They demonstrated discipline, tactical grasp of offensive
horsemanship, and great field archery to crush the best heavy infantry
in the world. The battle was fought completely on Parthian terms.
Denied any semblance of the initiative, the Roman legions were unable
to hold a position—or retreat from it. The Parthian arrows penetrated
shield and breastplate, destroying the legions as they stood in a hopeless formation.

Carrhae made Parthia a power in the world second only to Rome.
Scene of one of the greatest historical performances of the bow in
battle, Carrhae proved that any formation of foot soldiers could be
annihilated with arrows; that there was no necessity for closing with the
formidable swordsmen of Rome. The mystery is that future opponents
of Rome did not note the lesson of this battle. But the pattern of war
did not change in the Mediterranean; with the exception of the Parthian interlude, war was still fought under conditions favorable to the
Roman heavy infantry.

No great coalition of Eastern horse-archer tribes appeared against
Rome. A determined alliance of horse-archers, led by Parthia, would
have irreparably damaged Rome and changed the course of history.
But it was not to be, for Parthia was left without efficient leadership
for many years.

The surenas who led the Parthian horsemen at Carrhae was not
to live to bring more field triumphs to his nation. This remarkable and

anonymous man, so great in reputation and ability, was murdered by his own jealous king. The surenas was the true father of cavalry missile warfare. Had he lived a few years more, he might have caused a complete and permanent revision of the Roman school of heavy shock infantry. He might have strangled the reputation of the Roman legion before the beginning of the Christian Era. Rome might never have recovered had the Parthians continued with tactics as consistent and as deadly as they had used at Carrhae.

This Parthian surenas, not yet thirty when he died, was apparently a man of great personal magnetism. Had he been a king rather than a general, he might have united all of the tribes of western Asia into a crushing combination against Rome. For a few months after the Battle of Carrhae, the history of western Asia and the Mediterranean pivoted on this man. His death by an assassin's dagger may have been one of the most significant episodes of history. On the basis of but one battle, he takes his place as one of the great all-time captains of the bow. His fame is secure.

Parthia moved into a period of its history after Carrhae where the chronic need was generalship. The results of this lack of field leadership were reflected in later campaigns and caused the war to drag on for endless years.

In 51 B.C., a badly led Parthian army crossed into Syria where two Roman legions, reinforced survivors of Carrhae, refused them battle. The Roman troops retired to Antioch where the Parthians attempted the impossible use of cavalry in a siege operation against immense enemy walls which would have been a problem to the most expert specialists in the art of siege warfare. The Parthians became greatly weakened by the prolonged siege operation for which they were unprepared and unsuited. They were defeated in one small field action and forced to retire. There before the walls of Antioch, they were operating under impossible battle conditions for horse-archers. Had they bypassed Antioch, raided the countryside, and destroyed any enemy field force, they might have aroused all of the eastern provinces to rebellion, for the spirit and morale of the Roman soldiers was at a very low ebb. Never was Parthian leadership more inadequate than in this campaign.

In July of 50 B.C., the first war with Rome came to an end and the glitter of the legion was greatly tarnished. The fate of the eastern border provinces was still undecided, but the Romans did not make another effort against Parthia for several years.

When Caesar returned triumphant from Gaul, he put his mind to the task of eliminating Parthia. After nine years of absence from Rome, Caesar had brought his minor and somewhat indecisive campaigns in Spain and Africa to a close and was ready to turn his entire attention to Parthia. In February, 44 B.C., Caesar was engrossed in plans for a massive invasion that would destroy Parthia forever. His assassination in March of that year, on the eve of his intended departure for Parthia, prevented any immediate invasion of the troublesome power on the eastern frontier.

One of the great speculations of history concerns the possible outcome of these wars had Caesar personally led the Roman legions against the Parthian bowmen. Caesar was a great improviser in the field; he might have solved the problem that horse-archery presented on the dusty plains of Parthia. However, there is a better possibility that he would not have solved those problems. Caesar understood his war instrument, the cohort legion, but as we shall note later, the great man had had his own difficulties in Britain against missiles that were far inferior to the Parthian arrow. It may be fortunate for Caesar's reputation that he did not encounter Parthian cavalry and the composite bow in the wide open country of Parthia.

Four years after the death of Caesar, in 40 B.C., the Parthians considered themselves ready for a major attack on Rome. Two large forces of cavalry began operations through the eastern provinces. They had uniform success. Antioch fell this time to attrition and, with it, all of Syria and Mesopotamia except the single city of Tyre where the reduction of the walls would have required the services of a navy. For a short time, the authority of Rome disappeared in western Asia.

But the Romans had great recuperative power. They now took the Parthian threat very seriously and legions in great force entered Syria. Several minor victories went to Rome, culminating in a severe battle on the banks of the Euphrates where the Parthians made the error of conducting frontal attack on a hastily formed Roman defensive field position. This lapse of tactics gave the Parthians a severe mauling and cost them the province of Syria. The archers attempted to ride up a steep hill to the Roman line; they were systematically destroyed by slingers and hand weapons of the type the Romans used so well.

This battle of 38 B.C. is notable for two reasons. It was representative of the grave leadership deficiencies that appeared too often in the military history of Parthia. The encounter was also unusual in that it was one of the few occasions in history where the sling was the decisive battle weapon. This second great battle between the Romans and the Parthians is not described in the usual history book, but because of the part played by the sling, this volume has more than a passing interest in the action.

It was a day in early spring when a horseman wearing a plumed helmet of glittering bronze rode down to the bank of the river and dismounted. Across the Euphrates, to the east, a glint of bright metal had caught the eye of Publius Venditius, lieutenant of Marc Antony and commander of the Roman army in the field. As the Roman stood there, peering at the parched hills on the opposite bank, the faint reflection he had seen grew into a wide band of silver as the point of a detachment of Parthian cavalry, metal helmets blazing in the sun, came into view. Battle was imminent.

It was the fifteenth year of the war against the horse-archers of Parthia, and this Roman army stood there to protect the province of Syria from a Parthian invasion led by Pacorus.

Venditius had much to ponder as he watched that glittering column across the river. Only a few miles from where he stood, other legions of Rome had toiled across the dusty desert to find death against the Parthians in the first great battle of this dreadful series of wars. There was nothing to mark the battlefield of Carrhae now except a ruin of bleached skeletons and rotting leather armor.

Venditius remembered Carrhae, as did every other field commander of the legions. He knew the folly of trying to stand in the field against horse-archers. The glittering helmets across the river drew nearer. Venditius made up his mind quickly. A sharp command and the legions flowed away smoothly, each cohort perfect in discipline and alignment. Behind the dusty formation, a mob of men without armor followed in irregular order. They were auxiliaries, men wearing short white tunics and bearing primitive weapons.

The legions sought the safety of high ground, leaving the Parthian crossing of the river uncontended. Disposed in a hollow square, the auxiliaries in the center, the legions waited for the attack that soon came. Steel-tipped arrows, propelled by the composite bows of the Parthians, began to pierce the wall of shields. The Romans took the fire, closed their ranks, and waited. It was all that swordsmen could do. The whining arrows ripped through shields and armor and men. Inside the square, the men in white tunics, the *rorarii*, uncoiled their weapons and opened their goatskin ammunition bags.

The Parthian horsemen, accustomed to arrow practice without reprisal fire, became aware that the legion had developed a sting. Horsemen began to go down under the relentless shower of stones. Stunned, riderless horses screamed as they plunged on the field. The Parthian arrow flow slackened as it drew effective counterfire. Accustomed to deliberate bow practice at the expense of the legion, they began to grow unsteady. The greatest weakness of mounted bowmen —the tenuous nature and the restless temperament of horsemen and the difficulty of restraining them as a disciplined unit—began to assert itself.

Goaded beyond endurance, the undisciplined Parthians drove in, closing the range, to assail the steep slope where the Romans waited. The Parthians, trying for point-blank fire, closed in to hand-to-hand range. It was fatal.

The fight became a melee as the Roman infantry came within sword thrust of the enemy. The slingers left the hilltop and disposed themselves into small supported groups across the plain. The slingers of Venditius were not bothered by the logistics of supply. Their ammunition, inexhaustible in quantity, lay at hand on the rocky floor of the valley. It was a wild battle of twanging bow, thrusting sword, and darting spear—and continuous, arching volleys of smooth stone.

Pacorus plunged dead from his horse, his skull crushed by a stone, and the Parthians fled the field in disorder. It was a great defeat for the best archers in Asia. The legions had regained some of their lost prestige with the help of the simple weapon that had slain Goliath.

Never in history had the slinger appeared to greater advantage than in this Parthian battle with Rome.

The military and treasure-hunting aspirations of Marc Antony precipitated another general assault on Parthia.[2] The victory of Venditius in Syria had improved the morale of the legions, and now Antony planned an invasion in force to dispose of the Parthian threat for all time. In midsummer of 37 B.C., Antony approached the Euphrates at a point near the ill-fated crossing made by Crassus in 53 B.C. Finding formidable opposition massed to dispute the crossing, Antony turned north to Armenia where he planned to establish an operational base.

His first objective was the city of Praaspa in the kingdom of Media, a subject ally of Parthia. With a force of 16 legions, 10,000 cavalry, and 30,000 auxiliaries, almost 120,000 men in all, he began a slow advance.

The seriousness of the campaign is reflected in the fact that this was three times the force that Caesar had used in Gaul.

A baggage train of three hundred wagons was detached with a guard of 2 legions under Statianus, and Antony hurried on to Praaspa. He never saw his wagon train or the escorting legions again. Only the corpses of the slain greeted him when he returned upon belated advice that Statianus was under attack. He found a long line of burned wagons and dead onagers. More than twelve thousand Romans had been killed in the futile defense of the train.

Skirmishing and foraging operations failed to bring out the Parthians in full strength. In one of these engagements, the Romans killed eighty Parthians in a running fight that cost the deaths of several thousand legion soldiers. Severe disciplinary measures became necessary to sustain the morale of the troops.[3] The slaughter of Statianus had made the Roman soldiers fearful and unconfident. Antony had lost all of his siege engines in the destruction of the baggage train and he was unable to capture a city for use as a winter headquarters. Failing in an effort to bring the elusive Parthians to battle (in this campaign, the Parthians had reverted to proper tactics with the bow), Antony made a desperation offer to withdraw if the Parthians would return the Eagles and Standards lost by Crassus. Antony also included a demand for the release of the ten thousand Roman prisoners who had been settled at Merv. This offer was rejected by the Parthians, and Antony then began a slow retreat from the vicinity. As the initial stages of the retirement led through very rough country, he was not molested by the Parthians for two days.

On the third day, the Parthian army, in force, barred his path; the extended Roman column was punished severely by waves of archers. Antony ran for his life to the safety of the low hills of Armenia while the remnants of his legions dissolved in panic and flight. During every mile of the terrible rout, the Parthian arrows exacted their toll. Antony conducted eighteen separate defensive actions during the course of the retreat of 277 miles to Armenia. Every mile of the march produced Roman dead. Only by maintaining the old Macedonian *testudo*, the tortoise formation of overlapping shields, were the Romans able to avoid complete annihilation. For twenty awful days the legion felt the power of the composite bow, leaving thousands of dead and wounded along the route, with the kites and vultures blackening the sky above the Roman column.

This ambitious Roman campaign ended with a loss of thirty-five thousand killed. Antony was never able to set foot upon the soil of Parthia proper.

After the great victory at Praaspa, Parthia remained quietly on the defensive, holding Armenia despite a revolt in Media. In A.D. 37, after more than sixty years of desultory fighting and minor patrol actions, negotiations brought an official end to this second lengthy war with Rome.

About A.D. 107, the Parthian king placed his son on the throne of Armenia. Trajan, in a series of border engagements, restored the province to Roman control eight years later. Under Hadrian, an era of peace opened, with Rome in a passive role on all of its borders.

This peace was not to last for war flared up in A.D. 160, ending in a great Roman defeat at Elegia; again the resources of the empire were decisive with Roman victories in Syria three years later. In A.D. 200, the third Parthian war came to an end with the Romans in possession of their eastern provinces of Armenia and Syria. It should be noted that throughout the course of these border wars, the Roman armies did not venture into Parthia. All the engagements were on the soil of disputed border provinces. For two centuries after Antony's defeat, the waves of invasion and counterinvasion swept across the eastern provinces. Only Severus, in A.D. 195, was able to gain decisive victories in the border wars. He at last entered Parthia (the first Roman army since Antony's to do so) and captured the capital, Ctesiphon, slaughtering the men and carrying women and children as prisoners to Rome. In this period of Parthian history, Volgases, the Parthian king, was a weak and passive leader. He had abandoned the capital and its people, and he held the Parthian army in the field without giving battle. He survived the defeat by Severus by only ten years.

In A.D. 215, the Romans were double-dealing in Parthia. The emperor of Rome asked for the hand of the daughter of the Parthian king as he stood ready with thirty-two legions for a massive invasion of Parthia. The reply was sharp and negative.

"Such a union," the Parthian king responded, "could hardly prove a happy one. It is not fit that either family should sully its blood by mixture with a foreign stock."[4]

The Roman emperor made a second plea and was invited to Parthia for a conference. He came with an army—the first Roman army to set foot on Parthian soil for many years. The Parthians laid their bows aside. In a sudden treacherous attack, the Romans killed many of their hosts, and the king barely escaped with a few horsemen. The final war was underway.

Two years later, the armies of Parthia and Rome met for the last time on the field of battle. A vigorous king, Artabanus, was now on the throne of Parthia. Macrinius, the new emperor of Rome, had an army on the frontier and was threatened by a Parthian force that had crossed the frontier into Mesopotamia to the Roman provincial capitol of Nisibis.

Macrinius immediately sent ambassadors to the Parthian camp, offering to return all Parthian captives held in Rome. Artabanus rejected the Roman offer, insisting, in addition, that the Parthian cities destroyed by Rome be rebuilt and that Mesopotamia be ceded to Parthia. Refusing these terms, Macrinius prepared to give battle.

At Nisibis, in A.D. 217, a strong force of horse-archers assisted by a new corps of Parthian camel-lancers in full armor met a powerful Roman army that was well convoyed by Mauritanian cavalry. A terrible three-day battle developed with Roman casualties so great that they abandoned the field in full retreat after the first day. Brought to bay after a pursuit, they were engaged by the Parthians in a day of position fighting that resulted in stalemate. On the third day, the Parthians initiated a successful enveloping movement. The Mauritanian cavalry was dispersed, and the Roman infantry was enclosed within the familiar circle of wheeling archers. Parthian bow practice came into play and the Romans were soundly thrashed. The Parthian casualties were also heavy, but the Romans fled the field and took refuge in a fortified camp.

Behind the ramparts of this camp, Macrinius reopened peace negotiations. Artabanus relinquished his claim on Mesopotamia; the Romans agreed to restore all Parthian captives. In lieu of rebuilding the ruined Parthian cities, Rome agreed to pay Parthia an indemnity —an equivalent to at least $5 million.

These were expensive wars for Rome. Parthia had been able to cut off the trade routes to China. The classical Silk Road led from Balkh to Kashgar via the Alai Trough, 200 miles south of the formidable Pamir Range. The Parthians made fortunes by intercepting silk shipments and then releasing them to Rome at exorbitant prices. Silk sold in Rome at one time for the equivalent of $800 a pound. In order to make more of a given quantity of silk, the Roman women had two of each three threads of the weave removed to form a cloth that was no more than a silk lace. The revealing costumes made from this cloth were standard attire for the upper-class women of Rome.

At Nisibis there came to an end the most extended field operations ever to be conducted by the bow in war. It had begun at Carrhae in 53 B.C.; it ended at Nisibis in A.D. 217. For 270 years a people armed with the bow had stood off the greatest military power of ancient times. It was a great performance and it validated the composite bow as a major unsupported weapon.

The Rome that Parthia fought was not the decadent city of the later empire. This was the Rome of Julius Caesar and his immediate successors—representative of the greatest field armies the Romans were ever able to produce.

The result of these long wars had been the purchase of ignominous peace from Parthia. The Roman ambitions in the East were stifled. They had found it comparatively easy to get into Parthia; it had been much more difficult to extricate their armies. Of six great Roman expeditions, only one had been productive of favorable military result.[5]

The Parthians were the first great missile cavalry. Although, at times, they suffered from defective field leadership and tactical deployment of their troops, they pioneered the bow with the first all-cavalry army. They solved the problem of field arrow supply, and they demonstrated that the weapon could stand, virtually unsupported, against any other weapons or any formation of battle.

There on the banks of the Euphrates, the soft belly of the Roman legion was fatally exposed when it came into battle contact with the missile cavalry of Asia. The Roman military system that died in the desert had tried to fight a war with a tactical conception that had been invalid since the days of the spearmen of the Greek city-states. Actually, the heavy infantry tactics of the legion had been outmoded for three centuries when Rome began this series of wars with Parthia. Unsuspected military excellence had been developing on their borders. Nations were learning the art of economical mobile war with the bow.

But Rome did not change; the legion carried on—an anachronism in history—for almost four hundred years. The commitment to heavy infantry remained constant and the legion blundered through its many wars, blindly heading for extinction. The assumption of Oman and other distinguished military writers that heavy infantry was eliminated as the decisive arm at Adrianople in A.D. 375 will not stand historical inspection. The truth is that heavy infantry had ceased to be effective many years before the Christian Era. The manipular legion had failed in the Punic Wars; the cohort legion had been in constant trouble from the attacks of armored cavalry, from horse-archers, and even from the chariots of Boadicea in Britain.

The centuries between Carrhae and Adrianople had formed an indictment of the Roman military system.

In permanently halting the eastward expansion of Rome, Parthia had reaffirmed the archery tactics of Asia. It was a remarkable military effort these horse-bowmen made against Rome; they came very close to altering the history of the ancient world. They pointed the way to a more decisive and economical tactic of war, for they were the advance guard of the formidable men with the bow who were to terrorize Europe in later centuries. The equal of the Parthians in the prosecution of mobile war did not appear until the coming of the Mongols in A.D. 1200—twelve centuries later.

12

The Sunset of the Roman Legion

In the long period of warfare from the end of the Punic Wars in 146 B.C. to the conclusion of hostilities with Parthia in A.D. 217, the Roman legions were in continual and serious trouble on the frontiers of Rome. In 134 B.C., a slave war in Sicily resulted in the defeats of four Roman armies before the revolt could be quelled after two years of desperate fighting.

Twenty-nine years later, in 105 B.C., the Romans suffered the disaster at Arausio that was comparable to the defeat at Cannae. At Arausio, the legions of Mallius and Caepio were cut to pieces in the German forests. The savage Cimbri and the Teutons annihilated three Roman armies and captured a fourth. Rome retired from Germany after these defeats and never returned.

In 103 B.C., another war in Sicily required three years of hard fighting to restore order and this campaign was barely concluded when Pompey began, in 83 B.C., a war against Pontus, a minor kingdom. This little country, in the northeastern part of Asia Minor on the edge of the Black Sea, had been founded in 400 B.C. and was not a threat to Rome. Roman armies averaging a strength of more than one hundred thousand men were in the field for twenty years before the small country could be made into a province in 62 B.C.

In 73 B.C., Spartacus, a slave, escaped into the crater of Vesuvius where he built up an army of fellow slaves. He defeated ten Roman armies in three years in a war that taxed the government to its limits. After defeating Clodius and Varinius, Spartacus overran southern Italy. In 72 B.C., Cassius and Manlius were defeated as were two other

113

consular armies that were rushed into the field. Spartacus was surrounded finally at Calabria where he made a last stand, surrounded by several Roman armies. He was killed and six thousand of his followers were crucified along the road from Capua to Rome. Three thousand Roman prisoners were found alive and unharmed in his camp.

The cohort legion produced one success during this period—Caesar's conquest of Gaul. This action had started in 58 B.C. and was to continue for eight years before a sparse population of barbarians with no central government could be subjugated. This great area, taking in what is now Switzerland, France, Belgium, the Netherlands, and parts of Germany, was sparsely settled by some four million people, often mutually hostile and possessing no military history or tradition.

The Gauls used no missile troops excepting the casting of javelins at close quarters. The military practice of the barbarians was to charge in dense, disorganized masses to engage at close quarters with an inferior sword. Some of the Germanic tribes used the battle-ax. Caesar reported the barbarians' attacks as mad rushes into the waiting ranks of the legion. The cohort legion appeared to its best advantage against untrained irregular infantry of this nature.

The Helvetians recklessly expended their manpower in attacks in a dense phalanx and were quickly reduced after a few field actions that did little more than test the steadiness of the Roman ranks. The Belgae had no supply support and no tactics and the entire nation fell apart after a short resistance. Only Vercengetorix, the Arvernian leader who was almost a king, remained as a threat to Caesar although he had no official government behind his army. Vercengetorix fought the legions with hastily gathered forces representative of many tribes of Gaul. Although he won a battle, the only defeat sustained by Caesar in Gaul, Vercengetorix was unable to hold his tenuous force in the field. In 52 B.C., he was basely surrendered by his own people; seven years later he was executed in Rome as a part of the festivities of a Roman triumph.

The conquest of Gaul had been hardly more than a military incident, and it had not required the services of a Caesar. Although the campaigns have been invested with an aura of romance, Caesar himself dismissed the opposition with his famous, *"Veni, vidi, vici."* The quality of the opposition in Gaul was no test of any military school.

Elsewhere, where Caesar ran into missiles, he was not so successful. In 55 B.C. he turned his attention to Britain when he crossed the

Channel with but two legions, implying great confidence on the Caesar's part. He landed on the southwest corner of the island and was met
by determined resistance so effective that he abandoned the campaign
immediately after being followed along the coast by masses of chariots.

The following spring Caesar returned to Britain in force with five
legions and two thousand Bactrian cavalry, landing on the coast of
Kent. Cassivellaunus conducted a very able resistance against this
formidable force of forty thousand Romans. After a few meetings had
established the worth of the Roman swordsmen, Cassivellaunus dismissed his levies of infantry and relied solely upon a force of four
thousand chariots. Although this war vehicle had been outmoded for
three centuries, the baffling evasive movement and the shower of missiles was not solved by Caesar's cohort legions.

The Romans moved forward slowly, making no real progress. The
principal result of the raid was the capture of a herd of cattle. This
accomplished, Caesar returned to Gaul. Cassivellaunus had found, and
exploited, the fundamental weakness of the legion. Although Caesar
minimized the failure of these two unsuccessful attempts against Britain, they were positive defeats for the legion at the hands of missile
troops of barbarians. Caesar's expedition of 54 B.C. had been intended
to be a full-scale assault.

The Romans did not return to Britain for almost a century—not
until A.D. 43, in the reign of Claudius, when the legions renewed their
effort against the island. Eighteen years of severe resistance by the
Britons culminated in the revolt of Boadicea in A.D., 61. The queen
destroyed two legions with chariot-mounted missile troops. These
battles saw the legion reverting to the tortoise formation of Alexander
in desperate and futile defensive stands.

Although this was the end of organized resistance, the legions
were occupied for forty years in the reduction of a portion of the
island. A hostile and unconquered population was contained by Hadrian's Wall. This greatest defense line to be constructed by Rome was
seventy-three miles long. Begun by Hadrian in A.D. 123, it was completed by Severus in A.D. 210.

The cohort legion was eroding on other fields during this period.
In A.D. 9, Varus was overwhelmed on the German border with the loss
of all of his legions. Near Liege, the Gauls destroyed two legions of
Sabinius. In Africa, the legions of Albinius passed under the yoke in
shameful defeat. By A.D. 160, armored cavalry was showing its hand on

the Continent, and the German tribes were striding ahead of Rome with decisive armies of heavy lancers. The science of war had passed Rome by and their stubborn commitment to heavy infantry had brought the moment of climax.

The legion had become an outdated instrument of war.

In A.D. 251, the disaster at Forum Trebonii saw Decius and all of his men killed as he attempted to quell an invasion of the Goths. The sunset of Roman infantry, long delayed, was at hand. Dacia (modern Romania) was ceded to the Goths. The empire blundered on for another century as the giant economy died slowly. In A.D. 375, the Huns forced the Visigoths into Roman territory where they were given land by Rome in a last despairing attempt to set up a buffer against the increasing raids. The culmination of the Visigoth intrusion was the Battle of Adrianople where the legions huddled together like sheep under a storm of arrows that pierced shield and cuirass. There the legion waited for death at the hands of lance-bearing shock cavalry that broke into the Roman formation to complete the destruction. All the Romans died on the field, herded into a circle of death.

The legion had not been empiric during these centuries; it had been an anachronism, displaced in time for five hundred years. Rome had ignored other and better formulas for waging war and, inevitably, the empire paid the price. For centuries the battle wounds of the Roman legion had been salved by the almost limitless resources of the government. The legion itself had never been successful against major opponents with missiles.

Considerable space has been devoted to the organization, equipment, and tactics of the Roman legion in its various wars because the legion was the whipping boy that established the worth of two greater schools of war. It is apparent that the chroniclers of the legion have been far too kind in their assessments of its battle efficiency. Rome conquered most of the known world but the ultimate success of the long campaigns has obscured the deficiencies of the armed force that was placed in the field by the Roman Empire. The legions met but two major opponents in all of their long career. One of these, Carthage, they defeated after conflict for a century and a half, in the course of which they lost the majority of the battles. The other opponent, Parthia, humiliated them in the field to such an extent that Rome purchased a peace after a stalemate could not be broken. All the other opponents of the Roman legion were unorganized barbarian tribes or small nations without resources for prosecuting war. In many of these small wars, the decision was obtained for Rome by means of mercenary forces of Asiatic horse-archers who were hired as allies to produce a missile attack that Rome could not attain. Rome won the wars while the legion was losing the battles.

The Romans bridged a very interesting transitional period in military history, during which strong contesting schools of war were forming. The Romans were able to consolidate into a strong power before their heavy infantry commitment was forced to face a strong enemy able to exploit the weakness of the legion with superior weapons and tactics. When capable enemies did appear, the empire was so well established that it could absorb the successive military disasters and survive on momentum for several centuries. The Roman military system had always been faulty.

When the legion is considered solely as a battle agent with no allowance made for the inherent strength of the government that fed it, the formation cannot stand inspection. Historians become too preoccupied with the final results of the wars to properly evaluate the legion in battle.

The remarkable recuperative ability of the government is not difficult to understand when the size of the Roman Empire is visualized. Rome of the Christian Era possessed the only strong unified government in the world. A comparative figure will make clear the great resources and limitless manpower that made possible such rapid and continual replacement of battle-shattered legions. China, at the beginning of the Christian Era, had a population of 80,000,000. Rome of the same period controlled a population of 85,000,000. The city was capable of placing 750,000 troops in the field. This figure is believed to have reached as high as 900,000 at one period and the Romans usually had armies totaling 350,000 on the frontiers.

As early as 28 B.C., there were 4,063,000 Roman citizens of military age, seventeen to sixty. By A.D. 14, this figure had increased to 5,000,000. The population of the city of Rome was at least 2,000,000. In area, the Roman Empire was 2,500 miles by 1,200 miles—approximately the area of the United States.

This combination of resources, manpower, and centralized government completely negated the deficiencies of the legion in battle. No estimates of total Roman casualties can be made for those centuries of battle that resulted in a far greater percentage of defeats than victories. The Roman military system was unique. It seems incredible that a people so efficient in government, engineering, architecture, and law could not have developed a better field force than the legion.

The persistence of the Romans in accepting massed heavy infantry as the decisive force could be better defended were it not for the fact that two superior tactical schools had existed during the entire period of Roman expansion. The Romans had the benefit of the military experience of the heavy cavalry school of Alexander, modified by Hannibal to inflict defeat after defeat upon Roman arms. The Romans also had many sad experiences against Hun horse-archers as well as the debacle in Parthia that should have been used in an evaluation of their military system.

The Indictment of Heavy Infantry

The impaired mobility of shock infantry makes the arm capable of but limited independent action. The offensive power of heavy infantry decreases rapidly when such infantry acts alone against an organized defensive position. Against an active and mobile enemy, heavy infantry is helpless. When compacted by cavalry attack, heavy infantry disintegrates swiftly. To be decisive, heavy infantry must have adequate cavalry support and efficient and powerful missile strength. These the legion did not have.

The result was costly defeat, rarely a costly victory, and usually indecisive battle. The history of the legion contains a record of much frustration and aimless marching in futile attempts to bring an enemy to battle. The legion formation in depth had some flexibility in maneuver but it was fatally slow in deployment.

Offensively—against other heavy infantry—the legion was supreme. It was never able to generate much offense against active troops. It is strange that the Romans were never able to properly evaluate missiles and the horse. Because of this lack the legion had no offense or defense against opponents who conducted distant war. Legionaries could be ridden around and destroyed in an open field. They could be worn down by small war action. They could be decimated on the march by an enemy barely in view, and they could be held and starved when forced into a defensive position within a fortified camp in denuded country. When trapped in open country, the legion was usually destroyed when the opponents were horse-archers. Particularly dangerous was the inability of the legion to extricate itself from a field on which it had been beaten. Its long and plodding columns were the arrows' best target.

Although the Romans operated in a wide area as an offensive and aggressor force, Roman military thinking was dedicated to the defense. The legion bored slowly into a victim country with a fundamental strategy that was concerned with the occupation of strong points. The Roman legion on the march in hostile country was essentially a defensive unit en route to a predetermined strong point that was to be a pivot and base for a defensive action. The legion was, therefore, in the paradoxical position of conducting active armed invasion of a country by means of a series of defensive stands.

Although the legions controlled a great part of their world at one time, the pacification of Roman tributory areas was never complete. The Roman provinces were in a continual state of revolt and the countryside was controlled only by routine patrols in force. Gaul was never firmly held although Caesar killed or enslaved two million people. Everywhere, the Romans stood on the defensive with a tenuous hold on occupied countries.

In the face of hard contrary military facts, Rome retained its commitment to heavy infantry. The Roman system endured—curiously inflexible and never economical in operation.

13

The Huns: Fatal Experiment

Among the first of the horse-archers to attract the attention of the Western world were the mysterious people we call the Huns. They were a tribe, or tribes, of that confused scramble of races who left the deserts of Asia to propel themselves upon Western civilization. The Huns appeared in history in many periods and in many areas. Sometimes they were plunderers; again, they were allies of the people they had plundered. They were ever ready to wield their weapons against a nation or to sell their services as allies to that same nation. They were enemies of Rome as well as Roman allies; the bulwark of the missile offense of the Byzantines; mysterious raiders on the fringe of Europe; and a serious threat to Western civilization.

We will examine their inconsistencies and their strange military history that was to culminate in Attila's abortive attempt on Europe.

The Huns were a small, brutish people with flat, beardless faces. Everywhere they appeared they brought terror and revulsion. Early in their history they pushed into the lower Volga valley, moving slowly westward against the population of south Russia. The Ostrogoths, living around the mouth of the Dneiper, were forced into modern Hungary and then across the Danube into the Roman Empire. It was the pressure of the Huns, in the end, that brought about the fall of Rome.

In A.D. 432, the Huns were so dangerous that Emperor Theodosius paid King Ruas of the Huns an immense sum of money as tribute. When Attila succeeded to the throne, this demand for tribute was doubled.

Originally the Huns had been great horse-bowmen. They used a tremendous bow—constructed entirely of layers of horn—and they had leather whips for close combat. Their children were taught to ride upon sheep and to kill mice and birds with miniature bows.[1] The entire nation, women and children included, traveled with the army in felt yurts that were the equivalent of modern housetrailers. A strong rear guard protected the extraordinary caravans as they plunged across Europe.

In the years prior to Attila's ascent of the throne, the Huns had operated under a great captain of the bow in the person of Uldin. Uldin had saved Rome in the year A.D. 405 as an ally assisting to repel the invasion of a tremendous army of Slavs and Germans under the leadership of the ferocious Radagaisus. The small fur-clad Huns of Uldin had been given a Roman triumph by the grateful citizens. The alliance had provided a dangerous familiarity with Rome and the Huns soon took advantage of the weaknesses they had discovered within the Roman Empire.

Attila became king of the Huns in A.D. 433 and immediately extracted a greatly increased tribute and other humiliating concessions from Rome. From 434 until 441 he was occupied with the extension of his power in central Europe. In A.D. 441, he began an attack on the Balkans. Peace was made and Attila then turned his attention to Rome. The Hun tribute was increased in 443 and again in 447. In A.D. 450, Rome refused to deal further with the insatiable Hun and the stage was set for Attila's attack on the empire.

In A.D. 451 found Attila camped on the Rhine with a force that has been estimated at five hundred thousand men. This was undoubtedly an exaggeration; it was a common practice for Europeans to overestimate the numbers of Asiatic horsemen. Asiatic cavalry was so fluid and speedy that it was difficult to determine the size of their armies. It was also to the advantage of European generals, after a defeat, to exaggerate the quality and numbers of the opposition. It is doubtful that Attila had two hundred thousand men on this campaign.

Although the Huns are best known while they were under the leadership of Attila, their decline as a military power began with his ascent to the throne. In his youth Attila had been sent as a hostage to Rome during the period when the Huns were allies with Rome in the wars with Radagaisus. Although Attila had thoroughly despised Rome, some of the elements of the Roman military system had caught his eye.

The well-drilled and disciplined legion must have been an awe-inspiring sight to the young barbarian privileged to see the formation on parade in Rome. There was much that was orderly and glittering and precise about the legion that would appeal to a young nomad accustomed to the carelessly wild evolutions of Uldin's horsemen.

The tactics and military thinking of Attila became colored by this contact with Rome and, upon his rise to power, he immediately instituted certain changes in the Hun training and equipment for war.

There was much that was sound and reasonable in the changes that Attila made. As the Asiatic archers had become more and more in contact with the heavy cavalry of Europe, many features of the European school showed to advantage. In the confusion of battle in crowded city streets and in cramped and constricted positions, the Asiatic light bowmen sometimes had found themselves at a disadvantage against the broad swordsmen of Europe. The light archer required room for his missile attack. At close quarters, the light saber of the Asiatic soldier was inadequate.

To meet these new conditions of battle that involved the necessity for imposing shock against shock, the assault of city walls, and the bruising melees in the streets, Attila introduced a considerable body of heavily armed troops, mounted and afoot. In making this compromise, his army lost much in mobility and speed.

There was one factor that Attila failed to consider—the temperament of his people. The partial adoption of European arms and tactics was not destined for success. Although it brought a certain parity in hand-to-hand fighting, it also tempted the Huns, on too many occasions, to attempt to fight the battle on European terms. The gigantic European horsemen were more than a match for the small nomads in close combat, whatever the parity of weapons. Great defeats for the bow came when nomad horsemen accepted these conditions.

By temperament, none of the horse-archer tribes were fitted for siege operations or prolonged, indecisive field actions. They could not adjust to giving battle in a city street or on a formal, constricted field with enemies drawn up in battle array. Previous war, as waged by the Huns, had been based upon quick and decisive decision, accomplished by maneuver and a storm of arrows. They acted in contradiction to all their instinct and training when they made possession of a city or a field their objective.

Attila changed all of these age-old military customs of the Huns, and his army became a conspicuous example of the national inability of some races to adapt themselves to strange weapons and tactics. Attila learned that he could not make steady and disciplined heavy weapons soldiers from his levies of wild and restless horsemen. As a result, Attila's experiments, although they made him an object of horror, left only a vague imprint on history.

Let us observe his ill-conceived army in action in Europe. Attila crossed from his camp on the Rhine in A.D. 451; in a few weeks, he had captured Rheims and St. Quentin and was becoming a threat to Paris. At the city of Orleans, the military percentage caught up with Attila. The Huns won the original battle, fought in the open country that surrounded the town, and Orleans fell. In the orgy that followed the capture, Attila lost control of his army and they were surprised and severely beaten by a Roman army that marched in to the relief of the city. The first shock of the battle was in the streets of Orleans where detachments of Huns, experimenting with new weapons and unfamiliar tactics in European formations, were badly mauled by the expert Roman swordsmen. Trapped in the narrow streets by the legion, the Huns were no match for Roman infantry and, after taking severe casualties, the Asiatics fled the city in disorder.

In July of 451, a few days after the street battle in Orleans, the East met the West in one of the most important battles of history. It was a battle that could have been, and should have been, avoided by Attila. His troops were still unnerved by the defeat in Orleans. Had he been an expert tactician, he would have realized that the constriction of the battlefield at Chalons would place an intolerable burden upon his light archers.

In disputing the position at Chalons, Attila exposed his very inferior military judgment. He accepted battle on this plain that was hemmed on one side by the Marne River, choosing to risk the issue in a formal position battle against the greatest heavy weapons soldiers of the era. Had Attila chosen to apply evasive, harassing tactical maneuver against the relatively immobile army of Aetius, the possibilities would have been great that the Huns could have eliminated the only effective armed threat in the field against them. Instead, Attila chose to engage at close quarters.

The Romans of this period were not of the fiber of the legions of Julius Caesar, but they were still the best swordsmen in the world. They were commanded by the consul Aetius, a soldier who had experienced many changes of fortune in his career. Aetius at one time had been accused of intrigue and had fallen from the favor of Galla

Placidia, empress of Rome. Before being restored to grace, he had
been in exile for several years among the Huns. He knew the Hunnish
people intimately and was able to assess their performance under
varying conditions of battle. Aetius realized that the position at Chalons was ideal for the Roman purpose.

As will be noticed from the troop deployment, the battle situation
was highly favorable to the Roman tactical concepts of warfare. Aetius
must have surveyed that field with great satisfaction. The Marne River
prevented Attila's cavalry from circling the Roman left wing. A high
hill, held by a Roman detachment, menaced Attila's baggage train with
long-range missile fire. The two armies were drawn up in precise lines
—ready for the slaughter. Attila's mounted-archers might as well have
been infantry as they were denied the privilege of evasive maneuver
and could not apply the fundamental principle of economy of force.
The battle at Chalons was European position war in the best classical
tradition.

At dawn the Huns were in position. In Attila's rear were the ruined
ramparts of a long-abandoned Roman fort. Here the Hun marshaled
his chariots and his reserves to form a strong defensive position behind
his front line, and here Attila aligned his forces. The restless Huns
disposed themselves into a center that was led by Attila himself, supported by right and left wings.

A few hundred yards distant Aetius formed the orderly deployment that all opponents of Rome knew and feared. Aetius himself
assumed command of the left wing, in position near the bend of the
river. The Huns were nervous; there was no air of confidence in the
ranks as they waited for this test of battle on European terms. Attila's
field commanders had protested the field disposition. There were
mutterings in the ranks of the Huns; there was no scope for maneuver
in the narrow valley.

Neither army was willing to begin the attack. The well-disciplined
troops of Aetius sat impassively. The Huns became increasingly restive
and irritated by the delay. Occasionally, the nomads made wild sorties
in small force against the Roman line. Throughout the morning the
troops faced each other; the action was confined to a small missile
activity. It was not until late in the afternoon that Attila ordered the
Hun line forward.

The Roman center received the shock of the attack and held firm
in the face of the Hun arrows. The range closed rapidly; Attila became
subject to the age-old limitation of the bow at close quarters. The

conflict became hand to hand. In the melee, the Hun flanks folded and the Roman wings closed about the doomed center of the Hun army. Attila's archers, penned within a closing circle of steel, were overwhelmed by the skillful Roman swordsmen. The heavily armed infantry and armored cavalry of Attila went down before the precise maneuvers of the Romans who knew everything there was to know about the use of the pike and the sword. The pilum and the gladius came into methodical play, stabbing and chopping away the lives of the Huns.

Attila had no offense. His most potent weapon, the bow, had been deployed out of the action in the selection of this field, and he had neither the experience nor the science to set up a proper defense with his heavy weapons. The battle developed almost immediately into arms-length combat, and the Huns, broken into small units, were set up for the kill. There was no escape lane through the flashing swords. Tirelessly, the Romans cut them down. In a few short hours, Attila's dream of a conquest of Europe had faded. It is stated that the casualties of both armies at Chalons were 250,000 men; among the Huns, hardly a man was unwounded. Even in the face of possible overestimations, the battle at Chalons was a tremendous action.

The defeat at Chalons eliminated Attila as a serious threat to the West. Never a great military commander, the Hun general now abandoned entirely the principles of cavalry warfare for which Asia had been so feared and began a complete reweaponing of his army. He set up protection for his Huns with heavy armor; he instituted precise infantry movements with pikemen and javelins. The chief weapons became the spear, the ax, and the sword. His horse-archers became an auxiliary service and never again were the Huns able to wage effective mobile war. Attila's subordination of the bow to the status of a supporting weapon eliminated the last great threat of his horsemen.

Attila the Hun is one of the most greatly overestimated characters in military history. His principal claim to inclusion in any study of war should be an examination of his misuse of an army that had magnificent potential talent. The European tactics that Attila tried unsuccessfully to emulate were greatly inferior to his own great heritage from the deserts of Asia.

In history, Attila is known, inaccurately as a leader of one of the great waves of savage horse-bowmen who poured out of Asia. Actually, the Huns of Attila's period had long outlived their former greatness and were no longer representative Asiatic cavalry. Attila's army was an unsatisfactory compromise, merging of European and Asiatic tactics. He does not stand, nor should he be compared, with the great captains of the bow who preceded and succeeded him in history.

But the Huns were not yet finished as military archers, for on the death of Attila, they were released from the whims of this inadequate soldier and regained much of their lost stature in a new alignment of power—as an ally of the Byzantine Empire. When Attila died, the Huns reverted to their proper status as horse-archers. We shall see them in a much more favorable light as dependable and terrible light cavalry in the Byzantine armies of Belisarius and Narses.

14

The Byzantine Abandonment
of the Bow

The small, disciplined armies of the Byzantine Empire of the sixth, seventh, and eighth centuries A.D. represented the highest development of the art of war to reach Europe. The Byzantine army composition suffered from serious faults that were to prove fatal in the end but their efficient armored cavalry, supported by strong missile attack—an advanced concept of the use of the horse—stood as a bulwark for the fading Roman Empire for several centuries of severe field action. From their concept of the armed and armored man on horseback was developed the feudal knight of the ninth to the fifteenth centuries. The tactics and equipment of the Byzantine army heavy cavalryman were the patterns upon which the jousting knight of the Middle Ages was created.

Although the Byzantines remained constant in their reliance upon armored cavalry as the decisive arm, their army was subject to continual reorganization, assessment, and changes in composition. The history of the Byzantine military establishment divides readily into two periods, each of which will be considered.

The Byzantine Army—A.D. 500–A.D. 900

The Byzantine army was much more effective during this earlier period of their history. In this respect they resembled the Persians.

127

There was much less reliance on the infantry arm and, therefore, greater mobility. The Byzantines were able to present a strong missile attack with the use of heavy concentrations of horse-archers who were able to supply adequate support for the less active mailed horsemen. The order of battle utilized the essentials of shock, mobility, and fire-power to a remarkable degree and this army was uniformly successful against powerful opposition.

Byzantine armies of this period were small, efficient, maneuverable, and highly trained. They relied heavily upon Hun bowmen for missile support, and the Huns, recovered from their dismal experience under Attila, reached a high point of excellence as disciplined soldiers in their service with the Byzantines.

The sixth century produced outstanding field commanders in the persons of Belisarius and Narses as they led the Byzantines in a series of campaigns in eastern Europe against the Goths, the later Persian Empire, the Vandals, and the Franks. At the Battle of Daras in A.D. 530, Belisarius exploited the reliance of the Persians on infantry-archers and destroyed them with his armored cavalry and wings of Hun horse-archers.

At Tricameron, with a very small force of fifteen thousand men, Belisarius eliminated the Vandal threat with a determined charge of mailed cavalry supported by his Huns. Procopius has preserved the account that Belisarius made in his report of phases of the Byzantine battles with the Goths.

Belisarius reported:

In the first small skirmishes against these Goths I found that the chief difference between them and us was that our regular Roman horse and the Hunnish *Foederati* are all capital horsemen while the enemy had hardly any knowledge whatever of archery. The Gothic Knights used lance and sword alone while their bowmen on foot are always drawn up under cover of the heavy squadrons. So their bowmen are no good until the battle comes to close quarters and can easily be shot down while standing in battle array, before the moment of contact arrives.

Proof of the folly of reliance upon foot-archers and lance-bearing cavalry against horse-bowmen was also taught the Goths at the Battle of Casilium, where Narses had annihilated the Frankish horsemen who had ridden mailed to the eyes. The French cavalry, after scattering a small group of Byzantine foot-archers, had halted to receive the charge of the Hun horse-archers from the Byzantine wings. Rather than close with the Franks, Narses had halted his cavalry-archers when within good bowshot and had leisurely shot the Frankish army to pieces as it stood helpless, unable to close.

With a background of uninterrupted military successes, the Byzantines approached the tenth century and closed out this preliminary period of their history with decisive victories against fine armies of horse-archers. On numerous occasions they defeated the best of the Saracen cavalry, exterminating the army of Omar in A.D. 863 and repeating the lesson of shock combined with missiles in a series of actions against the Emir of Aleppo.

These Byzantine armies offered an excellent composition that provided the shock of heavy cavalry with the full support of proficient missile horsemen. Not since the days of Alexander had a European army been so consistent in the field. The Byzantines had been equally impressive against the fine Saracen bowmen. Their tactics had taken full advantage of the inability of horse-archers to withstand the shock of close combat. The Hun archers had first reduced the effectiveness of the Saracen bowman; the Byzantine heavy cavalry had then closed in to mop up under the covering fire of their own Hun archers. This early Byzantine army commands the respect and the admiration of military students because of their elastic and realistic use of the principles of shock and firepower.

The Byzantine Army—A.D. 900–A.D. 1400

In the light of the successes of the preceding centuries, it is difficult for the historian to rationalize the gradual trend toward dependence upon foot-archers that occurred in the second phase of Byzantine military history. The battle lessons taught by Narses and Belisarius were apparently forgotten as the emphasis turned to the application of pure shock. The only possible explanation for the Byzantine development of foot-archers is that the Huns became undependable or not available. It was the practice of the Huns to wander in and out of battle commitments and alliances and to abrogate treaties of such alliances. Whatever the reason, the Huns were not available as a part of the later Byzantine military establishment. It was a fatal loss. Their great horn bows, plied from horseback, were sorely missed, and the Byzantines suddenly found themselves with no adequate distant missile attack capabilities.

The only solution available to the Byzantines was the formation of a center of infantry-archers. It was not a happy transition. With their bows in the hands of infantry-archers, the Byzantines accepted a parity with the lesser armies of the later Persian Empire. This new Byzantine composition was to learn, as many nations of history have learned, that a center of infantry-archers could neither support nor act as a pivot for the operations of wings of heavy cavalry. The Byzantine army, as a result, developed a fatal lack of distant power that hastened the dissolution of the empire.

The small efficient armies that had once represented the Byzantine empire in the field now degenerated into compositions of awesome power that were fatally slow in maneuver and deployment. Relying completely on a multiplicity of weapons and excessive armor protection, the Byzantine army lost the dash and speed it had possessed in A.D. 500.

The Byzantine troopers of this later period were among the most heavily armed men in history. They were equipped with sword, dagger, bow, lance, and, quite often, the battle-ax. The men rode armored with a steel helmet and a mailed shirt that reached from neck to thigh. They were protected with metal gauntlets and steel shoes, and all the horses of the front line were encased in frontlets.

This decisive arm was supported by two classes of infantry. The first, the light armed infantry, were archers equipped with light, sleeveless coats of chain mail. The heavier class of infantry carried shield, lance, sword, and ax and were seldom in action except in the later battle stages or in exercises in rough country. In formal battle, the infantry held the center, supported on either wing by cavalry. Against enemy cavalry, the Byzantine infantry formed hollow squares behind their shields. The cavalry usually equaled, or exceeded, the total number of foot soldiers. The Byzantines now formed into two lines—a fighting line in the van and a support line in the rear. Behind these lines was a reserve to replace casualties and on either wing was a small and compact massing of horsemen to protect the flanks.

The wide-ranging activities of the heavy cavalry were now severely strictured and rendered exceedingly perilous by the absence of accompanying missile support from light horse-archers. The Seljuk Turks were soon to point up this battle weakness in the action at Manzikert.

The Seljuk Turks, although formidable horse-archers, were not among the foremost practitioners of distant war. During this period of their history, they were composed of elements of Bulgarian, Scythian, and Magyar peoples and, being in the process of organization, had no strong central government. They were great horsemen and fine archers with a composite bow of great power, but they were deficient in the knowledge of the tactical movement of troops in the field.

In the middle of the eleventh century, the Seljuks had made serious inroads on the frontiers of the Byzantine Empire, occupying many strong positions on the eastern border. A Byzantine army was in the field against them.

The Turks were "given to ambushes and stratagems of every sort."[1] They were expert in scouting operations and in feints to feel out enemy strengths and weaknesses. The Seljuks had difficulty in maintaining an army in being in the field for, whatever their own strength, they usually engaged in small detachment attacks with small groups of horsemen sweeping the flanks and executing limited charges when the opportunity was presented. Unable to use their great mobility to advantage as they confused mere movement with maneuverability, they were highly deficient in striking power and shock. Usually they were unable to apply the principle of economy of force because of this inability to conduct offensive maneuver. The Seljuks had never been able to stand up against determined heavy cavalry and they were not effective against steady infantry.

The Tactica of Leo described their composition:

> The Turkish horde consisted of innumerable bands of light horsemen who carried javelin and scimetar but relied most of all on their arrows for victory. In battle they advanced not in one mass but in small scattered bands which swept along the enemy's front and around his flanks, pouring in flights of arrows and executing partial charges if they saw a good opportunity. On a fair open field however, they could be ridden down by Byzantine heavy cavalry, who are therefore recommended to close with them at once, and not to exchange arrows from a distance. Steady infantry also they could not break and foot archers were their special dread, since the bow of the infantry archer is larger and carries further than that of the horsemen; thus they were able to have their horses shot under them and when dismounted were

almost helpless, the nomads of the steppes having never been accustomed to fight on foot. The general who has to contend with them should endeavor to get to close quarters at once.

As Leo had stated, the Turks dismounted were no more than third-rate infantry. Separated from their horses, they lacked confidence and seemed unable to defend themselves. Armies of horse-archers make greater demands upon leadership and discipline than do more stable, more easily controlled formations. Bowmen on fleet horses can have their unity destroyed by their mobility. Irregular bodies of horsemen can enclose the enemy, but the enclosure will have no substance unless the movement is calculated offensive maneuver. Aimless, rapidly moving bodies of horsemen, mutually unsupported, can present no real strength or offensive threat. One of the solid principles of war is the dictum that an army should not be moved unless advantage accrues as the result of the movement.[2] This the Seljuk Turks had not learned.

Because of these deficiencies in tactics, organization, and discipline, the Turkish effort against the Byzantines had been mere incursions for booty, usually conducted on the far fringes of the empire. The shattering defeat the Byzantines suffered at the hands of these irregular Turkish archers occurred at Manzikert, in the border province of Armenia.

Although the effects of Manzikert were disastrous, the Turks displayed little skill in their conduct of the battle. The tactical errors of the Byzantines and their lack of mobility contributed more to the Turkish victory than any excellence on the part of the wild horsemen of Sultan Alp Arsen.

In the spring of 1071, Emperor Romanus Diogenes moved an army of more than sixty thousand men to the eastern frontier of the empire in an effort to recover the citadels of Akhlat and Manzikert that had fallen into the hands of the Turks. Siege operations had recovered Manzikert and similar operations were in progress at Akhlat when the Byzantines collided with a Turkish army of more than one hundred thousand men.

The initial contacts quickly demonstrated the Turkish weakness for sustained attack against a determined order of battle. Alp Arsen was so impressed by the steadiness of the Byzantine army that he offered peace on a basis of immediate withdrawal. Romanus refused the Turkish offer and the armies were drawn up for battle.

In the preliminaries a small force of Byzantines had been destroyed when they made a rash attack on a body of Turkish cavalry. The Turks drew the force into an ambush and killed or captured them all. They made no effort to close with the enemy other than sending forward large bodies of archers who sent their arrows into the Byzantine camp at extreme range. The Byzantines suffered casualties from this storm of missiles and Romanus began a formal advance with his entire line after his skirmishers had been unable to close with the elusive Turks.

In the face of the Byzantine shock attack, the Turks drifted before the assault. Refusing action, they drew the Byzantines farther and farther from their fortified camp, which was not sufficiently garrisoned. After a long and irritating pursuit of the Turks, who continued to gall the column with arrows, Romanus ordered a retirement. While refacing was being accomplished, the Turks closed suddenly to point-blank range and interrupted the movement so severely that Romanus was forced to attempt the difficult maneuver of changing front while under fire. The second line defected and, the field was abandoned by the Byzantine reserves who retreated hastily to the fortified camp. The Turks then drove in an attack against the Byzantine rear, splitting the center from the right wing. As night fell, the right wing collapsed and fled the field.

During the frenzied maneuvers in semidarkness, Romanus allowed his left wing to become detached from the center; this wing was in turn destroyed in an independent action with the Turkish archers. The isolated center now came under final attack from the flanks and rear, and in complete darkness, the Turks rained unaimed showers of arrows in upon beaten and doomed men. Not a man of the center escaped.

Manzikert demonstrated the futility of the pursuit of horse-archers by heavy cavalry unless a river or lake or mountain formed a barrier against which the horsemen could be pinned. Romanus wasted his strength and destroyed his tactical formations in fighting highly mobile troops who waited patiently for an advantageous moment to strike. In doing so, Romanus invited general attack from an enemy that had shown small ability against a determined and organized defense. The destruction of demoralized troops in a night action was a battle situation best adapted to the small unit attacks of the Turks, and they conducted this assault with relative impunity.

The Seljuks, relying upon the bow as the principal arm, possessed the great speed that was denied the heavy horsemen of the Byzantines who were encumbered with lance, sword, ax, and bow in addition to their armor. Had the Byzantines held formation, the superior speed of the Turks would have been negated by their lack of offensive shock and the Byzantine cavalry would have had protection from their infantry-archers. Had Romanus elected to prepare a defense in the open field, rather than attempt retirement, the Byzantines could have expected the possibility of a stalemate that would have left their army intact and forced the withdrawal of this formidable Turkish raiding force.

Although the Byzantine Empire was to persist until the thirteenth century, the barbarian power in Asia Minor was to grow stronger and stronger until the mailed horsemen of Europe were to accept the loss of the holy land to the principles of distant war. As had been the case with the ancient Persians and others, the Byzantines had armored and equipped themselves out of existence with an unwieldy cavalry corps that had no proper missile support.

The dreadful and indecisive Crusades were to bring the two con-flicting schools of war into conflict.

15

The Bow in the Crusades

The desert archers were born of fanatacism. The Muhammadan conquests began in Arabia in A.D. 630, and for four centuries the green wave conducted a militant and successful religious war that engulfed Persia, Syria, and all of the Near East. Egypt fell, in turn, to the Muhammadan archers and then most of Spain and Africa. The Muhammadan advance into Europe was finally contained by Charles Martel at the great Battle of Tours in A.D. 732.

What had started as the mere vision of an opportunistic religious leader had resulted in full-scale conquests under the green banner of Mohammed. The fall of Jerusalem had aroused all of Christian Europe against the turbaned desert archers of Islam.

The First Crusade

Christian religious fanatacism set the stage for Saladin. In the eleventh century, the popes exhorted Europe to attack the Moslem world in an effort to recover the holy land. The result of the First Crusade had been the capture of Jerusalem by the Christians in 1099. The indifferent leadership of the Muhammadans had cost them the third most important city of Muhammadanism, for Jerusalem, along with Mecca and Medina, made up the geographical and sentimental bulwark of the religion.

The Second Crusade

The Second Crusade (1147–1149) was disastrous for European arms. Conrad's German army was destroyed at Iconium with that of Louis when their united armies failed to take Damascus. A million men had died in a two-year campaign that resulted in complete victory for the Moslems. But the Christians still held Jerusalem.

The desert men, all the way from Smyrna in the east to Cairo and Alexandria in Egypt, flexed their composite bows and waited for leadership. It came at last in the person of Saladin, who, in 1174, became sultan of Egypt and Syria. He swiftly consolidated the warring and sometimes mutually hostile desert tribes into a disciplined and strong striking force and, by 1186, the Moslem general felt strong enough to proclaim a *jihad,* a holy war, against the Christians.

The troops that Saladin assembled made up one of the great armies of history. To evaluate its efficiency, one must consider the high quality of the opposition. Saladin faced a Christian army of almost 250,000 men—the most ambitious force ever dispatched from Europe to the holy land—that had for its main offense the flower of European chivalry, tremendously powerful men in armor. At close quarters they were frightful antagonists. No other fighting men in the world could stand against them individually when they plunged into battle swinging their great broadswords.

To support these ferocious hand-to-hand swordsmen, the Crusaders had the crossbow, which for sheer power and penetration was the best missile weapon to be developed by man until the advent of firearms. The iron quarrels of the crossbow were murderous missiles; a man felt naked and defenseless under their fire for they could sheer through the best armor with ease. An attack on a column under the protection of expert crossbowmen was a venture of great peril. The Crusaders, strong at missile war during this period and invincible at close quarters, were antagonists to be feared and respected.

To oppose them, Saladin had his desert horsemen, armed with the composite bow and the scimitar. The composite bow had reached its full development in this period of history. It was heavily reflexed, constructed of horn, sinew, and wood, and assembled by great craftsmen. The pull was in excess of 100 pounds and the draw was assisted by mechanical means—varying systems of string pullers. The bows of Saladin were the forerunners of the Turkish bows of the Janissaries which were probably the most highly refined and expertly constructed bows in history. In addition to its great power, the composite bow could be operated at great speed. It was capable of launching three or four arrows while the more cumbersome crossbow was being wound. This advantage in speed of operations was offset to a considerable degree by the lighter quality of the arrows. The Saracen missiles had great difficulty in penetrating the Crusader armor, particularly when such armor was reinforced with felt.

At the jolting collision of close-order work, the Saracens were completely outmatched. Their light curved scimitars could not engage the broadsword of the Crusaders on equal terms.

The first battle for the repossession of Jerusalem was fought near Tiberias in 1187. Out on the hot and parched desert, a composite army of twenty thousand knights and crossbowmen met the archers of Saladin. It was a frantic and desperate battle fought by the Crusaders against light horsemen who drifted in and out of bowshot at will. The Saracens rode around the heavy cavalry of the Crusaders, who were unable to bring the Moslem cavalry within lance reach. The desert archers were seriously deterred by the whining bolts of the crossbow and suffered numerous long-range casualties. In the end, the operational speed of the composite bow turned the decision as heavy and accurate fire bit deeply into the armor of the knights. The Crusaders had not yet developed the protective measures that were later in vogue. A greatly overextended European line was subjected to a concentration of arrows and forced into a defensive stand. When night came, the Moslem cavalry flanked the wings of the Crusaders and enclosed them within a dry camp inside a ring of archers.

At dawn, the Crusaders began a desperate attack against the rain of steel-tipped arrows, but the swiftly moving horsemen of Saladin separated the knights from the support of the infantry crossbowmen. The scattered foot soldiers were shot down by the Moslems, and the knights, on ponderous horses, could generate no attack against the fluid Saracen line. In a last gesture of battle, the knights hurled themselves against the shifting enemy deployment that had overwhelmed them. They were forced into a close formation by the galloping rings of desert horsemen. Raymond, the Christian commander, was able to cut through the lines with a few horsemen to reach the coast and safety. The rest of the knights of Europe died on the field.

His assault tactics perfected, Saladin turned his attention to the investing of Christian strongholds. In rapid succession, he took Acre,

Sidon, Bereut, and Ascalon. Within a few months, the holy land was virtually in his hands and, in September, 1187, Saladin was before the walls of Jerusalem. A few weeks later, his mining operations brought down a section of the wall and the holy city fell into Moslem hands. The Muhammadan objective had been gained.

The Third Crusade

The loss of Jerusalem spurred the Christians to a Third Crusade. In 1189, when Richard Coeur de Lion came upon the scene, his mere presence was sufficient to raise the hopes of the Crusaders. Saladin met a worthy opponent in Richard, who was a bad king but a great fighting man. Richard had a flexible mind—in an inflexible age. He was not a great tactician, and he realized his own limitations in the handling of large bodies of men. Although he was a heavy weapons man of the Age of Chivalry that produced him, he knew also the value of the crossbow as an offensive weapon and in the protection of his columns. It was necessary to approach Richard's army with great caution as the harassing Moslems were soon to learn.

In the field against the agile Saladin, Richard was handicapped by the relative immobility of his heavy knights. He very carefully weighed the speed of fire of the composite bow against the superior penetration of the crossbow, and was able to gain a stalemate with the great Saladin.

It is not within the space limits of this book to detail the Third Crusade's long series of desert actions that followed the fall of Jerusalem to the Moslems. For three years Saladin contended with Christian knights led by Richard and Barbarossa but the Moslem did not have uninterrupted success against these formidable field commanders. Occasionally, his desert horsemen were defeated when they came into close contact with the European swordsmen. Saladin could not always use his most potent weapon to good effect. The necessity for assaulting strongholds that could be supplied and provisioned from the sea by Christian ships required services and equipment that no cavalry arm could supply. Saladin was forced to convert his light horsemen into siege troops and this necessitated hand-to-hand battle.

As the Third Crusade continued, Richard began to perfect defenses against the composite bow of the Moslems.

In 1191, Acre had been recovered by the Crusaders after a siege of two years, falling to the Franks on July 12. For some weeks after the fall of the fortress the Crusaders rested in the city, engaged in truce negotiations with Saladin. It became apparent, late in August, that discussion was useless and on July 22, Richard began the march to Jerusalem. A direct move was impossible because of the barrier of the Ephraim Range and Richard decided to set up a base at Jaffa. With that plan in mind, he began a march along the old Roman road that passed through Haifa, Akhlit, Caesarea, and Arsoulf. It was obvious that Saladin would harass the march and Richard had the problem of providing protection for a column several miles in length.

Nearest the sea he placed infantry guards and the baggage train; beside them, in compact bands, he spaced his cavalry equally along the line of march. On the desert side, the long column of infantry crossbowmen covered the entire length of the column. They required nineteen days for a march of eighty miles while suffering from the intense heat.

Bo-ha-Din's account of this march describes the events of the Moslem attack:

> The enemy moved in order of battle; their infantry marched between us and their cavalry keeping as level and firm as a wall. Each foot soldier had a thick hassock of felt and under it a mailed shirt so strong that our arrows made no impression upon them. They meanwhile shot at us with crossbows, which struck down horses and men among the Moslems. I noted among them [the Christians] men who had from one to ten arrows sticking from their backs, yet trudged on at ordinary pace and did not fall from their ranks . . . and so they marched until they finally pitched their tents on the farther side of the river at Caesarea.

The main attack on the Crusader line came near Arsoulf, led by Bedouins, Soudanese archers, and Turkish horse-archers. The knights' horses began to go down under the arrows but the counterfire from the crossbows severely punished the Moslems who had no protection from the iron quarrels. A series of charges by the Christian heavy cavalry applied shock that the desert men were unable to absorb and Arsoulf ended with a convincing Christian victory.

In this battle, the crossbow proved to be more than a match for the composite bow of the Turks. The light Turkish arrows could not penetrate the heavy felt and the chain armor that Richard had provided for his men. The Moslems, with their best weapon ineffective, were unable to muster sufficient offense to disturb the Christian heavy horsemen.

Saladin learned, as the Huns had discovered at Chalons, that assault on armored horsemen by light archers is not productive of result. Never again did Saladin risk his men in hand-to-hand frontal attack.

The crossbow made what was probably its most impressive battle appearance at Arsoulf. Its slow rate of fire was not a factor in an open-field engagement for the speed of the composite bow was negated by the heavy protection afforded the Christian crossbowmen.

On other fields, without a Richard to inspire them, the Crusaders were not so fortunate. Harenc, Tiberias, Acre, and Mansourah were great tactical victories for the desert horsemen. A second battle at Carrhae, fought on the same field that covered the brittle bones of the legions of Crassus, turned back history eleven centuries. This second battle again demonstrated the military fact that heavy troops must not be caught in open country by proficient horse-archers.

In the spring of 1104, Bohemud of Antioch determined to make an attack in force in Mesopotamia for the purpose of garrisoning the city of Harran (Carrhae). The countryside around the city had been laid waste and the Turkish troops in the ancient town were short of provisions. A Christian army of twelve thousand marched to assault the garrison. Deficient in missile weapons, the army was cut off in the desert by a Turkish army of ten thousand archers. Before the initial attack of the Franks, the Moslems gave way slowly until the Christian knights had been decoyed to a spot in the desert twelve miles from Harran.

Late in the afternoon, Bohemud had wearied of the fruitless pursuit of the swiftly moving Turks and ordered the knights into camp. The moment the Franks began to prepare a campsite, the Turks came with a rush, pouring in flights of arrows. The second Battle of Carrhae became a replica of the annihilation of Crassus. The Franks entrenched on a hill until nightfall and then began a slow retreat toward Edessa.

At daylight, the Turks were on their flanks. The Turks split the Christian line with intrusions in force until all semblance of formation was lost. Then at point-blank range, the bowmen deliberately shot down the struggling knights as the Christians made a futile effort to close with the sword. More than six thousand dead marked the line of the retreat of the mauled Christian army.

A consideration of the battles of the Third Crusade offers the possibility that these light desert archers of Saladin met the most formidable opposition ever encountered by troops relying principally on the bow. The Christians, particularly the powerful fighting men led by Richard, were tremendous men physically and were superbly mounted and equipped. Their missile weapon, the crossbow, proved to be at least equal in range and superior in penetration to the composite bow of the Moslems. In no other battles of history did the crossbow perform so well. A hit meant death or a severe wound; the light armor of the Saracens offered no protection against the crossbow quarrels.

In contrast, the chain mail and felt surcoats of the Crusaders and infantry-archers were almost proof against the light Saracen arrows. No greater defense against arrows was ever devised than this combination of chain mail and felt as used in the Crusades.

As individual or unit swordsmen, the knights of the twelfth century were a military class apart. There could be no question of the valor of these men or of the dreadful execution they were able to deal out at close quarters. The great Crusader sword, so heavy it can scarcely be lifted by a modern man, was a flashing instrument of terror that was able to shear through armor and flesh. It could decapitate a horse.

The horses that these men rode, although deficient in speed, were powerful in attack and trained for ferocity in battle. No light cavalry, wielding the scimitar, could stand against the Crusader heavy cavalry.

The Moslems, facing shock and powerful missiles, had only the mobility of their fleet horses and the possession of the initiative. Against the best-equipped Crusaders, the Moslem missile attack was effective only against the horse or an occasional chink in armor. It required swarms of arrows to inflict minor damage to the mailed men.

The effort produced by Richard in the Third Crusade represented the greatest concentration of force ever placed in the field by Europe outside the Continent. The fact that this array of 250,000 men was held to a stalemate reflects the genius of Saladin. His all-around excellence in the handling of all arms under varying conditions of warfare cannot be evaluated properly in a discussion of the tactical operations of the bow in war. The Moslem performed a miracle of organization and training as he converted his horsemen into proficient siege troops.

Such warfare is foreign to the experience or inclination of light cavalry, for such troops become restless in siege warfare and deteriorate rapidly. No commander of missile warfare until Mukhali, the great Mongol general of Kublai Khan, was able to make so successful a conversion as Saladin accomplished with his Saracens.

The static position war so often imposed upon Saladin by the nature of the work to be done tested his versatility and adaptability to the utmost. His army probably had a greater mastery of the combined tactics of Europe and Asia than any force in history until modern times.

The seacoast walled cities of the type constructed by the Crusaders in the holy land still command the admiration of military engineers. Tremendously strong fortresses with walls that still stand intact, they could not be softened by assault without extended preliminary sapping and battering by siege engines. These siege operations subjected the Moslems to the best weapons of the Crusaders—operated under the most favorable conditions. The crossbow, wielded from walls where the slow rate of fire was not important, was much superior to the composite bow. In the final action the soldiers of Saladin were forced into sword play with the greatest swordsmen in the world.

That Saladin more than held his own under these conditions of battle is a matter of historical record. After three years of battle, the Christian quest for Jerusalem ended in failure. The truce of 1192 left the Crusaders in possession of a small coastal strip. A quarter of a million Christians had lost their lives in a futile attempt to regain the holy city.

Jerusalem remained in Moslem hands until 1917.

The leadership qualities presented in the actions of the Third Crusade were of very high order—when the state of military tactical development in Europe is considered and the resources of the Saracens are evaluated. Richard Plantagenet has been sometimes maligned as a reckless, sword-swinging jouster who made an aristocratic pageant of war. However, his performance as a field leader does not justify such a casual dismissal of his military capabilities. Richard showed unusual ability in holding the components of his army in close cooperation with each other in positions of mutual support. He did not permit the maneuvers of the Moslems to separate his knights from the support of his crossbowmen; thus, he was able to avoid some of the disasters that overwhelmed less able commanders. Richard showed unusual ability in the handling of missile troops, for no commander of his age was able to use the crossbow so successfully. This, in itself, was a remarkable attitude for an aristocrat of the feudal age. The usual leader of armored knights in the Middle Ages was contemptuous of missiles and the men who wielded these weapons. Richard was not wedded to the cult of the sword and the lance.

Not the least of Richard's capability for war rested in his completely adequate defense against the Saracen arrows. No other commander of medieval heavy armored cavalry demonstrated the defensive ability of this king of England. Two centuries after Richard, the armed knights were dying in thousands, milling on reddened fields under lesser commanders as they fell helpless before the arrows of the Mongols. Under Richard, the knights of Europe reached their highest military potential.

An evaluation of the Saracen army has already been indicated. As a field general, directing the maneuvers of light mobile troops, Saladin rates as one of the great captains of the bow. His slashing operations against formidable crossbowmen and dangerous mounted and armored swordsmen were productive of successful military result. In evasive war of attrition—grinding down the quality of the enemy by raiding operations—he was unsurpassed. Against walled cities, he was more than adequate. When it is understood that the Crusaders were the most dangerous men in the world at close quarters and could not be ridden around with impunity and destroyed at long range, it will be seen that a field engagement against them was a severe test of discipline and equipment.

The army that Saladin commanded was, to the Christians, a mere coalition of reckless Muhammadans, held together by religious rites rather than racial bonds. Saladin demonstrated magnificent qualities of leadership in assembling them into a dangerous and steady fighting force. The great Moslem usually commanded the weaker center, leaving his strong right wing to one of his most experienced generals. Saladin was not physically strong and was often unable to stand the rigors of field service. He died two years after the close of the Third Crusade at the age of fifty-six. These two great adversaries, Richard and Saladin, developed a curious mutual respect for each other that bordered on affection.

16

The Feudal Knight: End of an Era

The Western European military establishment, circa A.D. 1000 was expressed by the gentlemen on horseback with lance and sword. For about four centuries these exponents of mounted shock were supreme on European fields during a period when the art of war was at a low ebb tactically in these areas.

It had been a cumulative influence that had set up this cult of the horse and the sword, for this was an age of ritual. Caesar had had a part in the arming of these feudal knights, for the memory of the great swordsmen of the legion was strong in Europe. The raw power that had been resident in the Spartan *hoplite* and the immobile steadiness of a sarissa-bearing pezetaeri of Alexander's phalanx had contributed to the creation in Europe of the iron knight in the saddle.

The Goths had had a part in the development of Western European chivalry. Large men physically, the Goths, too, had preferred the shock of headlong individual combat. The Byzantines, most heavily armed of all armored horsemen, had been the pattern and immediate prototype of the western European knight.

From the beginning, the knights had been a class apart—making their own rules of war; establishing a ritual for the possession of the sword; creating an aristocracy whose badge was exclusive use and possession of the horse. They glamourized and sanctified war as the most glorious of adventures, protecting their social class by an elaborate procedure of ransoms and words of honor and paroles. They bore honorable wounds from sword and lance with pride and arrogance and fortitude. Parading to battle with a great gesture, with painted shields

144

and a lady's red scarf affixed to their helmet, they set themselves up as the moderators and the designers of proper social military conduct. They shed their blood on ridiculous quests and crusades in search of dragons and damsels in distress, living to the full the childlike superstitions of their age, crossing the clanging drawbridges of their castles with a flourish of trumpets. They were careless and contemptuous of their lives and the lives of everyone else, slaying or maiming their best friends in tournament jousts between wars, making war a personal matter to be settled as individuals, dreaming of a castle to be felled, a rival to be slain, a woman to be seduced. Godlike men in fear of the Church, with ungodlike manners, they accepted rape and pillage and murder as the natural rights of a gentleman. Recognizing a king but refusing any real impressment of authority, they were proud, arrogant men on horseback.

There were pennants and banners and ribbons fluttering from lance heads. A retinue of servants cared for the riding horse, the charger, the courser, and the battle horse. A single horse rigged for battle was not sufficient; these men rode to war with a stable of beasts, each serving a particular need. The silent serfs walked beside them, unprotected from the hazards of battle and subject to slaughter if captured. It was a day of greatly privileged men who had formulated for their pleasure the rules of war. It was a day of champions, of doughty men meeting between the lines for single combat. It was a day when men rode alone before the enemy, inviting combat, according to the ritualized rules.

It was glittering; it was colorful; but it was not war.

This theater of western Europe was to have many centuries without effective missile threat to the mailed knights. The wars these aristocrats waged were all contests within the school they had created. As long as these knights remained in their own area of western Europe, they could rely upon the assumption that war would be fought according to their rules. It was only when they went on Crusades that they encountered missiles.

Here in their own small area the European knights fought through bruising, brawling centuries with lance horsemen opposed to lance horsemen in battles that ended with hand-to-hand work with the ax or sword. It was naïve war and fought by men with small tactics and minor strategy. For many years there was no threat to these iron horsemen except from the other iron horsemen who opposed them. There was no military science in Europe and no formal armies except levies carelessly gathered by the lord of a manor.

When the knights of the Middle Ages were not engaged with each other in their highly formalized battles, their opponents were Vikings, Saxons, and Danes who rushed on foot to attack with axes and swords. It was primitive war, hardly superior in tactics to the battles in the dawn of history in Sumeria and Babylon.

There had been but two interruptions to mar the complacency of these armored knights. Fortunately for the security of Europe, neither of these attacks against the feudal warriors by mounted missile troops had been supported by tactical efficiency or formal battle organization. The first of these intruders had been the Huns. A second incursion of horse-archers had occurred in the ninth century with the invasion of the Magyars. These were a people of great military potential—and small organization. They succeeded in setting up a small and brief horse empire in Hungary. Region, the historian, said of them, "Had their strength and perseverance been as great as their audacity, no race could have stood against them."

The weakness of the Magyars was their inability to sustain battle or a campaign because of their lust for plunder. Pitched battles with the Magyars were rare, as these people, intent on the looting possibilities, were evasive and badly disciplined. At Augsburg in A.D. 810, they ambushed a Christian army under Lewis of Bavaria but usually they could not be brought to decisive battle.

The Magyars seldom appeared as an army in being in the field. They spread across a territory like locusts, in bands of one hundred or less, supporting each other casually, occasionally combining for brief periods of combat in irregular unit formations. When their pack animals were well laden with loot they would retire to their Hungarian bases, fighting rear-guard actions if necessary.

To combat them, the wealth and the people of overrun nations would concentrate in walled cities—the Magyars were never able to develop any capacity for siege operations. The Saxons and the Thuringians took to the horse and built up large and successful levies of armored cavalry. With these forces, the small raiding parties of Magyars were cut to pieces when the terrain conditions were favorable for heavy cavalry. King Otto caught them in an unfavorable position for rapid maneuver on the banks of the Lesh River. The Magyars were trapped and destroyed in a decisive action. It was a conspicuous success for the European theory of heavy cavalry, and it reinforced the position of the knights as battle instruments.

This view that the iron men obtained of the bow in Magyar hands was misleading and dangerous. The fairly easy defeat of the Magyars gave western Europe an exaggerated confidence in heavy weapons that was to be rudely shattered when proficient horse-archers with well-trained offensive armies appeared on the scene in the thirteenth century. A century or two after the Magyars, the knights were dying in thousands before the arrows of the Mongols.

But up to A.D. 1200, the minor warning signals from Asia had been largely ignored, for the small contacts that these knights had had with missiles had been a Magyar invasion and the experience gained by Crusaders in protecting themselves from the light Saracen arrows. The commitment to shock cavalry persisted in Europe and the armored knights were not supported by any arm except ragged posses of halberdiers or pikemen, who were systematically slaughtered by rival horsemen in battles devoid of science. No school of tactics developed, nor was any school to develop for many years. It was not until the seventeenth century that Europe fielded a professional army.

The knights continued to be decisive on European fields until the day when they rode into the realities of the thirteenth century to find that the science of war had passed them by. In England, the silent yeomen discovered the longbow; in France and Spain and Italy and Germany, the crossbow contributed its weight to missile war; in Asia, the Mongols were flexing the composite bows in preparation for conquest.

And so to the fields of Europe there came, at long last, the stern principles of distant offensive war. No longer could the thrusting lance or the slashing sword control a field or survive on a field. Every hedgerow, every swale, every forested grove, contained a threat of death from missiles that ignored plate armor.

The iron-encased gentlemen on horseback found no answer.

17

The Mongol Horse-Archers

The Mongol horse-archers began their development as early as 700 B.C., for their kinsmen, the Scythians, are known to have had effective horse-bowmen by that date. Prior to 500 B.C., irregular formations of horse-archers from Mongolia were pressing against China. The third century before Christ saw the beginning of the construction of the Great Wall by Emperor Shih Hwang as a defense against the nomads of the Gobi. It was a futile defense but the wall was to be strengthened century after century—to reach its final form during the Ming dynasty in A.D. 1500.

Always the Tartars pressed against China. It was a war of centuries and with varying fortunes for the badly organized nomads. A great battle of 120 B.C. marked an invasion of China in such force that the Chinese victory produced Tartar casualties stated to have been ninety thousand. The centuries grew into a thousand years for, in A.D. 1004, the Chinese purchased a peace that had no meaning and no substance.

In A.D. 1200, China and the abutting Gobi Desert was a sealed world. The great forces that were developing in Asia were of no concern to the Near East and the Mediterranean. Western Europe was in a feudal age of knighthood. These areas, half a world away, knew nothing of the bitter conflicts that were waging in Mongolia and China, where war was developing into a matchless science as warring nomad tribes fought each other for supremacy.

This new warfare, *perfected* in the Gobi Desert from patterns that had been set up by Parthians and other early peoples, was war of maneuver, with fluid movements and extended pivots. It was a strategy

148

that was complete with fifth columns, espionage, dissemination of false rumors, and a liberal use of the psychology of fear. The tactical school made use of relatively small armies, superbly disciplined, trained, and equipped. War became an application of swift and relentless offensive.

The generals who developed this type of war were among the greatest in history. They supported their troops in the field with an amazing development of the science of logistics. Having mastered the art of fighting over degrees of longtitude, miles from a friendly base, they demonstrated that cavalry need not be attached to a base. They developed new concepts of ground and terrain. They understood the principles of survival in what they called *serious* ground. They originated iron rations of dried milk and powdered meat. Their tactical weapon was the composite bow, elevated to full dignity as a major weapon. With this bow they conquered, organized, and held a great deal of their known world.

Europeans of A.D. 1200, knew nothing of this fearsome development in the Gobi; least of all were they aware that 1162 had witnessed the birth of a son to the wife of a chief of the Yakka Mongols, on the fringe of the northern Gobi. Temujin was his name. In A.D. 1208 he became Genghis Khan, kakahn of the Mongols and the greatest conqueror in history.

The world was very large in A.D. 1200. Generations of Europeans lived and died in their own small valleys, never to get more than twenty miles from their homes in their lifetimes. There were tales told by the venturesome who had journeyed a few hundred miles—there was no other information about a great unknown world that rolled to mysterious horizons.

The Crusades had been the only large movement of men to affect Europe and these had been mere excursions into lands that were old in history and known to Europeans. The voyages to the holy land were hardly longer than the length of the well-traveled Mediterranean. Beyond the holy land stretched a great unknown vacuum without history, for Marco Polo was not yet born to tell his tales of Asiatic empires to incredulous listeners.

Europe could not know that the tactics of total war were forming in Asia. It was not until this terror, brought by small, disciplined groups of horsemen, was standing on the very threshold of Europe that the implications of this new type of war were realized.

It was with unbelieving horror that Europe viewed these Asiatic horsemen who were riding on the fringe of Western civilization. It was not that Europe was having its first view of such horsemen. Attila the Hun had paid them a visit; other Asiatic riders had flitted across the history of Europe—Scythians, Medes, Magyars, and Avars. But these had been the visitations of aimless men, raiding ferociously and then going beyond the horizon. They had been men without apparent purpose save plunder.

The men who came from the Gobi in the thirteenth century were a new and frightening breed. They swallowed whole nations at a stride. They did not plunder much for immediate gain; rather, they herded nations like fat cows, for repeated milking. These Mongols were men of terrible fixed purpose, organized into regiments and brigades that set out to conquer the world. These riders were not raiders; they had come to impose permanent rule upon Europe. Slaughter, looting, and rape were incidental by-products, not a part of the broad plan.

Never before in the history of the world had so perfect an application of armed force inflicted itself upon civilization. The Mongol armies created by Genghis Khan represented the highest level that the attack of man upon man had achieved.

This Mongol army was capable of subsisting in enemy country. It required no commissary. If food was not available, the Mongols simply abstained from food. They were able to take almost incredible physical punishment. Subotai, the great general of the khan, was once called from the field for an urgent conference. This remarkable soldier, then in his fifties, bandaged himself and rode twelve hundred miles in less than eight days; he then returned to his army to resume field operations.

This union of weapons and tactics and physical stamina was to stun the world. The efficiency of Parthians, Scythians, Huns, and other practitioners of mobile war had been only relative. Genghis Khan contributed grim talents of organization and iron discipline that were complete reevaluations of the science of war. All the wild horse-archers prior to Genghis Khan had been inclined to abandon battle (often when the enemy was on the verge of annihilation) for the more pleasant prospect of looting the opposing baggage trains and camps. On at least two occasions, badly beaten and demoralized Roman troops had almost escaped the Parthians, who had become preoccupied with looting.

Genghis Khan inflicted a dreadful iron discipline on his troops. No Mongol detachment ceased the business of killing in favor of a quest for loot. Even had a detachment been willing to risk the severe penalties for such an act, there would have been no prospect of individual gain. Mere battlefield possession of loot did not give any Mongol trooper title to that loot. The troopers looted when the battle was ended, on command, and all loot was equitably distributed among combat and other personnel, without regard to individual captures. The fletcher, the arrowmaker, the bowyer, and other craftsmen back in the Gobi had claim to a percentage of battle loot and captives.

The speed, stamina, and horsemanship of the Mongol army was not comparable to any other standards. In September of 1221, Genghis Khan, engaged in a pursuit, sent his army 130 miles over the rough mountain area of Afghanistan in two days with but a single halt. Batu marched one of his armies 180 miles in three days. Individual Mongols rode as far as 600 miles on a single pony in nine days. It was customary to send Mongol youths as replacements to armies 2,000 miles from the Gobi, with simple orders to find the army and report for duty.

In organization for battle, Genghis Khan was many centuries ahead of his era. His columns were task forces, complete in arms and equipment, information, interarmy communications, and tactical and stragetic planning. No field commander for many centuries after the Mongols had such complete control of battle situations that often involved triple columns in actions hundreds of miles apart.

The battle equipment of these Mongol cavalrymen permitted extended operations miles from any base of supplies. Each trooper carried the files, hatchets, small tools, and repair equipment necessary for the maintenance of his weapons in the field. His physical well-being was attended by the sleeping bags, tents, heavy sheepskin clothing, and field armor of boiled hide that were carried on the march.

The Mongol bow reached a degree of excellence in finish and workmanship. The pull of the bow varied from strengths of about 70 pounds to as much as 160 pounds. The bow was not standardized; the fact that it was a hand product of skilled craftsmen made uniformity neither desirable nor practicable.

This great recurving bow could kill at 300 yards and was stated to be effective against European armor at 200 yards. The extreme range of the Mongol bow may have been in excess of 600 yards although, at that range, the light Mongol arrow would carry but little striking energy. The soldier carried two bows and two or three full arrow quivers.

With the bow, the Mongols employed the lance, saber, and sometimes the mace. A few of the shock troopers were armed with a form of pike—with a hook on the end to engage an enemy horseman and pull him from the saddle. Particularly in the later Mongol campaigns, the army carried siege engines for reducing walls. Heavier siege equipment was usually constructed at the scene of the attack by Chinese specialists. What evidence there is indicates that the Mongols made quite extensive use of gunpowder in the form of hand grenades.

The Mongol horseman rode in a light armor of boiled hide, and after the successes in China, they made considerable use of the fine lacquered armor of Chinese manufacture. The horses of the front-line troops wore flaps of heavy leather on the shoulders and breasts. This protection was designed as much to protect the lungs of the horse in cold weather as for defense against missiles. The Mongol horse archer had a firm seat as the result of a stirruped saddle of wood, arched high in front and rear. The bowman could fire to either side or to the rear with great accuracy and speed.

On campaign, the Mongols carried one to three spare horses per man, mounting the animals in turn. Under stress or emergency action, the army could move eighty miles in a day and average fifty miles a day in a sustained pursuit for many days. The greatest massed horseback movements of record were made by the Mongols.

Tactically, a Mongol army on the move in enemy territory operated with wide screens to the front, to either flank, and to the rear. The main body moved on an extended front, often as wide as fifty miles for a tuman of ten thousand men. This force was tied together into a mutually supported offensive team by a remarkable courier system of interunit communication. The couriers heavily bandaged their vital parts and often rode a thousand or more miles to deliver a message.

The order of battle of the Mongols consisted of five ranks in a single line, with wide intervals between the ranks. The first two ranks were manned by troopers in leather armor who carried saber and lance in addition to the bow. The three rear ranks were unarmored and carried only the saber and the bow. When the attack was launched, the three rear ranks, passing through the armored men, began the assault with arrows. Not until the enemy was disorganized or in flight did the armored men go into the action with the lance.

The field maneuvers in the face of the enemy were based upon broad sweeps designed to conceal the Mongol strength (or weakness) and to mystify the enemy as to the objective. An enemy operating against the Mongols could not hope to engage until the situation was favorable to the troopers from the Gobi. The Mongol speed tactics made it possible to apply overwhelming pressure upon any cut-off portion of an enemy line. Mere number of the opposition meant nothing to the Mongols, who fought with consistency against superior odds.

The strategy of terror was important in their prosecution of war. They were specialists in espionage and in the infiltration of enemy country; they were masters of the simulated retreat to encourage the enemy to keep on the move. It was the custom of the Mongols, in the early stages of a campaign, to destroy the will of the enemy by the ruthless massacre of men, women, and children. A few survivors were allowed to escape to bear the news to other areas that resistance meant death.

Although the Mongols could, and did, lay successful siege to cities, they preferred to engage in the open field. If efforts to starve a city or the strategy of intimidation did not force surrender, they would then take up siege operations and storm the walls. This was often necessary in taking the large walled cities of China.

It was in the field of logistics that the Mongols compel admiration. Even under their severe conditions of battle on exterior lines, the Mongols seem to have solved the problem of arrow supply. This had always been the major problem of bowmen. The Assyrians and the Persians had adequate arrow supply because of use of the chariot where arrow storage facilities were ample. The horse-archers of the earliest period had often had attendants to manage the horses; they carried the spare arrows. The Parthians had provided for arrows by a system of pack camels held close to the arena of action. Parthia did not have the battle problems that confronted the Mongols. The Parthians fought on interior lines with the action confined to the homeland or an adjoining province. Furthermore, the Parthians engaged in no extended cavalry movements of months' or years' duration. Had they waged war far away, the Parthian camel train would have broken down.

In contrast, the Mongols did not fight from compact interior lines. They were usually deep in hostile country, constantly on the move, and engaged in frequent battle. Their highly mobile and efficient supply system has aroused the admiration of all military students.

Let us examine the field problems that confronted the Mongols.

Once an arrow is launched, it may not be recovered except under the most favorable combat conditions. Against enemy walls or a strong defensive position in the field, there can be no recovery of arrows. This problem of adequate arrow supply, for armies on campaign for months, or even years, was of critical magnitude. There could be no miscalculations. The number of missiles the Mongol trooper carried on his person is subject to varying estimates. Some authorities state that the Mongol archer carried two bows and sixty arrows; other sources hold the trooper responsible for possession of four bows and four hundred arrows. Certainly the horseman could not have departed on a long campaign with less arrows than the latter figure. These were carried on the trooper's back in a saddleside quiver and on his spare horses. Simple arithmetic gives us the astounding total of four million arrows required to supply one tuman of ten thousand men. Therefore, a representative field force of ten tumans (one hundred thousand men) would have had in their possession a field supply of forty million arrows!

The composite bow of the Mongols was no casual weapon that could be hastily repaired in the field. It was an arm highly susceptible to battle and use damage. In this respect, it had a much greater problem of maintainence than did the English longbow. It was imperative that an ample supply of reserve composite bows be carried in the field. The home manufactory was often six thousand miles distant.

The management, control, grazing, and watering of some thirty thousand horses was also the problem of each tuman of the Mongol army. It was no casual problem in an army that often moved sixty miles in a day. The Mongols undoubtedly used the wrangler system that was in common usage on the plains of the western United States in the nineteenth century. By no other method could this huge herd of horses be grazed, moved at the pace of the army, and held continually available as spare mounts. Under such a wrangler system, horse handlers would be detailed to guard the spare horses in alternate periods of movement and grazing throughout the night while the main army slept.

The Mongol horses were remarkable animals to be able to hold such a pace, day after day, on pasturage alone. They were fed no grain. The Gobi was bitterly cold in winter and many of the Mongol campaigns were conducted in snow. The Mongols learned early that the horse does not need shelter or pampering even in coldest weather. The Mongolian horse had long hair; when turned loose after a hard ride in midwinter, the sweat froze immediately and protected the animal with a glaze of ice that became effective insulation. The lungs of a horse will often freeze in very low temperatures; experience indicates that the lungs will freeze from the outside, inward, rather than as the result of breathing frigid air. If the breast of the horse is protected by a flap of sheepskin, no disabling from frosted lungs can occur.

The matter of food supplies for the troops was minor and much simpler in solution. The Mongols were trained to get along with little. They were supplied with meat—dried and reduced to a powder—and with a form of dried milk to supplement their forage efforts. Each Mongol trooper carried in his saddlebag a 20-pound slab of dried mare or cow milk. Each day he broke a half pound segment from this slab and placed it in his waterbottle. The day's ride would shake the mixture into liquid milk. The trooper thus had milk supply for forty days in his saddle bag. Worn-out horses supplied fresh meat occasionally and, in extreme situations, the Mongols opened a vein in a horse's neck and drank the blood.

The amazing self-sufficiency of these masses of horsemen moving out and sustaining themselves on prolonged expeditions is difficult for men of our age to understand or credit. It can be explained, in part, by the normal life of the nomad of the Gobi Desert in the thirteenth century. These Mongols were true nomads in a country where the community food supply was dependent upon the state of the grass and the luck of the chase. Privation, cold, and famine were no strangers to the Mongols—these things were a normal hazard of living.

The Mongol army was organized with the basic unit, the *tuman*, of ten thousand men. Each tuman was divided into ten *minghan* of one thousand men, equivalent to a regiment. Each minghan had ten *jaguns*, or squadrons, of one hundred men. The smallest tactical unit was the *arban*, or troop of ten men. The usual Mongol field army was three tumans, or thirty thousand men. Several tumans combined into an *ordu*, or army group, when on serious campaigns.

The numerical strength of the complete Mongol army has been grossly overestimated. There were hardly more than a million Mongols in total population. From this population was drawn an army that varied from about 120,000 men to a maximum of 200,000. In the latter stages of the empire, non-Mongol troops and impressed captives augmented this total, but the original conquests of Genghis Khan were made with not more than 200,000 soldiers. The largest Mongol army ever assembled was apparently that of Bayan, the great general of Kublai Khan. This was a force of 200,000 that conducted the conquest of the Sung in A.D. 1275. At the death of Genghis Khan in A.D. 1227, the Mongol army had a strength of about 130,000 men. It will be noted later in this chapter that Subotai raided Europe with a force of 30,000 men, and that he used a total of 150,000 men in the final serious attack against Europe.

The Mongol army was perfected in the field in the long series of campaigns against China that began in A.D. 1206, the year that Genghis Khan assumed power. The Mongols were successful in all of the field battles against the Chinese during the campaigns of 1206, but the walls of Peking stopped them. Two additional attacks in 1207 and 1208 produced no Mongol capacity for siege warfare, but a fourth attack by Subotai and Mukhali crushed the Chinese field armies and resulted in the capture of Peking by Mukhali. The Chinese conquest was not, however, to be completed during the lifetime of Genghis Khan. It was not until the reign of Kublai Khan in 1249 that control was effected. China was so formidable in a strength of walled cities and mere masses of numbers that the permanent conquest required more than forty years.

Meanwhile, ferocious intertribal battles were fought in the Gobi during this period of expeditionary efforts against China. Genghis Khan was uniting the people of the Gobi into a strong empire of nomads. There was also a major war with the Khwarzian shah who controlled a formidable Turkish army in Afghanistan.

The Mongol tactical school produced many outstanding generals —Jebei Noyon, Mukhali, Subotai, Hulagu, Batu, Bayan, and, in a later period, Timur. The field performances of these Mongol armies that threatened the world for two and a half centuries will be pictured briefly by an examination of a few of the major campaigns of Jebei Noyon and Subotai.

Jebei Noyon

Had this young general had a longer life, he might have developed into the greatest of all of the field commanders of Genghis Khan. His field ferocity was tempered by caution and he had the advantage of being closely associated, in joint operations, with the great Subotai. Jebei Noyon died on the return from the first European raid.

Jebei Noyon had a strange relationship with Genghis Khan. During the early wars that had resulted in the consolidation of the Mongol tribes, he had been a leader of the Issut tribe and had wounded Genghis Khan with an arrow in a desert affray. He had then transferred his allegiance and his tribesmen to the army of Genghis Khan. From the khan he received the name Jebei Noyon—Prince Arrow. He was the first of the khan's generals to make his way into China. With Subotai, he overran Persia and defeated the Russian princes. He was a specialist in mountain warfare and his ride across the Pamir Range makes Hannibal's crossing of the Alps a mere excursion by comparison. No more severe cavalry ride was ever made in the history of warfare. Jebei Noyon crossed the Pamirs in midwinter through the cleft between the Thian-Shan Mountains and the Pamirs, over the icebound passes of Kisil-Art and Terek-Davan at an altitude of more than thirteen thousand feet.

JEBEI NOYON AGAINST THE KHWARZIAN SHAH. In the winter A.D. 1219, Genghis Khan was engaged in the the preliminaries of empire building with an attack on the Khwarzian Turks led by the shah Mohammed. These Turks were a major antagonist with a large army of disciplined horse-archers. The Khwarzian Empire, occupying a portion of what is now Afghanistan and Baluchistan, was bounded on the east by one of the highest mountain chains in the world and was exceedingly difficult of access. Genghis Khan led the main Mongol force of about one hundred thousand men in an attack from the north, while Jebei Noyon was detached with three tumans (thirty thousand men) to enter the country from the east.

The ride of these thirty thousand is probably the most spectacular and remarkable cavalry movement in history if sheer severity of conditions is a criterion. The passes were piled high with drifted snow and treacherous sheet ice. Paths were literally beaten through the drifts with horses slipping and floundering in belly-deep snow in the face of icy winds. The pass, almost three miles high, became marked with the corpses of frozen soldiers and the carcasses of horses. The Mongols ate the raw, frozen horsemeat, leaving a trail of horse skeletons behind them. The terrible march was prolonged by severe storms that swept down from the Pamirs to immobolize the army for days.

It is difficult for us to visualize these horsemen, trapped for weeks in an icy pass, gaining a few miles a day and surviving to remain an army in being. It was spring when the decimated force came over the last pass and looked down upon the land they were to contest. Foraging detachments were dispatched across the valley to gather in cattle and supplies while the main army halted to reorganize and look to their weapons. The foragers were met by one hundred thousand Turks,

superbly mounted and eager for battle. In the clash that followed, the
Mongol foragers gave way, keeping up a continuous volley of arrows
as they retreated to the main body.

The battle was joined in the valley at the foot of the pass. The
wheeling, evasive movements of the Mongols were not matched by the
less active cavalry of the shah as the engagement developed on a broad
and shifting front. The issue was decided on a leadership basis. The
Mongols nullified the immense superiority in numbers enjoyed by the
Turks in a complete application of the principle of economy of force.
Overextended portions of the shah's battle order came under attack
by Mongols, who secured temporary superiority in numbers at these
points of the line. The archery fire began to concentrate upon the
Turkish center and the pressure became so severe that the shah was
in danger of capture. The battle in the Fergana Valley was one of the
great Mongol exhibitions of tactical field maneuver. All day long the
battle raged in a clamor of twanging bowstrings and the shrill whine
of arrows in flight. The Mongols never closed to hand weapon distance. They fought as archers should fight, with a destructive hail of
arrows at the greatest effective range.

At nightfall each of the armies retired from the littered field. By
dawn there was nothing before the shah except the bodies of the slain
and the burned-out embers of the Mongol fires. During the night the
Mongols had rounded up the cattle their foragers had secured and had
departed to keep their rendezvous with Genghis Khan before Samarkand. No reliable estimates of the losses in this battle exist.

Thus ended the Battle of the Fergana Valley. But the ride of Jebei
Noyon had only begun. He had covered eight hundred miles of the two
thousand miles that had separated him from the khan. He took up the
ride again after this temporary interruption of battle, receiving en
route a reinforcement of five thousand men to replace losses. The
magic of the khan's courier system was never more apparent. Separated by about twelve hundred miles of difficult terrain, the armies had
maintained contact. The khan had been informed of Jebei Noyon's
battle within a few days after the event by messengers on fleet horses,
bandaged against the physical punishment of awesome distance rides
at full gallop.

The army of Jebei Noyon pressed on, from high mountain valleys
through passes of mountain ranges with elevations of twenty thousand
feet. They had a rendezvous at a far place on the map and nothing—
not battle, hostile armies, weather, or altitude—could stand in their

way. Behind them, they left burning towns and the remnants of opposing field forces. There was something inhuman about this dreadful tenacity of the Mongols on the march. They were indeed androids.

Months later, the ride of Jebei Noyon ended at Samarkand. From that point, he was to continue on a joint effort with Subotai.

Subotai

This conqueror of thirty nations and the winner of sixty-five battles never tasted defeat. Subotai may have been the greatest general in history. In any estimate of the qualities of the generals of Genghis Khan, the name of Subotai is the brightest. Surnamed "The Valiant" by Genghis Khan, this grim tactician led the greatest raid in history ever undertaken by a cavalry force. Audacious and completely successful, Subotai maintained his force of thirty thousand in Europe for three years without reinforcement except for impressed conquered enemies and dependent upon foraged supplies. In the course of this great raid he killed more than one hundred thousand enemy soldiers, defeated a score of nations, and completed a march of more than six thousand miles before returning to the Gobi. This was Asiatic cavalry in its most tenacious and frightening aspect.

When Subotai completed this probing raid, plans were made in the Gobi for a general conquest of Europe; in this later general attack, Subotai's 150,000 men killed more than a million people in a long series of actions in Europe.

Subotai's Raid Into Europe with Thirty Thousand Men

While Genghis Khan was before the walls of Samarkand, his intelligence reported that Shah Mohammed had escaped to the south. The army of the Khwarzian shah was finished; 180,000 Turks had been killed in a main action on the Syr River. However, the campaign was not finished by Mongol standards. There could be no escape for a ruler who had dared oppose Genghis Khan. No war was considered won if the defeated ruler survived.

Subotai was called to the traveling yurt of Genghis Khan and received orders unique in military history. He was ordered to pursue the shah, across the whole world if necessary, until the monarch was captured or there existed proof of his death. To accomplish this destruction of one man, Subotai was given command of three tumans and the most tenacious manhunt in history was underway. Jebei Noyon was second in command.

The panic-stricken shah fled deeper into his domain. A few short months earlier he had mustered what has been estimated at four hundred thousand to oppose Genghis Khan. A few battles had reduced him to a status of fugitive. From Bokhara, he rode to Merv. From Merv, across the mountains to Nishapur. From Nishapur, west across the mountains and desert through Persia to end at last on an island of the Caspian Sea where he died of fright and exhaustion.

Behind him, the implacable tumans of Subotai rode, week after week, covering, at times, eighty miles in a single day, accepting the surrender of fortresses and defeating all organized field forces. At Teheran, an army of thirty thousand barred the path of the Mongol general. A few hours of battle and the inhabitants of the burned and looted city were massacred to the last woman and child. Subotai reached the Caspian in time to see the sails of the ship that bore Mohammed to the place where he died. Subotai remained there in camp until news of Mohammed's death was received. It had taken five months for the Mongols to wipe out an army of four hundred thousand men and efface an empire.

After a pursuing ride of two thousand miles, Subotai left his army on the shores of the Caspian under the command of Jebei Noyon and rode twelve hundred miles for a conference with Genghis Khan.

While resting his army on the shores of the Caspian and awaiting word of Muhammad's fate, Subotai had conceived the idea of a raid around the shores of the Caspian before returning to the Gobi. With his force of thirty thousand men, it could hardly be more than an incidental raid but it would open up the fringe of Europe and provide valuable data of the terrain and physical features of the unknown country for a future conquering army.

Securing the permission of the khan for the venture, Subotai returned immediately to his command and began the circuit of the Caspian Sea. The first victim in his path was the Christian nation of Georgia where a tremendous armed force was prepared and ready to leave for participation in the Crusades. The appearance of Subotai altered all plans for Georgian battle in the holy land. In one brief engagement, the Georgian heavy knights were annihilated by the Mongol archers. A feigned retreat led the Georgians into a prepared ambush from which few of the Christians escaped. It was hardly more than an exercise in field archery for the fleet and proficient Mongol bow-men. The Georgian knights, mailed men on ponderous horses, were helpless victims as the brine-dipped, steel arrowheads of the Mongols holed their armor with ease. East European knights died by the thousands in a fierce decisive battle.

The tumans rode on to enter the passes of the Caucasus. Every nonessential article of equipment was jettisoned as they toiled over the high passes on rough mountain trails. They traversed glaciers and deep, black gorges and came at last into the valleys of Russia. Here, exhausted and carrying no more than saddle equipment, the Mongols encountered a numerous and determined army of mountaineers massed for battle. It was a murderous struggle, with the Russians greatly outnumbering the invaders. Again the Mongols outmaneuvered the enemy, dividing the Russians into convenient detachments and systematically slaughtering them with long-range arrow fire.

The Mongols moved on—across the Don to the northern shore of the Sea of Azov, on into the Crimea and across the Dneiper to the edge of the principalities of eastern Europe. Before them lay Hungary and Poland and the bulk of Russia. Subotai halted briefly on the shores of the Black Sea to rest his horses and men. The cartographers completed their charts of the region traversed. Everything of interest had been noted and plotted. Every lake, every river, every straggling village or walled city, and every mountain pass had been located and mapped for the information of future Mongol armies.

Then Subotai turned north into Russia proper. For a period of several weeks he maneuvered rapidly in a country that swarmed with enemies; he finally formed an order of battle on the Kalka River against more than eighty thousand Russians. Again the bow in expert hands commited fearful tasks. The cumbersome Russian army was herded across the steppes like sheep; *more than seventy thousand were killed.* The great host of Russians was broken into fleeing segments; *and* there was no escape from the fleet Mongol horsemen. Whining arrows destroyed the enemy at leisure. In three weeks there were no surviving Russian field forces in the south. This small army of Subotai's was demonstrating that it was centuries ahead tactically of the cumbersome knights who had stood in their way. Europe was having its first dreadful preview of Asiatic war in the perfected bow tactics of Genghis Khan.

Then, in 1222, Subotai turned his army homeward. He was the bearer of the greatest news that Genghis Khan was ever to receive: The weakness of Europe had been exposed to view. The armies of the West

had been met and annihilated, and their military potentialities had
been carefully estimated. Subotai had found nothing to seriously impede the progress of his archers—Europe was ready, at any time, for
conquest and plunder.

It was on this return trip that the military career of Jebei Noyon
came to a close. He died in Turkestan while en route to the Gobi.

Subotai's raid must be viewed historically as the greatest of all
massed cavalry rides. Thirty thousand Mongols had pursued Shah
Mohammed for two thousand miles to the shores of the Caspian and
then, after a short halt, Subotai's force had continued on for more than
four thousand miles of extended reconnaissance and battle in eastern
Europe. Scores of peoples had been defeated in pitched battle by this
small force of Mongols who maintained themselves in the field for
more than three years. This raid put the final polish on the field tactics
of the Mongols. It justified to the fullest the grim tenet of Genghis
Khan that superiority in numbers meant nothing.

The military information gained on this raid was of incalculable
value. The weakness of European infantry and heavy cavalry had been
exposed for future exploitation by the Mongol horse-archers. The
technical difficulties of moving large cavalry forces over thousands of
miles of hostile country had been explored and solved by Subotai. The
Mongols learned what a field army needed—more important, they
learned what a field army did not need.

It was Subotai's raid that turned the thoughts of Genghis Khan to
a deliberate dream of world conquest. The ease with which the heavy
Russian armies had been destroyed marked eastern Europe as an
easier victim than China or the savage horsemen Genghis Khan had
subdued on his own borders.

Although Subotai's return to the Gobi in 1222 had crystallized
Genghis Khan's determination to conquer Europe, the Mongol khan
was not to see Subotai set forth again. In 1227 Genghis Khan died
while on a campaign against China, and delays in seating his successor
and further mopping-up operations along the frontiers delayed the
formal assault on Europe until 1236.

The grand plan of the invasion of Europe was charted by Subotai,
who visualized an eighteen-year campaign to destroy the West.

Subotai's Attack on Europe

In December, 1237, Subotai, with 150,000 men, crossed the Volga
on the ice after having consolidated Mongol gains in eastern Russia.

The consummate strategy of the Mongols was demonstrated by their concentration upon the forested areas of Russia in the preliminary operations.

The Mongols occupied Ryazan, destroyed the principality of Vladimir, and occupied Moscow, then a place of small importance. By the end of March, 1238, all of the northern Russian principalities had ceased to exist. Batu, grandson of Genghis Khan and co-leader of the attack on Europe, wrote to Ogodai, who had succeeded Genghis Khan on the throne, "By the favor of Heaven and good fortune, O Emperor my Uncle, eleven nations have been subjugated."

Then with the open steppes of Russia before him, Subotai began a deliberate campaign of terror. For two years his cavalry conducted operations of a vast scale. The tumans ranged wide on independent operations, combining whenever major opposition formed. It was a huge theater of war and the Mongols tested the Russian will to resist by the mass killing of armies and civilians. Kiev fell on December 6, 1240. This largest of the Russian cities was taken street by street by Mongol lancers as bowmen crouched on the roofs of captured houses and poured arrows into soldiers and civilians alike. All the male citizens of Kiev were killed; the women and children were sent to the Gobi. The fall of Kiev marked the end of the Russian resistance. Five years after the destruction of Kiev, Giovanni Carpini, legate of Pope Innocent IV to the Court of the Mongol Khan, passed through the city and saw "an enormous number of skulls and bones of slaughtered men lying on the plain." In Kiev itself, "which used to be a very large and thickly populated town, there was standing barely two hundred houses."

With the Russian resistance at an end, Subotai now divided his army into three groups. A northern detachment of thirty thousand men under Kaidu assailed the Poles and the Silesians. A southern wing under Kadan was sent to invade Hungary from the north. Subotai, with Batu, prepared to deliver the main blow against Pest and Gran.[1] In March, 1241, the Mongols prepared to move into Europe proper.

A sweep across the border into Poland resulted in three pitched battles that destroyed all resistance. The beautiful city of Cracow was looted and burned in March, and the stage was set for the decisive Battle of Liegnitz.

Moving on from the sack of Cracow, Kaidu's army of thirty thousand met a combined German-Polish army under the command of Duke Henry of Silesia. A mixed army of Silesians, Moravians, and Templars, far outnumbering the Mongol column, chose to make a stand in the open fields near the city of Liegnitz. The Mongols opened the battle at long range with arrows, routing an advance force put forward by Duke Henry. The heavy armored knights of the Christians then moved in to attack, advancing slowly across the plain against what seemed negligible resistance. The Mongol horse-archers gave way in feigned rout and panic that was so convincing that the knights lost formation rapidly as they pursued the supposedly fleeing Mongols. Suddenly the pursuers were the quarry as the Mongols turned suddenly and fell upon the extended Christian line. The knights' horses were shot from under them; dismounted, the cumbersome Templars floundered helplessly. They were shot down in thousands by Mongols who never came within lance or sword range. Duke Henry and more than thirty thousand of his army were left dead on the field.

Kaidu, a worthy captain of the bow in his own right, had in less than thirty days marched four hundred miles, won two pitched battles and captured four cities. Northward, as far as the Baltic Sea, Kaidu had left no threat to Mongol arms.

While these flanking operations of Kaidu had been in progress, the rest of the Mongol army in three wide columns had moved into Hungary. These forces concentrated near the Danube at Gran, on April 4, 1241. The center, under the personal command of Subotai, had ridden 180 miles in three days to make the rendezvous. On April 11, the column under Batu destroyed the army of King Bela of Hungary as another Hungarian army left the walls of Pest and moved out to give battle to Subotai. Subotai refused to cross the Danube and began a slow tactical retreat, followed for six days by the Hungarian army. On the banks of the Sajo River, Subotai selected his battleground, having made union with the wing of Kaidu.

The Hungarian army at the battle of the Sajo was the greatest European force ever to face the Mongols—more than one hundred thousand men took up a position to contest Subotai's crossing of the river.

During the night, the Mongols forded the stream in the face of severe opposition and made use of gunpowder for the first time in Europe. At five o'clock in the morning the Hungarian heavy cavalry attacked the Mongol line; Subotai fought desperately with the river at his back—a situation that the Mongols always sought to avoid. At seven o'clock the Hungarians were beaten off and they withdrew to the protection of a fortified camp. Having concentrated the enemy, Subotai encircled the camp and began to rain in thousands of arrows. At noon, the desperate besieged Europeans attempted a sortie led by the

Knights Templars. All were killed. When all hope seemed lost, it was suddenly perceived that an unoccupied gap had appeared in the tightly drawn Mongol lines. This apparent escape route seemed to be guarded by only a few archers. The Hungarians poured through this escape port against small resistance. The long column headed for the Danube and safety.

Then the trap was sprung.

From all sides, fleet horsemen appeared to block the flight. It was the old Asiatic strategy designed to keep the enemy on the move and facilitate the recovery of arrows. For two terrible days the slaughter of the fleeing Hungarians continued without cessation. The retreat became rout and the Europeans degenerated into a panic-stricken mob. Eighty thousand Hungarians died in the Battle of the Sajo River. In the succeeding battles for Pest, another one hundred thousand fell, and Hungary was finished.

On the same date, April 11, 1241, the Mongol southern wing under Prince Kadan eliminated Transylvania as a threat. Eastern Europe as far as the Danube was conquered. Russia, Poland, Lithuania, and Hungary had been beaten down; only in Saxony was there an army left to oppose the Mongols.

The conquered territory soon learned that this was no mere raid for plunder. The Mongols had come to stay. Eastern Europe was to be Mongol—a tributary territory of the Gobi. In little more than a month all of the land between the Baltic and the Danube had been occupied.

In December, 1241, Subotai crossed the Danube. Austria was to be the next victim of the grand plan. Western Europe was to be a conquest of the future; the immediate plan called for consolidation of the gains in the East. The Mongols began the sorting and grading of the women captives and the assembly of craftsmen laborers for transport to the Gobi.

Before the conquest of Austria began, a messenger rode into the camp of Subotai in February, 1242. The rider had brought important news from the Gobi. Ogodai, the second khan of the Mongols, had died on December 11, 1241. The call had come for the *kuriltai*, the grand assembly that was to convene to select a new khan. It was mandatory that all Mongol leaders be present. The conquest of Europe could await the pleasure of the new occupant of the throne.

The next morning the threat to western Europe was ended for all time as Subotai turned his army and headed for the Gobi.

It was thus by a mere accident of history, the death of Ogodai, that Europe was saved. With Russia and Hungary as bases, in a few months Subotai would have stood on the shores of the English Channel. There was nothing in the European military organization to stop him. The conquest would have been complete and all of the Western world, as we know it, would have been altered. The death of Ogodai was thus one of the most significant events of history; had he lived for but one more year, the interest of the Mongols would have remained directed west instead of east. When Ogodai died, the house of Genghis Khan broke into disagreement and Mangu, the new khan, turned his attention to China. Batu remained in Russia to build up his own Golden Horde on the steppes. As the years passed, the Mongols developed independent and sometimes mutually hostile empires while China was united into a nation by Kublai Khan, who had small interest in Europe. Northern Persia came into being as a nation under Timor, a descendant of Genghis Khan. A Mogul empire was created in India by Babars. The power of Islam was destroyed in the holy land. The Mongols did what the Crusaders were unable to do, for under the new masters, Palestine became accessible to the Christians.

This renewed interest of the Mongols in China and the Middle East and India that resulted from the death of Ogodai was one of the most significant episodes in all history. All of Europe was prostrate before the troops of Subotai, and would have been taken with ease.

The influence of Genghis Khan's empire of the bow became permanent. The Mongols opened up and reshuffled the world, making it smaller as they consolidated warring tribes into strong nations. His conquests benefited Europe in increased scholarship, geographical curiosity, and availability of information that had been the sole property of Asiatics. The European mind expanded as the result of the march of the Genghis Khan's bowmen. But while opening up the world, the Mongols established themselves as the most terrible destroyers in all history. These nations were consolidated at the expense of nineteen million lives. These were big wars, these cavalry campaigns of the thirteenth century that brought nationalism to half the world. No other wars in history can compare to them in magnitude.

It may be said that the bowmen of Genghis Khan first brought the principle of total war to the world. These were not wars where the defeated nation paid indemnity and concluded hostilities with a treaty that left it sovereign. The empire of Genghis Khan was unique in its ability to survive, in one form or another, for many centuries after his death. The nations subjugated by the Mongols never regained their former freedoms. They were transformed into new nations and governed by dynasties set up by the descendants of Genghis Khan.

The Mongol army elevated the bow into its greatest role as an offensive weapon; it was used by cavalry as the decisive arm. The Mongols may have been the greatest soldiers of all time.

18

The English Longbowmen

Northern and western Europe had borrowed the bow, chiefly as a hunting weapon, from Arab invaders of Spain. In the beginning of organized warfare on the Continent, the bow had been used in war without distinction. Nowhere on the continent of Europe, except at the gateway of Asia, had the bow attained any status as a major weapon.

The wild tribesmen of Europe had fought with the ax and the broadsword, taking the field in undisciplined mobs. The outstanding characteristic of the armies of ancient Europe had been the lack of discipline. War was hardly more than a raid in force and there were few organized governments. In A.D. 1000, Europe had hardly attained a state of military efficiency equal to that of ancient Assyria.

Although considered to be an inferior weapon, the bow had undergone considerable development and was used casually by many of the tribes on the Continent. Its mechanical variant, the crossbow, came into general use in the tenth century, and William the Conqueror used both types of the bow at the Battle of Hastings.

Meanwhile the military establishments of Europe slowly assumed the medieval pattern as we have already detailed. The sword and lance became the weapons of the gentleman; the individual combatant, the armored knight, dominated the field. The ragged peasants carried the pike and the halberd and were mere supporting posses,[1] fighting with small science and no tactical formations.

But the bow was on the horizon in Europe.

By A.D. 1100, the crossbow had become a weapon of dreaded efficiency in the battles of the Crusades against the Saracen composite

168

bow. Armored knights on European fields were beginning to go down under the iron bolts in Continental battles. The old order was undergoing imperceptible change.

Across the Channel in England, the first great company of European archers came into being. No greater foot-bowmen have ever wielded the bow in war. The magic resilence inherent in yew wood produced a variant of the self bow that was one of the great bows of all time—whatever the construction, material, or design. The pull has been variously estimated at 90 and 160 pounds.

Very few, if any, of these great bows have survived the years. One, believed to have been that of Little John, is said to have been preserved at Cannon Hall. It was last strung in 1715, at which time it was used to kill a deer. The dimensions of this bow are believed to be 6 feet 7 inches in length with a 5-inch circumference at the grip. It is constructed of spliced yew and is strongly reflexed—not the usual construction of the longbow.

Three unfinished bowstaves were recovered in 1841 from the wreck of the *Mary Rose*, lost in the Thames during the reign of Henry VIII. The average length of these recovered staves was 6 feet 4 inches. No other specimens of the longbow are known to exist.

The yew for the English longbow was seldom of local growth. Most of the wood came from Italy, Spain, Crete, and Mesopotamia since a warm climate produced a superior wood that was harder and more finely grained. The Spaniards in the fifteenth century denied the English the import of Spanish yew by destroying the trees.

The English developed stockpiles of foreign yew wood by specifying that four staves (later ten) be included with each butt of wine imported from Greece and Italy. This expediency was not sufficient to supply yew wood for the national military needs and after unsuccessful attempts by English bowyers to fashion composite bows of inferior English yew wood glued to strips of ash and elm, the longbow began to decline in popularity in England. The decline was hastened by the invention and gradual acceptance of firearms.

As a military weapon, the longbow was a very sturdy arm and subject to few operational hazards. The bow seldom broke while in battle use. Treated with resin, wax, and tallow, the longbow was virtually waterproof. The strings were sized with water glue and whipped with fine thread.

This weapon first appeared in war at the Battle of the Standard in 1138, and its service ended in 1688 when it made its last battle appearance in Scotland in a local war. In the early years of the reign of Elizabeth, the longbow had commenced to decline in popularity. Only twenty men in one hundred of the trained bands were carrying the weapon. The danger brought to a head by the invasion of the Armada produced only 800 archers from the ten thousand men levied in London, and these were poorly trained.

Although the longbow was one of the contributing factors in the decline of the medieval armored knight, there were many reasons, tactical and ritualistic, to deny it acceptance as the major weapon. The caste system of England of the thirteenth and fourteenth centuries made any proper application of the bow to war an impossibility. The yeomen who carried the bow were of little importance. It was presumed that the highly expendable yeomen would die in battle. Routine of war was proscribed and formal. The archers were disposed on the field in accordance with custom and form and tradition rather than any application of efficient tactics. Actually, the English archers were dangerously exposed men in battle and were considered to be a mere holding posse maintaining an action until the propitious moment arrived for a charge of the knights. They were given no real protection in battle and were quite often ridden over by impetuous English knights eager to charge. The bowmen were never intended to be decisive. This was the privilege of the aristocracy.

Furthermore, there was a knightly stigma attached to the arrow wound. The bow was a peasant weapon in inferior hands. To be slashed with a sword or skewered on a lance was the proper death for a gentleman. The ignoring of this fact has magnified the importance of the longbow in English military history. Except in a few battles between people of the British Isles and a small campaign or two in Spain, the longbow appeared in but one major war—and this war it lost. The English battle experience with the bow was identical with that of earlier nations who had made some use of the weapon in the hands of foot soldiers.[2] Ancient Persia and England each won great initial victories with the bow, but as the military experience of their enemies increased, the tactical school of bowmen on foot, weakly supported by heavy cavalry, proved unproductive. As will be noted later in this chapter, the British tactical employment of the longbow was unsound as it depended upon blunders and indecision on the part of the enemy. The English were never willing to evaluate the longbow properly or to provide it with proper tactics and support.

In the spring of 1346 an expeditionary force under the direct command of Edward III crossed the Channel for battle against France. The Hundred Years' War with France had started the year before with tentative preliminary engagements. The invading army of Edward was, in the description of the day, "a great army of souldiers well appointed," of whom possibly seven thousand were archers out of a total force of about twelve thousand men. Edward landed his troops in the northwest corner of Normandy and began a movement to the east, with Calais as his objective. When he reached Rouen, he found that the French had destroyed the bridge across the Seine. After some aimless maneuvering in the face of a French force twice his strength and commanded by Philip VI, Edward retired to Abbeville where he found a second French army of twelve thousand men drawn up to dispute his passage of the Somme.[3] There was no choice but to fight at the ford.

The English archers cleared the riverbank and the army crossed the stream only a few hundred yards in advance of the main French army under Philip VI. At the village of Crecy, Edward came to bay.

Here, in a strong position on the slope of a hill, Edward made his troop disposition and prepared to fight. The English force—seven thousand archers, two thousand mounted men-at-arms, and some three thousand irregular Welsh and Irish infantry—were disposed in a prepared defensive position. The horsemen were dismounted and drawn up in three divisions as pikemen. At the foot of the slope, a right and left flank was formed by additional dismounted men-at-arms. In the center, in the open field, and in front of the dismounted horsemen, the archery strength was thrown out in an extended battle line, with staggered ranks, like men on a chessboard, to give each archer space for wielding his weapon. On one wing was a slight rise of ground on which other archers were disposed.

The archers in the open stood in the herse formation, two hundred to a front and some thirty men deep. In their front, they dug small holes a foot in depth to impede the advance of the French horsemen. The Irish and Welsh formed flanking wings on either side of the horsemen and bowmen; they were armed only with long knives. Their battle capacity was limited to the execution of fallen French knights.

This battle order placed a great burden on the bowmen, who were exposed to the full force of the expected French cavalry charge and were permitted no room for successful evasive action. This was a disposition that had had considerable lack of success when used by the Persians at Marathon. It staked everything on the ability of bowmen to stop heavily armed troops in an open field, with no provision for evasive retreat. Edward was not a tactician. Had he been, he would have placed his archers along the low hills, where they would have had some protection against enemy heavy cavalry. It is apparent that Edward considered his longbowmen as expendable and that all he expected from them was the infliction of whatever casualties they could accomplish in the short period before they were overrun. The real battle effort would be the charge of his own heavily armed knights. These dispositions completed, Edward waited attack.

It was late afternoon, Saturday, August 26, when Philip appeared before the English position. A thunderstorm broke, followed by heavy rain. The longbowmen unstrung their bows and protected the strings under their clothing. The storm cleared and six thousand Genoese crossbowmen began the attack. They opened too soon with a volley of bolts that failed to reach the English line. The longbowmen waited for killing range. According to Froissart, "Then they stepped forward one pace and let fly their arrows so hotly and so thick that it seemed snow." The crossbowmen of the French released but one volley before they were overwhelmed by the clothyard shafts of the English. Fumbling with their clumsy, slow-firing weapons, the Genoese died by the hundreds, pinned to the ground by the dreadful flow of English arrows. The vulnerability of the crossbow to wet weather conditions contributed to the ineffectiveness of the weapon.

The heavy lines of French cavalry rode over their own crossbowmen as they spurred their horses against the steady English archers. Horses went down, screaming and plunging on the field. The unhorsed knights, weighted by heavy armor, fell in waves before the steel-tipped arrows. On the flanks, the French tried to ride around the arrow storm, seeking a lesser antagonist, the heavy English cavalry in the rear. But the weight of the attack was broken by the bowmen.

Night ended the slaughter and, under its cover, the French withdrew, leaving one thousand five hundred noblemen dead on the field and "thousands of inferior people."[4] The English loss was only a few hundred men. The participation of the English gentlemen-at-arms in this battle is reflected in the casualties they suffered at Crecy. Two knights and about thirty other horsemen fell in the battle.

Crecy was the first major contest on European soil between the armored knight and the yeoman archer. It sounded the death knell of chivalry. Never again would the mailed knight be supreme in battle.

The Battle of Crecy is a study of superlative field archery and indifferent tactics. No individual battle performance in history can excel the archery of the longbowmen standing in that open field against the charge of mailed knights. Those dramatic moments, in the face of a range that was closing rapidly, may have been the greatest individual field performance with the bow. Edward won the battle because of the ability of his archers to prevent French charges from generating sufficient power to carry through to the objective. It was asking more of the yeomen than should have been expected of any infantry-archer. The English archers at Crecy, using their bows from an exposed front-line position, were perfect examples of unhurried precision under great pressure. The tactics of Edward were incorrect and dangerous. Exposed in open country as the archers were, the battle could have been lost in the first half hour had the French continued the attack with resolution and determination.

Although Crecy bulks large in the imaginations of historians because of its implications of doom for the armored horsemen, the English victory was no more than a preview of a tactical school that was to depend too greatly upon stupidity and irresolution on the part of the enemy. The English assumed that this stupidity on the part of the French would continue and that the tactics at Crecy would invariably produce victory. A pattern of deliberate defensive war was developed in which the English sought a site to be defended and there awaited attack. As no movement was contemplated, the meager arrow supply of the yeomen could be supplemented by the issue of all the field reserve. In such circumstances, the yeoman could be supplied with many more arrows than he could conceivably carry into any offensive action and the battle usefulness of the bow was thus greatly prolonged.

This position stand of archers, with a pile of arrows on the ground before each bowman, was theoretically sound upon superficial examination; actually, it was dangerously unsound as it was subject to too many assumptions as to the behavior of the enemy.

1. The tactic presumed that no unexpected attack would be made and that the English would always have time to complete their defensive dispositions and issues of materiel.

2. The tactic presumed willingness of the enemy to give battle at the site selected by the English.

3. The tactic presumed enemy irresolution and lack of determination in pressing home an attack of heavy cavalry.

4. The tactic presumed that the longbowmen could stop, under all conditions, the attack of horsemen during the very few minutes before the yeomen could be overrun and destroyed.

These presumptions were valid during the first stages of the Hundred Years' War. The French performed as expected. The English *did* have time to prepare defensive positions. The irrational feudal code, did, as expected, goad the French on to an attack on a selected English position. The French *were* irresolute in the attack on such a position. Most important of all of the assumptions made by the English, the longbowmen did stop the French attacks before defensive sites could be overridden.

The original success as the result of these presumptions of the English was fatal in the end. The presumption that these conditions would continue to be present proved erroneous. There was shortly to come a time when the French would correct their deficiencies and develop a superior psychology of battle that was to negate the great English longbow and again demonstrate that the bow was not an infantry weapon.

When that time did come, the English lost the war. They had no opportunity to prepare a defensive site. Occasionally, they were unable to contain the French attack with arrows at point-blank range and the magnificent English archers then died by the thousands. When favorable conditions no longer prevailed, the English lack of proper tactics for the bow caught up with them. The aristocrats were never willing to accept the tactical concepts that are mandatory when the bow is used in war. A superior weapon cannot be in ritualistically inferior hands or subjected to inferior tactics to support a social preemption of so-called superior men. This the English never learned until it was too late. In the possession of the longbow the English had the superior weapon, but they were not willing to coordinate it in battle, as an equal, with the activity of the mounted knights.

Ten years later, at Poitiers,[5] the English defensive placement of troops still remained effective as the French pattern of war had not yet changed. The Black Prince was in the field with a raid that was destructive, even if in small force. The English army in France consisted of about seven thousand armored horsemen and attendants, about three thousand longbowmen, and about one thousand auxiliary light troops. To cut off this raiding force, King John of France assembled an army of possibly twenty thousand men[6] and on September 17, 1356, at Poitiers, he intercepted the Black Prince as the English king was hastening to Bordeaux with his plunder.

The English had a full day to prepare a defensive site on ground interspersed with thickets and hedges, behind a barrier of thorn hedge that was protected by a shallow ditch. It was a strong position that should not have been attacked by the French. The French had the initiative. They could have outwaited the English, starved them into surrender, or forced them to attempt a retreat to the coast. But again, the inadequate French leadership was goaded into impetuous attack, although not fully informed as to the actual location of the English army.

The examination of French tactics of this period is completely bewildering by modern standards. The truth is they had no tactics other than the impetus of a bull rush. At Poitiers, the French had the small English army in a hopeless position. All that was necessary was to wait. Instead, the French chose to attack the strong English position.

The ground being unsuitable for a cavalry charge, the French king dismounted a large number of his knights and sent them forward as infantry. They began an advance over rough ground, greatly encumbered by their armor. The advance was too slow for the impatient king. He ordered a frontal charge with the remainder of this cavalry. The French horses, weighed down by the rider and 140 pounds of mail and weapons, moved very slowly and they were shot down without difficulty by archers concealed in the hedges.

The line of dismounted knights, moving heavily, continued the attack and were virtually annihilated by bowmen who poured in arrows at point-blank range. At this stage of the battle, an entire French division deserted the field and the battle was lost.

The French had reacted true to their feudal instincts and again the English defensive site had stood up under an ill-advised and badly planned attack. Had the French pressed home a third charge, they might have defeated the English at Poitiers. In the heat of the second attack, the position of the English archers became critical as they had expended the last of their arrows. The archers had discarded their bows and plunged into the battle with hand weapons to help turn the tide.

The French loss, about twenty-five hundred men, would have

been far greater had the English possessed an adequate supply of arrows. A third attack would have overrun the English and assured a French victory.

The Hundred Years' War dragged on. In 1415 the English took advantage of the reign of an imbecile king of France to renew demands for the return of Normandy. To enforce that demand, Henry V began the crossing of the Channel on August 10, and after thirty days of energetic campaigning, he captured Honfleur to control the valley of the lower Seine.

His army much depleted by the campaign, Henry began a retreat to Calais, finding the bridge down and a hostile population in his path. The French destroyed their own countryside and the English army, famished and weary, found themselves trapped near the castle of Agincourt.

At Agincourt, the English had a mere six thousand effectives to meet a French force that has been estimated as high as sixty thousand. (All figures of strength in these early campaigns are suspect.) In a narrow ploughed field, bordered by hedges and thickets, Henry deployed his small force. Again the archers were placed in the front line. On this occasion, they were protected by sharpened stakes 6 feet long, set in the ground at an angle. On either flank the cavalry massed to support the center of English longbowmen. Behind the archers, the main body of dismounted knights formed a strong rear center.

The ground was soft from repeated rains and influenced the French to try a repetition of their tactics at Poitiers. All the French heavy cavalry was dismounted and drawn up in three strong divisions, one behind the other, separated by intervals of 200 to 300 yards. Two bodies of lighter cavalry remained mounted and were held on either wing in the first line, designed to overrun the English archers.

The French, although greatly superior in numbers, then lay back in this disposition. The two armies watched each other for several hours. When it became evident that the French were going to outwait the starving English, Henry ordered his bowmen forward. Advancing slowly over the rough ground, the archers began to launch their shafts into the compact French lines. The wing cavalry of the French then moved forward, the horses in mud to the fetlocks. This French charge —if it can be called a charge—was ineffective because of the soft footing. The longbowmen delivered terrible punishment to the French, and then withdrew as the heavy English cavalry closed on the French line.

For a few moments, the fighting was hand to hand until a well-timed charge of the English horse broke the front line of the French. In this manner, by successive charges against the second and third French divisions, the English knights succeeded in fighting their own checkerboard form of war with success. The archers began to take a fearsome toll of the scattered French knights who were hopelessly bogged in the deep mud. Six thousand French were left dead on the field; the English loss was negligible. At Agincourt, the longbowmen were not under the tremendous pressure they had withstood at Crecy. The significant development at Agincourt was the fact that the English archers again expended all of their arrows early in the battle and were forced, in the latter stages, to engage as light infantry with ax, mallet, and pike.

On these three battles, the English built their great reputation as military archers.

Theoretically and tactically, this golden era of the longbow left everything to be desired. Europe was still struggling with elementary principles of war and no technically sound army existed in the Western world. Because of the quality of the competition they met in the early stages of the Hundred Years' War, English archery was decisive against the stumbling French opposition. As we shall note shortly, the English archer could not win against determined and efficient enemies.

As individual archers, the English brought the self bow to its state of greatest development; in the matters of organization, tactics and logistics, they lagged far behind the professional soldiers of Asia of the same historical period. It is well that the English, with their ritualistic tactics, did not meet the Asiatic composite bow in the hands of horse-archers. Had they met the Mongol bowmen, the history of England would surely have been altered.

Although the longbow attracted great historical attention as the result of these three battles, the reign of the weapon was to be brief.

The English victories in these three great exhibitions with the bow occupy much space in history, but we are inclined to forget that the English *lost* the Hundred Years' War to France and that victories of English bowmen occurred only in the earlier years of the war when French leadership, morale, and tenacity in attack were mediocre. It did not take the French long to exploit the battle weakness that was inherent in the English deployment and use of the bow. Under later leadership, the French defeated the English longbowmen with ease and won the war. Although Crecy, Poitiers, and Agincourt continue to make romantic reading in the history books, the military fact remains that grave deficiencies in tactics, supply, and composition led to the ultimate defeat of the English armies in France. The English had a major weapon—the best weapon of the period—but they were unable and unwilling to develop it into a decisive arm.

In the later stages of the war the French fought under the inspired leadership of Joan of Arc. When subjected to relentless or surprise attack, tactics instituted by the Maid of Orleans, the English found their infantry-archers unable to contain such attacks or to defend themselves as light infantry. The weakness had been there all the time badly obscured by the easy early victories.

The English commanders in the Hundred Years' War had not devoted sufficient time to the reading of their own history. Wallace's archers had been ridden down and destroyed at Falkirk in 1298. The English longbowmen at Bannockburn had been scattered and slaughtered by cavalry.

As the Hundred Years' War continued, the lesson of what infantry-archers could, and could not, do became increasingly plain. At Auray, in 1364, the English archers were overrun and forced to their daggers and clubs in a desperate survival battle. A strong French attack under shields had penetrated the English line and rendered the bow useless.

The failure of infantry-archers as a pivot was demonstrated again at Bauge, in 1421. Here the English cavalry ran away from their archers in an ill-timed pursuit of the French. The French cavalry evaded and returned to destroy the longbowmen. In 1420, at Jargeau, Meung, and Beaugency, the army of Suffolk was destroyed by pressing French attacks, the vigor of which demoralized the English and made the longbow impotent.

In 1429, Joan of Arc surprised an English army on the march near Patay. They had no time to prepare their traditional position defense. The archers were engaged in cutting stakes when the French cavalry overran them. Practically all the longbowmen were killed and a third of the Talbot's army was killed in this battle.

Although the longbow had begun to fail in battle as early as 1364, the English persisted in their dependence upon a defense based upon foot-bowmen. They found the French of later years a greatly improved foe. The sudden French attacks in the open field and against marching English columns reduced the great longbow to unimportance. At Formigny, in 1450, the French broke the herse formation of English archers and annihilated them. More than 80 per cent of the English army were killed in this decisive battle.

At Castillon, in 1452, the desperate English emulated the Persians at Plataea and sent longbowmen in waves against a strong French position. The archers were skewered on lances and were blown to pieces by the fire of primitive cannon. The Hundred Years' War came to an end.

The fifteenth century experiments with gunpowder in war were developing on European fields. As early as the thirteenth century, the *arquebus*, a very primitive firearm, was influencing war tactics on European fields. These early weapons were inaccurate, laborious to load, and short in range but they were able to gradually supplant the bow in Europe.

The English defeats in France hastened the demise of the longbow. By the sixteenth century men were standing in rigid lines, firing into each other at a range of 50 yards—the effective limit of the new firearms. War formalized into a new pattern when the bullet became the chief missile. The phalanx warfare, depending upon heavy infantry, became the pattern of European war.

The casual reader of history will point to the English longbowmen as conspicuous examples of the success of infantry-archers in battle. This is not a correct assumption. The character of the opposition must be considered during that short period of great English victories. Not only were the French unsteady in attack at the beginning of the Hundred Years' War, their cavalry was among the most unwieldy in history. The French knights, mounted on the equivalent of dray horses, were unable to maneuver. Furthermore, the French presented a final, almost ludicrous development of knightly chivalry. They dreaded the bow as much for its lowly social implication as for its deadly efficiency. In 1356, after Poitiers, the French organized a corps of longbowmen who became so expert that they were *disbanded by the nobility.* The French, after years of social jousting between gentlemen, were unable at the beginning of the war to face the stern realities of battle against yeomen archers.

Equally important in this assessment of the English as military archers is the military fact, ignored or dismissed, that the English yeomen were technically not infantry-archers at all. A glance at their organization and equipment will quickly establish that the longbowmen were actually light infantrymen, carrying the bow as a subsidiary weapon.

The English archer carried a sheaf of twenty-four arrows tucked under his girdle or in a leather bag. When standing in a fixed defensive position, this arrow supply was augmented by issues of reserves from supply carts. But as we have seen, the yeomen found that they could not always stand in such a prepared defense site and there is nothing to indicate that the English archer had more than twenty-four arrows when faced with a surprise pitched battle or when attacked on the march as happened at Patay. Of this sheaf of arrows, eight were feathered for extended ranges.

No serious or prolonged operation against a determined enemy could be sustained by archers with so few arrows. To correct this, the English armed their bowmen with pikes, axes, or heavy mallets. Therefore, the longbowmen of the English, although they acquired great reputations as archers, cannot be said to have carried bows as the major weapons. Although the bow was their most *effective* weapon, and quite often decisive, no *major* weapon can be limited in serious action to a battle life of a few minutes. Throughout their careers, the yeomen depended heavily, in moments of great peril, upon other hand weapons. They must be classed as light infantry, *armed additionally with the bow.*

It must be remembered that the usual sheaf of arrows could not be decisive except under certain ideal conditions of battle. These conditions were usually out of the control of the archers as they depended upon the enemy's irresolution. At a very early stage of any serious and prolonged action, it became necessary for the longbowmen to discard their bows and resort to hand weapons. If the issue was still in doubt when the yeomen had expended the last of their arrows, their sole remaining contribution to the battle could then be only as light infantry.

It seems obvious that the English archer was not favored with a tactical school that properly utilized his bow nor was he supported by any system of supply that would enable him to remain in action as an archer. This tactical misuse that the English made of the greatest weapon of the era has been obscured by the overevaluation of the few initial successes that obtained under ideal conditions of battle.

When the longbowmen met good infantry, determined in attack and tenacious on defense, the shortage of arrows was fatal. The longbow could inflict tremendous casualties for a few minutes but when opposed to disciplined troops, willing to accept initial casualties, the yeomen were destroyed by their own inability for remaining in action.

Heavy cavalry, well led, could overrun the English archers, as it did on many later fields. Had the yeomen been true infantry-archers, carrying the bow as their sole weapon and possessing an adequate arrow supply, this would not necessarily have been the case. Reliable infantry-archers, sufficiently equipped with arrows and given room for evasive movement, could, and often did, stop good heavy cavalry. The English archer, with insufficient arrows, was immobolized in a defensive position, with no capacity for movement. He had the option of stopping the charge or dying in his tracks. The military percentage caught up with the English longbowmen because the bow cannot be used with efficiency in such a situation.

Fortunately, the English archer did not have to meet efficient missile cavalry. Against mounted-archers, the longbowman would have been annihilated in short actions.

It seems, therefore, that although the yeomen were capable of delivering accurate and devastating missile attack, their inability to sustain fire destroyed them whenever they met major opposition.

The longbow of England occupies an ambiguous position in the history of war. One of the great weapons of all time, its battle use was so severely limited that it was never able to demonstrate its true and full effectiveness, even in the great victories in which it appeared. The great defeats for the longbow have been too carefully minimized.

Today the English longbow is remembered as a deadly and beautiful weapon of great romantic appeal. There is something irresistibly attractive in the picture of the yeoman drawing his great bow. In actual military use, it was a weapon stigmatized by its contact with the so-called inferior men of lowly birth. The bow was so undervalued by the medieval world that its use was extinguished by primitive firearms whose projectiles remained inferior to the arrow for more than three centuries after the passing of the longbow in England.

An analysis of the English military tactics of the fourteenth and fifteenth centuries indicates that it is not possible to assign these armies to any of the great tactical schools. The English military system of this period was unique. Although the cult of the horse as it had existed in England of that period had counterparts in many earlier civilizations, the majority of these earlier peoples had had a much more realistic approach to war. The Macedonians, the armies of Hannibal, the Persians, and, to some extent, the Assyrians had all made use of infantry-archers supported by heavy cavalry. But all of these peoples had placed a much higher evaluation on the bow than had the English.

The English system of war can possibly best be compared to the Persian effort although the comparison with Persian infantry-archers is forced. Basically, the English used a corps of foot-archers to support knights who fought mounted and occasionally dismounted. In the later stages of a battle, these knights mounted to attempt a decisive blow. Tactics and custom dictated that the bow was not to be the decisive weapon. All troop dispositions clearly indicated that the bowmen were expendable. It was almost as if the English gentry had suddenly found an unwanted and embarrassingly powerful weapon in the hands of low-born yeomen. By the standards of the aristocracy of this period, the bow was considered a dangerous weapon when in the hands of inferior people who might be tempted to inflict the weapon against the high-born. There was much historical precedent to validate that feeling. Rome had not permitted victorious legions inside the city walls except for the brief observances of triumphs. The legions were considered too dangerous and capable of assuming too much power.

In England the cult of the horse had ingrained the noble class with an acute distaste for missile war. It was not considered wholly correct for a peasant yeoman to bring down a French knight with a shaft, even though that French knight was an active field enemy at the time. The pageantry and ritual of war were more important in the eyes of the English gentleman, than was the destruction of a gentleman opponent by a ragged peasant. There were dangerous social implications involved.

The gentlemen of this period fought a protected war. If the gentry could survive the original shock of combat with their enemy peers or the arrows of the posses, they were usually treated in defeat as honored prisoners of war and as valuable objects for ransom. The slaughter of gentlemen knights on the field of battle was not an approved practice, financially or socially.

In contrast, defeated enemy bowmen or infantry were slaughtered on the field or taken into virtual slavery. Infantry, in medieval times, were no more than the padding of the show, mere levies furnishing the backdrop for the posturing of the knights. Often the aristocracy expressed displeasure after a successful battle that "so few of their own rascals had been killed."

Into this situation that had featured knights in full armor, attended by halberdiers and grooms, came the yeomen of England with a terrible and destructive weapon that was antisocial in all of its implications. It was incredible and it was not in accordance with form and tradition that these ragged peasants should presume to stand in the field against armored gentlemen.

It is understandable, therefore, that the English were never willing to provide adequate supply or tactical support for the longbow. War was pageantry; it offered no proper setting for the longbow. Equally illuminating was the refusal of the knights to demean themselves by conducting any operation that was designed to protect or conserve their archers. The longbow was possibly viewed as a weapon capable of altering the feudal society.

Certain it is that the English gentlemen were unable to face with realism the changing aspects of pageantry war.

19

The Plains Indians

No consideration of the horse-archers of history or the operation of the bow in war would be complete without a look at the American Plains Indians. This section of the book is concluded, therefore, with a short discussion of the Asiatic school of war as practiced to a limited degree in the United States in the nineteenth century.

In the Western Hemisphere, the bow was never developed to its highest level either as a weapon of war or in physical construction. The Indians of North and South America were isolated from the civilized centers of world population. With the exception of the Aztecs, the Mayas of Mexico, the Aymaras of Peru (who made use of gold as a ceremonial metal), and certain tribes of North American Indians who made limited use of copper, the Western Hemisphere was in a Stone Age culture.

The wars in North America had been mere raids of a dozen or a few hundred warriors or chance encounters of hunting parties when in pursuit of game. There was no formal government above a tribal level in most instances, and there was no science of military tactics. There was no tradition of formal war as we know it. The American Indians had not been subject to discipline nor had they developed any weapon to be used exclusively in war save a stone war club. The knife, the bow, and the lance were weapons of the chase and utilitarian in character. The development of missile weapons had been greatly retarded in the Americas. The Central and South American Indians had preferred the atlatl, as did certain tribes of the Eskimos. This weapon had been in disuse in Europe and Asia for many centuries. The tribes of South American Indians had possessed a form of the longbow, often as much as 12 feet in length. Along the Amazon River this weapon had shared popularity with the blowgun.

The various tribes of North American Indians had had little in common and had usually distrusted each other. There were a few cases of casual tribal cooperation as expressed by the Erie Confederacy and other minor tribal alliances, but in general the American Indians operated as individual clans with very little control over their actions.

In some sections, the bow had gradually evolved into an effective and formidable weapon. In the southern portion of North America—in what is now Georgia and Florida—the Narvaez expedition found the Indians in possession of a very strong bow "as thick as the arm," the chronicles state, "of eleven or twelve palms in length." This bow was credited with a range of two hundred paces, and the reed arrows, tipped with flint and sometimes of fire-hardened cane, could penetrate the Spanish armor. The accounts read: "Dead Spaniards showed their corpses traversed from side to side with arrows; and for all some had on good armor, it did not give adequate protection." The flint arrowheads achieved remarkable penetration; the cane heads splintered and found openings in the armor.

The composite bow had been known to the Americas for some centuries prior to the arrival of white men. Although not so highly refined as the Asiatic bow, the American bow was often reflexed and was a weapon of considerable power. The typical Indian bow was about 4 feet in length and constructed of wood, horn, bone, and sinew or a combination of these materials. Sinew-backed ash bows were popular Plains Indian weapons. When the material was available, one of the best Indian bows was constructed of laminations of the horn of the mountain sheep spliced with heated deer sinew. The range of the average Plains Indian bow was 150 to 175 yards, but the Indians preferred shorter ranges for hunting.

The tribal affiliations of the bowmen could easily be determined by an examination of the arrows. Various tribes would consistently use lance-point heads, barbed points, or triangular points, and the shafts and nocks of the arrows always showed distinguishing tribal marks. All Indian arrows were steadied in flight by three rows of clipped feathers set into slots for a distance of 5 or 6 inches along the neck and below the nock.

The arrows were usually distinctively painted, not only with the private mark of the owner but also with the tribal colors and patterns.

The length of the arrow was usually standardized as the distance between the armpit and the ends of the fingers.

The American Indian, after centuries of Stone Age culture, moved abruptly into the Iron Age when his aboriginal privacy was invaded by white men. There was no slow and steady evolvement in his weapons of native manufacture. In one instant of time the Indian had flint arrowheads; in the next, his arrows were tipped with iron and he was clamoring for firearms.

By 1580, the escaped horses from Spanish expeditions had multiplied on the plains into great herds and life became much simpler for the Indians. They were then able to follow the buffalo and to take up the nomadic existence of their Asiatic forefathers. They developed a mode of life that was almost idyllic as they settled into mobile villages. That mobility was the Indian's greatest protection against enemies. No valley was of sufficient importance to warrant a desperate struggle for its possession. The Indians were free to move at will across the horizon to another valley.

Thus, dimly, the Indians accepted the military precepts of Asia. They became elusive targets, avoiding position war and disdaining permanent possession of any piece of ground. The bow came into more favor, for with the union of horse and man, archery assumed new importance in hunting and warfare. With the bow, the Indians developed a few simple war tactics as they began to make hostile contact with white soldiers and fur traders and trappers. When the white men began serious encroachment on the Indian hunting grounds, the Plains aborigines found themselves in an undeclared but formal war. Such a war was foreign to all of their experience or inclination.

The undisciplined Indians were never soldiers, but they were peculiarly adaptable to informal combat, which had been a part of their daily existence. Immediately following the Civil War, the generals of the cumbersome military establishment of the United States had found themselves opposed by a quasimilitary force of Indians, mounted with bows in hand, that was to prove to be more than a match for white soldiers. The Indians were not willing to stand in line to be shot at and they were too speedy and elusive for the American bogged-down dragoon operations to be effective.

It took a great nation, inexhaustible in manpower and using all of the weapons of modern war, more than forty years to subdue a few small tribes of Plains Indians. The total population of western horse

Indians—men, women and children—was hardly more than fifty thousand. The contest was finally won as much by the destruction of the buffalo as by force of arms. In the course of these small battles, the Indians inflicted casualties at a ratio of 5 to 1. With limited firearms and never enough ammunition, the Indians depended upon the bow, mobility, elusiveness, and a native knowledge that war of position for a piece of ground was too expensive. The Plains Indians gave our clumsy concept of cavalry a severe demonstration of the virtues of mobile missile war.

The cavalry experiment in the United States had been of very late development. The original American conception of mounted troops had been a dragoon arm that was not cavalry at all but rather a commitment of heavily armed, mounted infantry. These dragoons, equipped and trained for infantry action, simply rode on horseback to the scene of the battle and there dismounted to fight on foot.

There was never much change from this original concept. In the 1880's the United States reorganized its dragoons and mounted rifle regiments into units that were called cavalry, but the new arm existed in name only as the training, traditions, and tactics remained virtually unchanged.

As this so-called cavalry arm of the United States developed slowly, the pistol and carbine replaced the rifle and a rudimentary school of mounted tactical operations came into being. The manuals of cavalry tactics of the period reveal that the principal emphasis was upon salutes and courtesies to officers and to headlong charges with the saber. Most of the infantry tradition was retained.

Much that is romantic and careless has been written about our cavalry force that was pitted against the Plains Indians. The actual performance of this arm is quite another matter. History has shown us that our cavalry in the 1870s was made up of badly trained recruits who were indifferent riders and worse marksmen. Cavalry is not mounted infantry that can be dismounted at will and placed efficiently within a defense position. Some horrendous disasters befell our mounted force when this was tried.

The stern military mandate is that cavalry is deficient on defense and must not be forced into a defensive action except in extreme emergency as when no other course is possible. The horse cavalry arm had severe limitations. It was equipped and armed for mounted offensive action and was not usually effective when forced into a dismounted defensive stand or into a limited dismounted offensive or holding action.

There is not space in this book about the bow to discuss the weakness of the American dragoon commitment. Let it be sufficient to state here that a true cavalry arm possesses great speed, great endurance and tenacity, heavy firepower in missiles, and great maneuverability. Mounted units, not being adaptable to dismounted defense situations must remain mounted, in defeat and in victory. Their capacity for movement is their only defense when overmatched. These were principles that were never learned by the leaders of United States horse soldiers on the plains. The result was a leadfooted, inept mounted force that was unable to execute the mission of cavalry and were thus subject to continuous disaster.

The American Indian, on the other hand, possessed speed, endurance, tenacity, horsemanship, and maneuverability. The Indians consistently avoided close action and, usually, dismounted action. The entire history of the Indian Wars demonstrates that the Plains horsemen were wary of infantry soldiers and cannon as these were military ingredients that were capable of making a deadly defensive stand. In contrast, United States cavalry forces were always considered by the Indians to be a minor opposition, easily evaded or decoyed into an ineffective defensive stand. In every respect, except in numbers and in formal battle training, the Plains Indians were very creditable exponents of mobile missile war.

They fought and retreated, to fight again. They lived off the country. They moved whole villages in an hour. They refused battle or offered battle at will, and they retained the initiative. They used every means of concealment and they made the terrain work for them. They could seldom be brought into hand-to-hand conflict.

The Plains Indians may have been the greatest natural horsemen of all time, excepting neither Parthians, nor Mongols, nor Scythians, nor Huns. They rode fleet little horses of great stamina, far superior animals than the tender, grain-fed horses of United States cavalry that were selected for conformation and appearance value in parades.

Although possessing these great advantages, the Indians had severe military weaknesses which led to their final defeat. They had small talent for unit action. Superstitions handicapped them in war. As they would not fight at night, defeated enemy could go into concealment in the daytime and retreat in safety by making forced marches at night. Messengers, using this device of night travel could, and did, traverse Indian country in comparative safety.

The importance that the Indians attached to *coups* resulted in the incurring of needless casualties. It was thought to be an act of great merit to close with and touch armed enemies with coup sticks in senseless gestures. Sometimes the Indians refused to fight at all if the omens were not favorable or if they had recently violated a taboo. A mere lack of war paint would dissuade them from giving battle. They were casual warriors, wandering in and out of an engagement at their convenience. If the restraint of discipline was imposed upon them, they would withdraw from the fight and sulk in their tents.

The greatest handicap of the Indians was the simple lack of manpower. The greatest concentration of troops they were ever able to assemble—and that under great pressure—was at the Battle of the Little Big Horn. An estimated one thousand five hundred warriors formed an irregular army, the highest expression of organized battle the Indians were ever to develop. This battle was the last appearance of the bow in formal war.

The bow had bridged millennias of time. It had had a long span of usefulness through years that began on the Sumerian plains and the Egyptian desert, to continue through the fields of Mesopotamia and Europe and the Gobi, to end, against riflemen, in the parched hills of Montana. It was fitting, in the face of all of that history, that the bow should win its final battle.

The general situation and the opposing forces having been particularized, we will scarcely do more than touch upon the Battle of the Little Big Horn and then only in terms of the result. The battle itself holds a vivid place in history and Custer's Last Stand has been debated in many books.

On June 25, 1876, Custer's Seventh United States Cavalry neared a great concentration of Indians encamped on the Little Big Horn River. After preliminary probing maneuvers with his command divided into four detachments, Custer made an attack on the Indian village. The cavalry was badly mauled. However, only the detachment led by Custer personally—some 290 men—was completely annihilated. The other units effected a union and escaped after taking severe casualties. At the close of the battle, less than half the Seventh Cavalry survived.

After repulsing an attack by Major Reno and severely beating his detachment at a hilltop stand, the Indians concentrated upon Custer's command and succeeded in isolating it on a bare hilltop in a bad defensive site. The final elimination of Custer and his men was accomplished by arching flights of arrows launched by bowmen from the cover of sagebrush and ravines. The Indians had few rifles and less ammunition although, in the final stages of the battle, they had available a considerable number of captured Springfields. Custer's position was not overrun. There was no concerted charge until the final mopping-up operation.

The Sioux and Cheyennes, under unusually fine leadership by Crazy Horse and Gall, utilized an effective barrage of indirect arrow fire, supported by some riflery. The soldiers at the Little Big Horn suffered severe casualties from seldom-seen Indians; concealed archers employed the bow effectively. The reprisal fire of the cavalry was so weak and misdirected as to be astounding; the Seventh Cavalry had no capacity for the infliction of casualties.

Although many of the Indians at the Battle of the Little Big Horn dismounted during the operation incidental to the envelopment of Custer (after he was contained in a state of immobility), their horses dragged long ropes, making the animals easy to recover and available for immediate remounting.

The Sioux and the Cheyennes made full use of the conditions under which the bow had advantage over the gun. They sprayed the target area with unaimed concentrations of arrows, without unduly exposing themselves to return fire. The disproportionate casualties reveal how the slaughter was accomplished; it is supported by Indian accounts of the battle.

The Sioux and Cheyennes apparently lost less than fifty men at the Battle of the Little Big Horn. The Indian loss has been stated to have been thirty-nine Sioux and seven Cheyennes killed. It is quite evident that the offensive effort of United States cavalry (operating within a defensive perimeter in a typical dragoon action) was incredibly weak. Six hundred armed men were able to inflict only negligible losses on the Indians while losing three hundred.

Custer was not the only general to underestimate the power of the bow. Little Big Horn was no more than another display of the power of mounted missiles when combined with great mobility. Although the finest performance of the Asiatic theory of mobile war to be enacted by the American aborigines, it was only a larger expression of the many chilling episodes of the plains wars that were to give the United States a new appreciation of the effectiveness of mounted missiles.

The lead-footed, unwieldy, and inadequately fire-powered dragoons of the United States were given a severe lesson in the virtues of true mobility, maneuverability, stamina, and evasive action during the wars against Indians. These battles on the plains virtually completed the war service of the horse cavalry arm and the Indians were finally broken by the application of infantry, Gatling guns, and quick-firing Hotchkiss cannon.

The American mounted service, miscalled cavalry, remained dragoons to the end.

Part Five

THE IMPACT OF THE BOW
ON MILITARY TACTICS

20

Evaluation: The Crossbow, Longbow, and Composite Bow

The Durable Crossbow

The crossbow, in its various modifications, had a strange and lengthy history. It was first used as a hand weapon as early as 1200 B.C. by the Chinese who developed a repeating model which carried the bolts in a magazine.

This Chinese repeater crossbow was a remarkable weapon of advanced design. It propelled two bolts simultaneously which were presented through a wooden magazine that contained twenty-four featherless quarrels about 8 1/4 inches long. The magazine turned on the stock to load the projectiles. The quarrels used by the Chinese were of bamboo, tipped with metal heads, and sometimes poisoned. They had an extreme range of about 200 yards and an effective range of approximately 80 yards. According to Chinese annals, one hundred men could project two thousand quarrels in fifteen seconds. The bow itself was constructed of bamboo, laminated and glued in strips for additional strength, and the string was of rawhide.

As a hand weapon, little was heard of the crossbow other than in China until it appeared as the ballista, a huge instrument employed against walls, and from walls, by many armies of antiquity. In this form, the weapon was highly effective, representing the first *precision* casting of a large projectile. It was far more accurate than the catapult, mangonel, or trebuchet.

The ballista, was refined into an enormous crossbow, as much as 15 feet in width across the arms. Usually constructed of iron, it was capable of propelling javelins as much as 12 feet long with great force and accuracy. This tremendous tension machine was wound by a windlass that was manned by as many as four men. The pull of such a great bow was several thousand pounds. The javelins it cast were winged with thin strips of horn. The ballista could also cast a shorter iron bolt that weighed as much as 5 pounds.

Procopius reports that during the siege of Rome by the Goths an armored Goth, sniping at the walls of the city from a tree, was pinned to the trunk by a ballista bolt penetrating body and armor. There are stories of javelins passing through the bodies of several men as they stood aligned in formation.

As a standard weapon of siege warfare, the ballista was used by Romans, Goths, Byzantines, Chinese, Mongols, and other people. In its period, it was the most successful development of the large projectile arm. Procopious describes the ballista development that was used by Belisarius:

> They have the general shape of a bow but in the middle there is a hollow piece of horn, lying over a straight iron stock. When wishing to let fly at the enemy you pull back the short strong cord that joins the arms of the bow and place in the horn a bolt, four times as thick as an ordinary arrow, but only half its length; men standing on each side of the *ballista* draw back the cord with little devices; when they let it go, the horn rushes forward and discharges the bolt, which strikes with the force of at least two arrows, for it breaks stone and pierces trees.

Following its initial use as a hand weapon in China, the crossbow, or arbalest, seems to have survived only as the ballista until its reintroduction as an infantry arm some centuries later. The crossbow's history is most interesting as the weapon passed from many periods in which it enjoyed great favor to times when it was regarded as an offense against humanity. On several occasions the Church took positive action against the weapon, deeming it barbaric and inhuman. However, this ban had little effect, and the weapon remained in war use, with considerable esteem, for many centuries after the Christian Era.

It reappeared in Central Europe in the tenth century and was first carried to England by the Normans. The crossbow was always strongly identified with Spain, France, Germany, and Italy; it was an important missile weapon in England from the days of the Conquest until about 1290—in parallel use with the longbow. It was the favored weapon in England for hunting, with the point of the bolt sometimes poisoned with white hellebore. Two kings of England, Rufus and Richard the Lion-Hearted, were killed by bolts from the crossbow. Richard was slain in France in a minor battle, and Rufus in a hunting accident in the New Forest in England.

Modifications

The crossbow appeared in many variations and modifications. A mechanical instrument, the principal developments and alterations were concerned with the method of drawing the string. The modifications are:

bent by unaided hand
bent by cord and pulley
bent by belt and claw
bent by screw and handle
bent by goatshead lever
bent by windlass and ropes
bent by crane
bent by lever fixed on a block
bent by light wooden lever

The crossbow was capable of projecting many types of missiles. The quarrel or bolt, usually about 15 inches long, was constructed of wood or iron. It was usually feathered or vaned with wood, although it was sometimes devoid of any stabilizer. Round stones were sometimes discharged as were lead pellets. A barreled type of crossbow cast unfeathered bolts.

The military quarrel was usually winged with leather in two vanes, although, sometimes, the material was horn or wood. The bolt winged with feathers was usually reserved for hunting.

The size of the military crossbow varied greatly. The English weapon was small, some 24 inches in breadth, with an overall stock length of about 18 inches; the bolt was usually about 9 inches long. The crossbow used by the French was somewhat larger. Specimens from the field of Agincourt are described as possessing arms 32 inches in breadth with a total weapon weight of 15 pounds, a formidable weapon. The point-blank range of the French crossbow was estimated to be 70 yards. Elevated to 45 degrees, it could propel a bolt about 350 yards. As we have noted elsewhere, the weapon lost efficiency rapidly in wet weather because of the impossibility of protecting the string.

Most powerful of all the crossbows were the Genoese adaptations of the fifteenth century. Weighing 18 pounds, they had arms with a breadth of 38 inches and a tremendous pull of 1,200 pounds. The arm was wound by a detachable windlass, and it propelled a bolt 14 inches in length that weighed 1/4 pound. Such a weapon had an extreme range of more than 450 yards. At 100 yards the penetration was frightful against any form of protective armor. The shock and jar of the discharge was very great. The Genoese crossbow was very slow in operation; it was a heavy and unhandy weapon.

Judged on the basis of projectile velocity, accuracy, and range, it will be seen that the crossbow was at least equal to, and possibly the superior to, the best hand-drawn composite bows or the English self bow. The French considered their crossbows to be highly effective at 150 yards and able to kill or seriously wound at more than 300 yards. The bolt could kill a horse at 50 yards.

This missile weapon earned the respect of every opponent who faced it. The Saracens feared the crossbow. Even the Mongols, most expert of all composite bowmen, avoided the crossbow when possible.

Weaknesses

Frightful as the weapon was, the crossbow could not usually stand up in a field operation against the longbow or the composite bow. Eight serious weaknesses reveal themselves when the weapon is evaluated for military use.

1. The mechanical operation caused a rate of fire so slow as to be fatal when the weapon was employed in the open field against troops possessing other types of hand-drawn bows. The longbow or the composite bow could propel at least three arrows while the crossbowman was discharging a single bolt.

2. In many modifications of the weapon the bolt was easily dislodged from the groove in which it lay during the heat of battle. A crossbowman, in an awkward or unnatural position, could not discharge the weapon at all. Any tilt of the crossbow—in some types—could dislodge the bolt.

3. The crossbow weighed from 12 to 18 pounds. No infantry soldier can carry a weapon of that weight to advantage.

4. More serious than the weight of the crossbow was the excessive projectile load. The weight of a crossbow bolt was much greater than that of an arrow. This weight was badly distributed as the bolts were short and difficult of access in any type of quiver or case.

5. When carried by troops in column, the crossbow was a most unwieldy weapon. Carried across the shoulder, its projecting arms made close-order movement impossible. In action, the crossbow required wide intervals in the ranks as it was discharged from the horizontal position with the long arms extending on either side of the wielder.

6. The crossbow was quite susceptible to weather conditions. In wet weather the iron was subject to rust. In cold weather iron was unreliable under great stress and subject to breakage.

7. The crossbow not only required well-seasoned wood for the stock but the quantity of iron it contained was in direct competition with the metal needs of armorers and the manufacturers of hand weapons and horse equipment. The most effective quarrel was also made of iron. The crossbow, therefore, presented demands upon the national economy out of proportion to the actual field worth of the weapon.

8. The greatest weakness of the crossbow was the vulnerability of the string to conditions of weather, to battle, and use damage. It was almost impossible to protect the string from dampness. The silk strings thickened when wet and could not be used. String breakage was frequent because of the tremendous tension that was built up by the strong pull. No string could be manufactured by any technique then available that was reliable under tensions of as much as 1,200 pounds.

Advantages

On the other hand, the crossbow had certain battle advantages over the composite bow and the longbow although these were not sufficient to give the crossbow a parity.

1. The crossbow required less strength to operate since the string was drawn by mechanical means. Crossbowmen could be developed from personnel not fitted for the operation of other bows.

2. The iron crossbow quarrel possessed great morale-shattering value. The bolt inspired fear and respect. The wounds it inflicted were

frightful, and the long-range penetration of armor exceeded the best penetration achieved by other types of bows.

3. The crossbow was easier to aim. Some were equipped with simple sights. The training of a crossbowman was a relatively short operation in contrast to the two years required to make a reasonably accurate longbowman.

4. The crossbow, although unwieldy, was more effective than the ordinary bow as a club for close combat. Devoid of bolts, the crossbowman was, to some degree, still armed.

The crossbow was used in England until the beginning of the fourteenth century, and it was effective on the Continent until its abandonment by all armies, circa 1525. The ballista survived as a siege weapon until about 1535. Used from walls, where the rate of fire was not critical, the crossbow and the balista were always superior weapons.

In the Far East, the crossbow was used until a much later date. The Chinese used the weapon against the British in 1860 and during the war with Japan in 1895. As late as World War II, certain soldiers in Tibet and other sections of inner Asia were using the crossbow. In fact, the crossbow has never gone out of use in Asia and the Pacific islands. It is still used in many island groups of the South Pacific and is doubtless in use today by the Tibetans against the Communist Chinese invaders.

Not usually appreciated is the fact that the crossbow had a considerable period of use in the Western Hemisphere. It was used by the *conquistadores* of Spain in Mexico and Peru. For many years the Potawatomi Indians of Wisconsin had this type of bow and it was in use as late as 1865.

The English Longbow and the Composite Bow of Asia

Inevitably, comparison must be made between the English self bow and the composite bow of Asia. The two weapons reached their peaks of development and design at identical periods of history. Genghis Khan had been dead but a century when the longbowmen shattered the French knights at Crecy. Agincourt was fought only a decade after the death of Tamerlane. The Mongol Empire was at its crest during the Hundred Years' War in France.

These two greatest weapons of the Middle Ages never met in battle as the English used the crossbow when opposing the Saracens in the Crusades. Had they met, the outcome would have depended upon tactics and position, rather than a comparison of superiority, for each of these weapons was deadly. Tactics would have determined the range under which the armies made initial contact. Terrain would have determined whether or not the mounted maneuver of Asiatic horse-archers would be limited. Two great tactical theories would have faced their supreme test.

The English were committed to defensive war in a prepared position. The Mongols were disciples of offensive distant war, and would never have committed themselves to a frontal attack on a prepared English defensive site. They would have been content to control the countryside, with the English under tight surveillance, until supply needs forced English movement. Such movement would have resulted in the destruction of the longbowmen.

Had English and Mongol armies met on a field for preliminary maneuver, the English would have had no time for the construction of a field defensive position of their choosing. They would have been *forced* into a hastily constructed position because of inability to evade the fast-moving Mongols. The Mongols were soldiers with great battle patience, fully aware of their ability to destroy slow-moving enemy columns.

Considering the two weapons solely as basic instruments of destruction in the hands of determined men, the following conclusion might be drawn:

1. For short-range accuracy, a slight edge should go to the clothyard arrow of the longbow. It was longer, heavier, steadier in flight, and less subject to air currents and minor physical obstructions. However, the advantage was theoretical rather than real, for the lighter Mongol arrow possessed sufficient accuracy for all practical short-range purposes. At a range of 200 yards, men exposed to the fire of the two weapons would have been unaware of deficiency in either arm. In wooded country of low visibility, the English arrow would have broken through leaves and small twigs and been less liable to deflection. This advantage would have been partially negated by the greater ease of handling the shorter composite bow in such country.

2. In long-range effectiveness, a decided edge must be given to the Mongol bow. In open country, at extreme range, the English longbow-

men would have been denied a target while under pressure from the longer-ranging Mongol arrows. Operating as infantry, the English would have been unable to close to effective range for the longbow. The composite bow of the Mongols could discharge an arrow at least 600 yards, and greater ranges have been recorded. At 400 yards, the Mongol arrow would have retained sufficient energy to have inflicted crippling wounds. The Mongol arrowheads of iron tempered with brine were bitter missiles at long range. Mongol archers were equipped for long- and short-range warfare. They carried a variety of arrows adapted to specific battle problems. The English longbowmen also had specially feathered arrows, but they would have been under fatal handicaps at extended ranges.

3. The composite bow was susceptible to weather conditions. Moisture is inimical to horn, sinew, and glue—all relatively absorbent materials. Reducing the amount of these materials in the bow—as the Mongols sometimes did—to secure an all-weather weapon reduced its efficiency. The Mongol bow—whatever its proportion of horn, wood, sinew, and glue—was a fair-weather weapon. When exposed to damp for lengths of time, it had to be reconditioned by exposure to heat— either flame or bright sunlight. Only when thoroughly dry was the composite bow completely effective.

In this respect, the longbow was greatly superior. The English bow was virtually waterproof from applications of tallow, resin, and oil. The very fact that it was used in the damp, humid atmosphere of the British Isles shows it to have been largely unaffected by weather or dampness.

4. Another point for consideration is accessibility. Mongol troopers on the move usually carried the bow unstrung unless they were in hostile country. An unexpected encounter in low visibility would have seriously handicapped the Mongol archer. Stringing or bracing the composite bow was a fairly lengthy process and not one to be accomplished while under enemy pressure. The need to dismount the bow required special equipment or an assistant. When possible, the composite bow was always warmed before bracing.

5. The strongly reflexed Mongol bow was a magnificent weapon, but it was complicated and subject to many disorders. The virtue of the longbow was its simplicity and easy availability. A parallel may be drawn between our present-day reliable single-shot pistol and the more efficient but less reliable semiautomatic, which must be protected from sand, mud, and excessive moisture if it is to function at all.

As an all-weather weapon, the longbow had that same position of being reliable at the expense of its efficiency. It was easy to brace and positive in action. Reliable under practically all combat conditions, it required no artificial treatment to maintain its level of efficiency.

The tremendous power that was built into the composite bow, which stood at great tension when merely strung and under terrific tension when drawn, made the weapon susceptible to battle and use damage. The slipping or breaking of a string was almost certain to destroy the weapon as it violently sought its reflexed position. Such a casualty could damage the composite bow beyond the possibility of field repair. Occasionally, it would reverse itself when in process of being strung. Even minor damage was difficult to repair, requiring the services of an expert bowyer. Any loosening of the bonding between the materials would render the bow useless. In contrast, minor casualties to the longbow such as a split in the material or a breakage of the ears could be fished or otherwise reinforced to make possible an impaired use of the weapon.

The replacement of Mongol bows lost in action was a major problem of the Mongol supply service. All rear-guard members of the tumans were instructed, under penalty of death, to retrieve bows and other equipment. The necessity for this stringent rule can be understood when it is recalled that it required two years, or more, to construct the Mongol bow.

Although the Mongol bow had a much stronger pull, the physical effort required to draw the bow did not exceed, and may have been less than, that exerted in drawing the longbow. The Mongols used various devices of string pullers and other mechanical means; the most common was the thumb ring. Any of the methods permitted them to draw the bow with the muscles of the entire arm and shoulder. The string of the longbow was drawn back by the fingers, without mechanical aid. The Mongol bowman carried a minimum of sixty arrows and often as many as four hundred. The English longbowman, with his usual issue of twenty-four arrows, would have been outsupplied. Sustained firepower would have belonged to the Mongols, who could have remained in effective action long after the yeomen had exhausted their arrow supply.

In the final analysis, the comparison of the two bows becomes a discussion of two types of war rather than two types of weapon. The bow is a weapon of movement and movement implies cavalry. The

English military establishment did not possess sufficient tactical refinement to have enabled them to successfully engage the proficient and talented Mongol horse-archers. The Mongols would have respected the longbow but, after having established its capabilities and its limitations, they would have exploited the English with superior tactics and destroyed the yeomen in rapid and decisive field actions.

Had Subotai brought his horse-archers into contact with the infantry-bowmen of England, the yeomen would have been overmatched, outmaneuvered, and annihilated.

21

The Infantry-Archer:
The Tactical Problem

We have seen that as an infantry weapon the bow was subject to grave and sometimes fatal weaknesses, whether it was used as the decisive arm or as a supporting weapon. In guerrilla warfare—in rough and concealing terrain—the bow could be used with great effect by foot-archers, but the very nature of the weapon prevented its full exploitation by infantry in formal war.

With the exception of the Akkadians, who operated in a period of history prior to the taming of the horse, no nation was able to make a completely valid adaptation of the bow for use by foot-archers. The value placed on the bow by the various tactical schools varied greatly, but very few of the significant military powers relied upon foot-archers. The few nations making the attempt found themselves confronted by tactical problems that could not be solved.

The use of the bow as an infantry weapon was usually a condition that was dictated by circumstances rather than by any positive desire to create such an army composition. There were many factors that could influence the decision to form a corps of infantry-archers and they were, for the most part, not dictated by military judgment. National economy had to be taken into consideration; cavalry was an expensive arm. On occasion, a national emergency did not allow sufficient time for the training of proficient horse-archers. Sometimes, the bow type was not adaptable to horse-archery. Very often, the ritualistic or social aspect (as already discussed) prevented the arming of horsemen with the bow.

The two outstanding exponents of foot-archery were the Persians and the English and in neither case was the choice based upon military considerations. The Persians used the foot-archer because they were unable to control the horse properly during the period before the invention of the stirrup. The English employed the foot-archer because the bow was not the weapon of a mounted gentleman. The type of bow used in England was a minor contributing factor, for the English had the shorter Welsh bow available that would readily have adapted itself to horse-archery. Neither Persia nor England were able to achieve the battle effectiveness of the bow with consistency. They won great victories, but they lost their wars.

Let us consider foot-archers in their relationship to the tactical problems they created. There were military responsibilities that the bow could not accept. Attempts to force such responsibilities on the weapon resulted in the greatest historical defeats for the bow.

Infantry-archers as a pivot

A center of infantry-archers hampered, rather than assisted, when wings of heavy cavalry were used as the decisive arm. Foot-bowmen could not operate successfully as a pivot for the maneuvers of mounted wings, for the center pivot must not be too closely attached to such wings.

If cavalry was to have freedom to roam widely on attack and reconnaissance missions, there could be no question as to the stability of the center. The center had to be able to defend itself and remain in being under all conditions of battle and without the necessity for protective action on the part of the cavalry wings. Philip of Macedon solved this tactical problem and gave his cavalry full maneuverability by concentrating heavy infantry in the center, supported by foot-archers. Philip increased this protection of the center by adding additional highly mobile light armed infantry.

As a pivot, the infantry-archer could never take the place of heavily armed swordsmen or pikemen. An unsupported center requires shock power and ability to protect itself at close quarters. Foot-archers had a proper place as a supporting missile arm for this center.

When the center was composed solely of infantry-archers, there was no assurance that it could remain in being. Infantry bowmen could not be left unsupported in open country when facing a determined enemy, whether that enemy was heavy infantry, shock cavalry, or mounted missile troops. A sustained attack could only result in the overrunning of the foot-archers and the disruption of the center. The Persians learned this military truism at the hands of the Greek spearmen who displayed the fortitude necessary to close, in open country, against arrow flights. The English were taught the same lesson by the French in the latter stages of the Hundred Years' War. The armored knights in the Crusades learned that separation from their center of crossbowmen meant the loss and destruction of the total force.

Inability to keep up with the attack

A center of infantry-archers could only result in loss of the initiative because of their inability to present the weight of their missile attack to a distant enemy. Under such conditions, the bow was completely out of the action. To be effective, the bow must be able to deliver missiles to the enemy, wherever that enemy may be. When supported by a center of infantry-archers, shock cavalry on the wings could not offer a sustained offense.

Inability to prolong the action

Not the least important weakness of the bow in the hands of foot soldiers was the inability of the archer to carry sufficient arrows for an extended action. The story of all of the battles fought by infantry-archers was one of frantic efforts to pluck expended arrows from dead animals or men—sometimes at a very early stage of the action. The archer under heavy pressure, when attempting to stop a charge, could deliver as many as twelve arrows per minute. A small exercise in simple arithmetic will show that this archer could not remain in severe action for more than a few minutes with any supply of arrows that he could conceivably carry. A heavy quiver of arrows is a galling weight. No foot-archer could be expected to carry more than fifty or sixty arrows —a supply that even under conditions of deliberate aimed fire would be expended in no more than ten minutes of severe action. Such limitations did not apply to the horse-archer who could, on long campaigns or in serious action, carry as many as four hundred arrows. The horse-archer also possessed the further advantage of being able to remove himself from a critical area when his arrows were expended. The foot-archer in such a circumstance stood and died.

No prolonged offensive movement or long-continued defense could be made by infantry-archers.

Arrow recovery on the field

Usually the arrow supply of foot-archers could not be augmented by the recovery of discharged missiles. There could be no recovery from a defensive stand. When engaged in a limited offensive action, the relative lack of mobility and the precarious control of the initiative made arrow recovery a slow process when it was possible at all. Here again, the horse-archer, controlling the initiative and able to keep the enemy on the move, was able to effect a considerable recovery of arrows.

The exit of the bow in Europe was hastened by the simple military fact that the bow was not adaptable to the type of war that suited the European psychology. The inherent tactical problems were as much a contributing factor as was the introduction of firearms. Actually, firearms were no threat to the bow as a projectile weapon for more than five hundred years after the use of gunpowder became common.

As European nations were never able or willing to develop sound tactics for the bow or to develop effective use of the horse in war because of the social implications that were attached to the animal, the military thinking that dictated the abandonment of the bow was probably sound. Since it was unthinkable that the horse be used as a vehicle for a bowman and since no gentleman would condescend to draw the bow in war, it was sound practice to equip the common man with a musket. The early musket at least had the virtue of being a good club in a close action.

Defense against the bow

Reserved for final consideration is this greatest of all problems that faced the armies of yesterday. There was no reliable defense against the bow—except another bow. During the centuries that the

ground tactics in a wilderness, was a sound lesson that invalidated European formal tactics. The British tactics continually violated the principles of maneuver and security and resulted in many shattering defeats in the Indian wars that preceded the Revolution and in the earlier battles of that war. In forest operations, the rudimentary American commitment to "small war" won victories at Bennington and Saratoga but, in the formal battles, the Americans too often followed the principles of European position war.

It is quite probable that more men were killed by the bayonet in the revolutionary war than by musketry and artillery fire combined. The Hessians quite often finished the battles with stolid bayonet exercises within the American line. This was a strange and inept war. Some military writers have asserted that internal political rivalries between Tory generals and a Whig government in England made impossible any application of the true British strength. When some of the battles of the war are analyzed, the postulate seems credible—as the Tory generals, on many occasions, displayed an amazing unwillingness for effective offensive action against the American colonists. It is certain that a large segment of the English population opposed the war.

When the United States was created and independence was gained, we began the prosecution of the succeeding minor wars of our history with a complete application of the principles of European formal war; our military commitment was organized on those lines. In America, as it had been in Europe, it became correct to present formal battle lines, fully exposed to fire. All of the earlier experiments in rapid movement and concealment were ignored. Our military organization developed its small stature in minor battles of the War of 1812, the Mexican War, and in minor preliminary skirmishes against Indians in the West. There were no important land battles in any of these wars. We had a Seminole war in Florida that was a classic example of complete frustration.

When the Civil War inflicted itself upon our nation, we were firmly grounded in the dreadful tactics of position war. The West Point curriculum of that period had developed no effective leadership, for it was concerned mostly with studies of Vauban's siege methods, fortification engineering, Hannibal's envelopment of the Roman legions at Cannae, and preoccupation with the frontal assault tactics of infantry. This was the last American war where infantry would attack in the open, in dense formations. The armies could offer nothing in the field

other than the thin line of Frederick and the massed battalions of
Napoleon; it was all the military science they had. There were no
adequate maps and no intelligence service; information about the
enemy was furnished the North by the Pinkerton Detective Agency.
Leadership on each side was too often uninspired, dogmatic, and
indecisive. Using tactics that were savage and outworn, masses of men
were hurled at each other. There was little element of surprise and, on
occasion, great armies floundered, unaware of the other's presence.
The Union army at Shiloh was completely in ignorance of the Confederate position when that army was encamped within two miles of them
on the evening before the battle.

These European tactical conceptions produced enormous casualties. The total casualties at Shiloh were twenty-four thousand. The
seven-day battle cost thirty-six thousand lives. It was after this battle
that General Butterfield appropriately devised the bugle call "Taps."
Antietam produced twenty-one thousand total casualties; Fredericks-
burg, eighteen thousand; Chancellorsville, thirty thousand. At Gettysburg, seven thousand men were killed in a single day. In the one
summer of 1864, almost one hundred thousand men were killed or
wounded in battle. One of the most terrible statements in military
history was that of Burnside after he had launched a series of useless
frontal assaults against the Confederate position at Marye's Heights.
"I felt that I had to do something," Burnside said. He lost twelve
thousand men in a single day and accomplished nothing.

The price of these tactics produced ghastly figures. The Union
forces lost 138,154 men killed during the war, with a total dead of
359,528 and a wounded toll of 280,040. Confederate losses, less accu-
rately recorded, were about 75,000 killed in action and a wounded toll
of about 200,000. (All casualty figures furnished by the United States
Department of Defense.)

Tactics were not greatly improved in World War I, particularly in
the European armies. The British bled themselves to death in gigantic
infantry operations in the early years of the fighting. The United States
suffered casualties of about 257,000 killed and wounded, and the
majority of these losses were incurred in about two months of fighting
in the Argonne Forest.

It was after this war that a loosening and opening up of tactical
maneuvering became the rule. In the intervals between World War I
and World War II, the German General Staff began extensive studies

of the campaigns of Genghis Khan and the Mongol mandate of total war. These ancient Asiatic concepts of firepower and maneuver were finally accepted by the Western military minds. The German *blitzkrieg* was simply a version of the tactics of Genghis Khan that had been developed as early as 500 B.C. by the Chinese general Sun Tzu. World War II produced wide sweeps and the rapid movement of tank columns with the armies not greatly concerned with flanks as there were virtually none.

As the result of this adaptation of original tactics developed for the bow many centuries ago, the ten million men mobilized by the United States during World War II carried out gigantic offensive operations against enemies in prepared defensive positions. In the joint operations against the Germans in Europe and the Japanese in the Pacific, the United States Army suffered battle deaths of 235,000. Additional naval casualties of 39,000 and marine dead totaling 19,000 brought the total of Americans killed in action to a figure just under 294,000.

Terrible as these casualties were, considering the number of troops engaged and the improvement in weapons, World War II becomes the most economical in human lives of any of our major wars. The killed-in-action figure is hardly larger than the total killed in action, North and South, in the Civil War.

Although frontal attacks were conducted on many occasions against the Japanese and, occasionally, the Germans, the emphasis was not on position war in World War II. The greatest battles were wide sweeps of tanks in rapid maneuver. Had this great conflict degenerated into position war, American losses could have been more than a million killed.

All of the Western armies were far too dilatory in adopting the principles of Asiatic economical war of motion with missiles. Many centuries of carnage passed before the full influence of the bow tactics were to be reflected in the open-field movements of modern offensive missile armies. And so it may be said, with the considerable support of history to validate the statement, that the bow, the original precision weapon, is still potent in influence on modern battlefields. This most remarkable of weapons has never been retired in entirety to the walls of museums to accompany the halberd, the pike, the atlatl, the spear, and the sword.

The principles of mobile war with missiles, our inheritance from Sun Tzu in 500 B.C., saved us thousands of lives in World War II.

Notes

Introduction

1. This is an arresting statement and necessarily requires considerable documentation. In the seventeenth and eighteenth centuries, flight archery was the national pastime of the Turks and some remarkable casts were made.

The authorities:
Sir Robert Ainslie, "Anecdotes of Turkish Archery," 1797.
Sir Ralph Payne-Gallwey, "Projectile Throwing Engines of the Ancients," 1907.
Cantimer, "The Othman Empire."
Moseley, "Essay on Archery" 1792.
Hein, "Bowyery and the Sport of Archery among the Osmanli."

Ainslie quotes the following records:
By the Sultan Selim, two arrows driven measured 972 yds., 2 - 3/4 in.
By Bilad Aga, one arrow, 804 yds., 2 ft., 2 in.
There are records of at least eight shots, all over 700 yards. Ainslie was British ambassador to the Ottoman Port and states he personally saw Selim shoot the two arrows and that he witnessed the measurement. These records were all established with the 160-pound bow, shooting 26-inch arrows with the use of the *siper*, a grooved horn or ivory about 6 inches in length that was strapped to the left arm and thus permitted the arrow to be drawn several inches within the bow. The arrows were very light and tapered, weighing slightly more than 1/2 ounce.

Payne-Gallwey wrote: "It is beyond question that in the 17th and 18th centuries flight arrows were shot from 600 to 800 yards by certain famous Turkish archers." He adds: "The achievements were engraved on marble columns at the ancient archery course near Constantinople and these records are still in existence."

216

Chapter 1

1. "I would", said Franklin, "add bows and arrows as good weapons not wisely laid aside. Accuracy is as great as the musket [a very conservative statement], with the advantage of no smoke and easy procurement."

2. Breechloaders prior to the Sharps were subject to dangerous gasleakage.

3. Clarence Ellsworth, in the Southwest Museum leaflet "Bows and Arrows," estimates that five thousand soldiers were killed by the arrow in World War II. The bow, in various forms, was used extensively in Asia all during that war.

Chapter 5

1. The Spanish square of the fifteenth century, 50 men wide and 40 men deep, continued the tradition of massed infantry. The Swiss phalanx of pikemen dominated European fields for many years. Gustavus Adolphus in the seventeenth century approached parity with the Roman legion of 200 B.C. Using the legion as a model, he formed infantry lines six files in depth, supported by wing cavalry. Frederick the Great created a thin line attack three files in depth. Napoleon used a perpendicular attack of massed battalions 40 men deep and 40 men wide. All of these European acceptances were only modifications of the Roman legion.

Chapter 6

1. The Chinese and the Egyptians were familiar with the bow during this period. Egypt appears to have relied upon chariots as the decisive arm after 2000 B.C. and upon infantry spearmen before the advent of the horse. The Chinese had both the crossbow and the self bow at this early date but infantry spearmen were the decisive troops.

2. The chariot was a war vehicle as early as 2000 B.C. There are many obscure references to indicate that the Kassites made use of the horse prior to the rise of Assyria. The Mitanni were also great charioteers. There are many candidates for the honor of having first mastered the horse. The use of the horse in earliest times that was made by the Chinese, the Kharri, and the Cimmerians cannot be evaluated.

3. *Ibid.*

4. Egyptian compound bows were recovered from the tomb of Tutankhamen, proof that this weapon was used as early as 1350 B.C. Photographs of these Egyptian bows were provided by Abbas Bayoumi, Director General of the Cairo Museum.

5. Rawlinson, *Seven Ancient Monarchies.*

6. History has shown that no more than 7 percent of a total population may be diverted to the armed forces without developing serious economic and agricultural weaknesses.

7. The destruction of Assyria was abetted by severe raids made by Scythians.

Chapter 7

1. Mitchell, in *"World's Military History,* demonstrates that the chariot occupied 6 1/2 by 10 feet of space. Carrying the archer and driver, it offered the missile power of one man. The same space occupied by infantry archers presented the missile power of twenty-eight men.

2. The relationship of national temperament and adaptability to various weapons is a study not yet explored. As in the pursuits of peace, there are natural adaptabilities to war. There are natural swordsmen, archers, or spearmen; it is difficult to accustom such soldiers to other weapons. See Chapter 13 for the failure of Attila to convert his horse-archers to heavy weapons soldiers.

Chapter 9

1. A Mongol general properly evaluated the stirrup when he exhorted Genghis Khan to proceed to victory and glory, to give no thought to his last days, "as long as boys are born to grow into men and as long as iron stirrups hang together."

Chapter 11

1. "The enemy was so rapid in their movements that it was impossible either to overtake them or to escape them when pursued; the arrows sped faster than sight could follow and penetrated every kind of defense." Rawlinson, *History of Parthia.*

2. Crassus, Antony, Caesar, Nero, and Trajan had all been interested in the legends concerning the treasure of Darius, rumored to have been buried near Ecbanta (now Hamadan) during the retreat from Arbela in 331 B.C. The treasure, worth millions, has never been found. It shared prominence with the military effort in all the Parthian campaigns.

3. "Some of the soldiers behaved so ill that he [Antony] was forced to punish their cowardice by decimation." Rawlinson, *Op. cit.*

4. *Ibid.*

5. Although Parthia was never an offensive threat to Roman security, the horse-archers had made necessary a concentration of Roman strength on the frontier. At least eight legions had permanent stations there in addition to large field forces.

Chapter 13

1. Parker, *"One Thousand Years of the Tartars."*

Chapter 14

1. Leo, *The Tactica.* A remarkable volume by Leo VI, Byzantine emperor A.D. 886–912.

2. Sun Tzu, *The Art of War* (500 B.C.).

Chapter 17

1. Prawdin, in *The Mongol Empire* evaluated the tactics of the Mongols in Europe with these remarks: "Not more than 150,000 Mongolian riders invaded Europe but these, led with consummate strategy and accustomed to work on a large scale, to cover distances incredible to Europeans with a speed that the mail clad and cumbersome chivalry of the European Middle Ages could never dream of, could in one day set more than 50 miles of country in flames, and on the next be ready to fight a decisive battle at such a distance that the foe could never believe them to be the same army."

Chapter 18

1. Posse, the medieval word to designate irregular auxiliaries, survives in a contemporary meaning as "sheriff's deputies."

2. The English, on occasion, mounted a few bowmen as rudimentary cavalry, the *hobilars.* These troops were not horse-archers but rather bowmen mounted on horses to permit them to keep up with the knights when on raiding operations. The very construction of the longbow prevented its mounted use. Horse archery requires a bow not longer than 4 feet. The original Welsh bow, short and very strong, was the only English modification of the self bow adaptable to mounted archery. The

English should have developed active cavalry to support the bow. This was not done.

3. Froissart states the French force contained 20,000 cavalry and 6,000 crossbowmen, plus auxiliaries. Possibly the French force totaled 30,000. Perce states that the French casualties were 36,000, an obvious overestimate.

4. The French loss totaled about 10,000.

5. Poitiers, the Roman Linonum, is one of the oldest towns in France. The town has been the scene of some of the most decisive battles of history. Near this village, the Frankish army of Clovis defeated and killed Alaric in A.D. 507. In A.D. 723, Charles Martel destroyed Saracen invaders near the town.

6. The French strength is subject to dispute. Froissart gives it as 40,000. English sources state the French force as 8,000 horse and 3,000 infantry.

ADDENDUM

The Construction of the Composite Bow

The composite bow was short-limbed and far more complex than any variant of the self bow. Upon a skeleton of wood, preferably maple, strips of horn were glued to the belly of the bow. The back of the bow was layered with sinew in hot glue. When these materials had been bonded, the bow was bent in the reverse position to form a complete circle and was left lashed in this position until the reflex action was complete. The Eastern peoples were very particular in their selection of wood, horn, glue, and sinew.

When made under the best conditions and by expert bowyers, the wood was seasoned for many years—sometimes as long as forty or fifty years. The glue was made from tendons, simmered and jellied in hot water. A second type of slower-setting glue was made from the skin of the palate of the sturgeon.

Of particular importance was the quality of the horn used. Eastern peoples preferred the horn of the carabao, or water buffalo, for its elasticity and uniformity. The sinew was obtained from the Achilles' tendons of cattle, preferably those of the steer. These tendons were dried, scraped, and reduced to fibers by pounding.

There were many manufacturing operations necessary to complete a bow, with great intervals of time between the various operations. The bowyer worked on many bows simultaneously; to complete all operations required as long as five years.

Skilled workmen were apprenticed to the crafts of bowyer,

fletcher, arrowmaker, stringmaker, nocker, and arrowhead maker.

The length and weight of the bowstring was very important. When strung, the composite bow carried the string about 8 inches from the grip although this distance varied with the individual bow. There was an exact ratio between string weight and bow weight, about 1 to 30. Thick strings were used in war bows, thin strings for distance casting.

The bowstring of Asia was usually constructed of raw silk saturated with a mixture of beeswax, resin, and fish glue. Payne-Gallwey states that the loops were often made of twisted sinew spliced to the raw silk string. The knots forming the loops were very carefully tied with an unusual arrangement of the strands that provided perfect symmetry.

The usual Eastern arrow had a large foreshaft that tapered toward the neck and was steadied in flight by the feathers of the cormorant, pigeon, swan, or eagle. Many types of arrows were in use—arrows for point-blank work, for distance casting, for piercing armor, for incendiary use, and whistling arrows for purposes of signaling. The Turks had as many as ten types of arrows.

The Asiatic Horse

The only true wild horse in the world is the tarpan of Inner Mongolia. Other so-called feral horses are merely tame horses gone wild. Many modifications of the tarpan were present in the armies of antiquity. Prominent were the large and powerful Nisaean horses, ridden by the Medes, Persians, Parthians, and other early horse-riding peoples. This horse was often white and may have been the royal horse of Genghis Khan. Certainly the Nisaean horse pulled the chariots of the Assyrians, Persians, and Egyptians.

The Libyan horse, another cross-breed from the tarpan, was the animal used by the cavalry of Hannibal; from it developed the Arabian strain.

The Mongol horse, the true tarpan, was a shaggy unkempt animal of great endurance. It stood about thirteen hands high and was self-sufficient in any weather. This great enduring horse contributed much to the success of the Mongol cavalry operations. Chapter 17 refers to some of the extraordinary rides that were made by couriers of Genghis Khan.

The Turks

The Turks, superlative archers and mentioned in many periods of history, are people of great mystery to the archaeologist, ethnologist, and historian. A. L. Kroeber, in his *Anthropology*, speaks of the Turks as follows:

> By the early part of the 7th century before Christ, iron had become common enough in China to be taxed . . . this lateness of iron in the far east indicates a strong possibility that the Chinese did not enter the Iron Age through their own discovery but were led into it by the example of Mongol or Turkish peoples of north central Asia.

The Turks were in central Asia for many centuries before they became identified in history with Muhammadanism.

Harold Lamb, quoting Czaplica, Koelle, and Vambery, mentions that in the fifth century a clan broke away from the mass of people called Hiung-nu and settled in the Golden Mountains between China and the Gobi Desert. Its families were called Turk, meaning "helmeted people." The Chinese called them the Tou-kie. These were not the Turks of Constantinople. In the beginning, some of the dialects were similar to Mongol. At any event, there were the Turks, in the back door of China.

Drawing largely from Chinese annals, European scholars have given to most of the other great clans—the Uiguirs, Karlucks, and Black Cathayans—the designation of Turks. Leon Cahun and Arminius Vambery accepted the Tartars as Turks. All of these so-called early Turks were pagans.

One cannot accept a narrow classical view in considering these very ancient people. One supposedly eminent classical scholar objected to the reference to Turks in the period circa 350 B.C. as made in this book, preferring to accept as Turks only those Muhammadan peoples in the vicinity of Constantinople from about A.D. 1450. This, of course, is a ridiculous assumption that cannot be supported by either history or anthropology. Quite obviously, this scholar prefers to remain anonymous rather than have his views regarding Turks made public. Actually, the word Turk is inclusive in its scope, for it covers many ancient races of men who lived in central Asia centuries before recorded history.

The Egyptians

By 1600 B.C. the Egyptians had a very heavy composite bow of a peculiar triangular shape. The arrows had heavy bronze heads and were capable of penetrating a thick slab of bronze. Used by charioteers and foot-archers, they were highly effective weapons in the desert wars with the Hittites. With the composite bow as his major weapon, Thutmose III built Egypt into a great empire. These great bows of the Eighteenth Egyptian Dynasty have physically survived to the present day. The excavation of the tomb of Tutankhamen brought to light magnificent specimens of the composite bow as it was used in Egypt three thousand years ago. Tactically, the Egyptian army seems to have been organized with a center of infantry-archers, supported by wings of charioteers. With the possible exception of the Assyrians, who may have used the same type of bow, the Egyptians probably had the best bow of this extremely early period. It is doubtful if their bow was improved upon for several centuries as it was in every respect a superior weapon.

The Scythians

The Scythians are an ethnological mystery. The word Scythian may be a generic term to designate many related tribes of early nomadic horsemen. Some authorities have identified the Scythians as the Cimmerians from the Black Sea area. They probably had close kinship with the Parthians, Medes, and Persians.

The Scythians are credited with having produced what may have been the first effective missile cavalry as early as 700 B.C.—possibly as early as 900 B.C. Early descriptions of the Scythians are not flattering. Herodotus describes them as a people gross in habits with large, fleshy bodies, soft, swollen bellies, and scanty hair. A more attractive picture mentions Zarina, a Scythian queen, who has been described as a rare beauty.

Whoever they were, the Scythians were a strange people. They were also an elusive and well-traveled people, for they irregularly bob in and out of history. They appear as raiders, as paid mercenaries, and as allies of many peoples. We know that they possessed a fine bow and were expert in its use. The Scythians were not credited with individual bravery in war, but they were formidable because of their ferocity and their great mobility.

The Babylonians

The Babylonians occupied the stage in the Near East for a brief period. Their main arm was cavalry, and their bow is believed to have been identical with, or similar to, the Assyrian bow. It was a curved bow, somewhat short—measuring less than 4 feet in length when strung. The bow had knobs at either end over which the bowstring was passed. Its arrow was about 3 feet long. The Babylonians also used the chariot in support of the masses of infantry-archers. Their tactics were similar but quite inferior to the formations of the Assyrians. They were not a significant military state, and fell easily to the Persians.

The Cretans

Little is known of the military efficiency of this nation, except the fact that the Cretans possessed the bow. Hundreds of bronze arrow-heads have been found in the ruins of Knossos. Their archery was apparently not very effective as histories of early antiquity mention that their arrows would not penetrate armor. The Cretans depended upon a fleet to keep enemies at bay.

The Janissaries

This elite corps of young Christian soldiers in the service of the sultans of Turkey were among the world's finest archers. The Turkish composite bow of this period was probably the finest bow ever to be made. It was expertly constructed of horn, wood, and sinew, and it could kill a man in armor at ranges in excess of 250 yards. The pull of this bow was 100 pounds and more. The arrow was released with the ancient Mongol loose which made use of the thumb ring. The Janissaries were among the last soldiers to use the bow in formal war. Many specimens of this Janissary bow remain in existence, the product of a great school of master bowyers.

Philippine Bowmen

There was, and is, wide usage of the bow by bush Negritos and Indo-Australian mountain people of the Philippines as represented by

Bilaans, Subanos, Tirurais, Manobos, and Tagbanuas. The Philippine bow is usually about 5 feet long and is constructed of palma brava, a durable, black, palm wood. The bow is usually reinforced with wrappings of bejuco vine or strips of bamboo. These bows may have pulls of as much as 40 pounds. The arrows are of reed or wood and usually have detachable heads bound to the shaft by a length of hemp fiber. Upon piercing game, the iron head detaches and the dragging shaft impedes the movement of the wounded animal in the thick jungle.

South Pacific Island Bows

Many of the islanders of Micronesia, Melanesia, and Polynesia use the bow—usually an inferior weapon. They are usually simple stave bows constructed from species of local palm. Several of the island groups of the South Pacific have native populations using the crossbow.

South American Bows

The South American Indian bow is usually a fair development of the self bow. They are remarkable chiefly because of their extreme length. Some of the bows of this area reach a length of 12 feet. Such a bow would be unwieldy in operation and it would be difficult to bring out the full capabilities of the weapon with any method of hand-drawing.

Chinese Bows

The Chinese composite bow was a superior weapon. It was usually constructed of laminated bamboo, reinforced with horn and sinew and sometimes with strips of iron. Some of the Chinese bows had pulls in excess of 150 pounds and were capable of penetrating arrows through any armor of the period. The Chinese had the composite bow at least two thousand years before Christ. The bow was a revered ceremonial weapon in China during the Han dynasty, and beautifully manufactured vermilion bows were awards of honor.

Korean Bows

The Koreans had a very strong composite bow with which they defended themselves against the Mongols. The Koreans were always difficult and tenacious enemies. Although Korea became a part of the empire of Genghis Khan, it was never strongly held. The mountains of Korea offered very difficult terrain for the Mongol horse-archers.

Index

Acre 138
Adrianople, Battle of 112, 116
Aegusa Islands, Battle of 89
Aetius 123 fol.
Africa 15
Agincourt, Battle of 176
Akhlat, Battle at 132
Akkadians 53
Alaric 220
Albinus 115
Aleppo, Emir of 129
Alexander 70, 72, 74
Alp Arsen 132
American Indians 19, 200
  arrowheads 21
  tactics 212
  see also Plains Indians
—North 184
—South 18, 184, 226
  bow 226
American Revolution 14, 24, 213
Antioch, Battle of 104
Antony, Marc 38, 107, 108
Arabs 5, 19
Arausio, Battle at 113
Arbalest 20, 196
Arban 155
Arbela, Battle of 74

Argonne, Battle of 214
Aristocracy 182
  see also Social and class implications
    of horses
Armenia 107, 109
Armor 22, 25
  felt 26, 140, 141
  quilted 25
  silk 26
  see also Mail, Chain; Mail, Plate
Armored cavalry, School of 39, 71
  Byzantine 127
Arquebus 179
Arrows
  bronze 225
  flint arrowheads 15, 21, 186
  Indian 185
  iron 186, 202
  obsidian 21
  penetration 21, 22, 23, 25, 200
  precision missiles 21
  protection against 22, 25, 26, 140,
    141
  poisoned 22, 197
  recovery 153, 208
  supply 102, 209
  velocity 22
  wounds 22, 25, 199, 202

Arsouf 140
Art of War, The xi, 42
Artabanus 110
Assyrians 55 fol.
  arrows 58
  bows 58
  stirrups 80
Athens 64
Atlatl 13, 15, 184
Attila ix, 120, 121
Augsburg, Battle at 146
Auray, Battle at 178
Austria 165

Babars 166
Babylonians 225
Bactrians 60
Ballista 20, 33, 195 fol., 200
Bamboo 18, 195, 226
Barbarians 114
Battering ram 55
Battle-ax 114
Batu 151, 163
Bauge, Battle at 178
Bayan 48
Bayonets 213
Bela 164
Belgae 114
Belisarius 128, 196
Big Fifty Sharps 14
Black Prince 175
Blitzkrieg xi, 215
Bo-ha-Din 139
Boadicea 115
Bodkin 22
Bohemud of Antioch 140
Boomerang 13
Bow
  Byzantine abandonment 127
  Crusades 135
  defense against 208
  evaluation 195
  first appearance in war 53
  musket compared 23

origins 13
types and modifications 17
Breech-loading rifles 14
Bridle 81
Britain
  Caesar 114
  see also England
Bronze
  arrowheads 225
  swords 96
Brown Bess musket 14, 24
Bullets 23
Burnside, Gen. 214
Butterfield, Gen. 214
Byzantines 76, 144
  abandon bow 127
  cavalry 77
Byzantine Empire 127

Caepio 113
Caesar, Julius 6, 39, 95, 97, 114
Calabria 114
Caltrops 35
Cannae, Battle at 90
Carpini, Giovanni de Piano xiii, 163
Carrhae, Battle of 101, 103, 140
Carthage
  cavalry 85
  military system 88
  Roman legions 116
Casilium, Battle of 128
Cassius 113
Cassivellaunus 115
Castillon, Battle at 179
Catapults 33, 98
Cavalry 77
  Asiatic 6
  Assyrian 57
  Byzantine 127
  Carthaginian 85
  European 78
  light missile 79
  Macedonian 72
  Mongols 148

Parthian 99, 105, 111
Persian 62, 63, 69
Poitiers 178
Roman 98
Scythian 224
United States 187, 189
Cavalry, Armored (school): *see* Armored cavalry, School of
Centurions 97
Cestrosphendens 35
Chalons, Battle at 123 fol.
Chamfrons 69
Chariots and charioteers 217, 218
  Arbela, Battle of 75
  Assyrians 56
  Babylonians 225
  Britain 115
  horse 222
  Persian 62, 69
Charles Martel 135, 220
Cheyenne Indians 190
Chiliarchy 35, 36
China
  arrows 21
  composite bow 226
  crossbow 195, 217
  Mongols 156
  principles of economical warfare 6
  Tartars 148
  Turks 223
Cimbri 113
Civil War, U.S. 213
Claudius 115
Clodius 113
Cohort legion 95
Commandos 15
Communications
  Genghis Khan 47
Companions of Alexander 41, 72, 74, 76
Composite bow 6
  construction 212, 221
  Crusades 136

Egyptian 16, 224
Mongols 154
Nisibis, Battle at 111
range 21, 202
Turkish 9, 225
types and modifications 18
velocity 22
Confederate Army 214
Conquistadores 26
Conrad 136
Cracow 163
Crassus 95, 101, 103
Crazy Horse 190
Crecy, Battle of 171
Cretans 225
  bronze arrows 225
Crossbow 20
  advantages 199
  Crusades 136
  evaluation 195
  longbow compared 200
  modifications 197
  weaknesses 198
Crusades 25, 201
—*First* 135
—*Second* 136
—*Third* 138
Ctesiphon 109
Cuirass 98
Custer's Last Stand 189
Cyrus 60

Dacia 116
Daras, Battle of 128
Darius 64, 69
Darius III 74
Darius, Treasure of 218
Dark Ages 4
Darts 87
Datis 64
Deception
  Genghis Khan 43
Decius 116
Dragon

Parthia 101
Dragoons 71, 212

Economical war, Principles of 1
  Sun Tzu 6
Economy of force 30, 45
  Genghis Khan
Edward III 171, 172
Egypt 60
  bow 16, 21, 217
  composite bow 224
Elegia, Battle at 109
Elephant corps 89
Energy
  Genghis Khan 48
England
  Caesar 114
  cavalry 78, 219
  crossbow 200
  infantry archers 206, 207
  longbow 17, 169
  poisoned arrows 197
Epaminobdas of Thebes 36
Eratosthenes 3
Espionage
  Genghis Khan 48
Europe
  cavalry 78
  Dark Ages 4
  Subotai 159
  tactics 211
Evasion xi
  Genghis Khan 46

Feathers
  American Indian arrow 185
  composite bow 222
  crossbow 197
Felt armor
  Conquistadores 26
  Crusades 140, 141
Fergana Valley, Battle of 158
Field control
  Genghis Khan 47

Firearms 179, 208, 211
  bow compared 14, 23
  see also Muskets; Rifles
Flaminius 89
Flexed composite bow 19
Flint arrowheads 15, 21, 186
Food supplies
  Mongols 155
Forum Trebonii 116
France
  crossbow 198
  Hundred Years' War 171 fol., 207
Franklin, Benjamin 14, 217
Frederick the Great 217

Gall 190
Gambesons 25
Gaul
  Caesar 114
Genghis Khan 5, 6, 8, 10, 14, 42 fol.,
  149 fol., 155, 156
Genoese crossbow 198
Georgia (Russia) 160, 161
Gettysburg 214
Gladius 87
Gobi Desert 148, 156
Golden Horde 166
Goths 116, 128, 144
Gran, Battle of 164
Grand Phalanx 36, 71
Granicus, Battle of 74
Great Wall 148, 156
Greece
  knowledge 3
  Marathon 33, 64, 67
  shock infantry 32
Gunpowder 14
Gustavus Adolphus 217

Hadrian's Wall 115
Hand weapons 9
  see also Firearms
Hannibal 85
Hasdrubal 91

Hasta 87
Hastati 96
Hastings, Battle of 15, 168
Helvetians 114
Henry V 176
Henry of Silesia 163
Herse formation 171
Hessians 213
Hetaerae 41, 72
Hiung-nu 223
Hobilars 219
Holy Land 135
  see also Jerusalem
Honfleur 176
Horse 39
  American Indian 188
  Asiatic 222
  cavalry 78 fol.
  Byzantine 127
  Crusades 141
  earliest use 217
  European use 211
  Mongol 154
  Parthia 100
  social aspects viii, 40, 182
  Spanish in North America 186
  warfare, introduced into 55
  see also Cavalry; Tarpan
Horse-archers
  Huns 122
  Mongols 148
  Parthians 219
  see also Armored cavalry, School of;
    Cavalry
Horse armor
  Byzantine 130
  Persian 69
Horse collar 56
Horse equipment 80, 100
Horseshoe 81
Hundred Years' War 171 fol.
Hungary 163, 164
Huns 116, 120
  cavalry 77

Iconium, Battle at 136
India 166
Indians, American: *see* American Indians
Impeditus 98
Imperial Horse Guards 41
Infantry 8
  archers 205
  Assyrian 56
  Carthage 88
  Persian 61, 63
  Roman 97, 118
Infantry, Shock (school): *see* Shock infantry, School of
Iron Age
  American Indians 186
Iron weapons 55
Islam: *see* Muhammadans
Issus, Battle of 74

Jaguns 155
James I (Eng.) 22
Janissaries 9, 225
Javelins 87
  Roman legion 96, 98
Jebei Noyon 156
Jerusalem
  Crusades 135, 136, 138, 139, 142
Joan of Arc 178
John (Fr. k.) 175

Kadan 163, 165
Kai-feng-fu 48
Kaidu 163
Kalka River 161
Kassites 55
Kentucky rifle 14
Khmers 41
Khorassan 60, 100
Khwarzian Turks 157
Kiev 163
Kisil-Art 157
Knight-errant 41
Knights 127, 144, 182

Crecy 172
Crusades 137, 207
  Hundred Years' War 175
Knights Templars: *see* Templars
Knossus 225
Korea
  composite bow 227

Lance cavalry 72, 76
Legatus legionis 96
Leignitz, Battle of 163
Leuctra, Battle of 36
Lewis of Bavaria 146
Leo 131
Libyan horse 222
Little Big Horn, Battle of 189
Logistics 8
  Mongols 153
Longbow 17, 169
  crossbow compared 200
  range 201

Macedonia 71
Macedonian War, Third 35
Macrinius 110
Magyars 78, 146
Mail, Chain 22, 25, 41
  Byzantine 130
  Crusades 141
Mail, Plate 22, 25, 41
Mallius 113
Maneuverability
  Genghis Khan 45
Mangu 166
Maniples 87, 95
Manlius 113
Manzikert, Battle at 132
Marathon, Battle of 33, 64, 67
Marching records 97
Mass 29
Mau-Maus 15
Medes 58, 60, 61, 68, 100
Mesolithic Age: *see* Stone Age, Late;
  Stone Age, Middle
Metaurus 91

Millarian Cohort 95
Miltiades 65
Minghan 155
Missiles
  see also Arrows
Missile war of motion, School of 8,
  42, 215
Mitanni 217
Mobility 38, 212, 215
  see also Maneuverability
Moderation
  Genghis Khan 46
Mogul Empire 166
Mongolia, Inner 80
Mongols ix, 8, 21, 42 fol., 201
  bowmen 5
  cavalry 77
  composite bow 19
  horse-archers 148
  missile war of motion 42
  silk armor 26
  tactics 219
Moscow 163
Moslems 141 fol.
Mounted Shock, School of 75
Mounted war 77
  see also Cavalry
Muhammad, Shah 157
Muhammadans 5, 135
Mukhali 156
Muskets
  American Revolution 14
  bow compared 23

Napoleon 217
Narses 128
Narvaez 185
Nero 91
Night fighting 212
Nile Valley 16
Nineveh 58
Nisaean horse 222
Nisibis, Battle at 110
Normandy 171, 176
Normans 15

North America
  see also Indians, American

Objective 29
Offense 29
Offensive warfare 10
  Assyrians 59
Ogodai 48, 163, 165
Oman 111
Omar 129
Onagri: *see* Catapults
Order of battle
  Crecy 171
  Macedonian 72
  Mongols 152
  see also Phalanx
Ordinarii 96
Orleans
  Roman legion 123
Orodes 101
Ostrogoths 120
Ottoman Empire 9
  see also Turks

Pacorus 107
Paleolithic times 13
Palma brava 18, 226
Pamirs 157
Panic 23
Parthians viii, 4, 60
  arrows 101
  bow 100
  cavalry 6, 7, 77
  military system 99
  Rome 94, 116, 219
Parthian campaign 94
Patay 178
Patience
  Genghis Khan 47
Peking 156
Pelasts 72
Penetration of arrows 21, 22, 23, 25, 200
Persians 60, 166
  bow 62

infantry archers 206, 207
  Macedonian battles 74
Pest, Battle of 165
Phalanna, Battle of 35
Phalanx 33
  Athens 64
  Greek 7, 35, 36, 65, 66, 67, 71
  Macedonian 36, 71
  Persian 69
  Roman 87
  Sumerian 53
  Swiss 212
  Theban 36, 71
Philip VI (Fr.) 171
Philip of Macedonia 36, 70, 71, 73, 75, 206, 209
Philippines
  bow 225
Pikes 87, 96
Pilum 96
Plain stave bow 17
Plains Indians 21, 23, 184
Plataea, Battle of 64, 67
Poisoned arrows 22, 197
Poitiers, Battle at 174, 220
Poles 163
Pontus 113
Position war 6, 7, 35, 212
Potawatomi Indians 200
Praapa 107
Principes 87, 96
Principles of war 29
Procopius 196
Psychological effects of arrow wounds 23
Publius 102
Pull
  Chinese 226
  composite bow 19
  Janissaries 225
  longbow 169
  Mongol 151
  Philippines 226
  Selim 216
Punic War, First 89

Punic War, Second 85, 89, 92
Punic War, Third 92

Quarrels 195, 197
Quilted armor 25

Radagaisus 121
Range
  American Indian 185
  composite 21, 201
  crossbow 195
  Janissaries 225
  longbow 21, 201
  Mongol 151, 201
  musket and bow 14, 24
Raymond 137
Records
  marching 97
  see also Range
Recurving bow: see Reflexed bow
Regulus 89
Reflexed or recurving bow 19
Rein 81
Reinforced stave bow 18
Richard the Lion Hearted 20, 138,
  139, 142
Rifles 14
Roman camps 98
Roman Eagle 97
Roman Empire
  fall 5
Roman legion 4, 8, 39, 86, 212, 217
  Cannae 90
  Carthage 85
  last years 113
  Orleans 123
  Parthia 94
  Phalanna 35
  shock infantry 32
  Trebia 90
Romanus Diogenes 132
Ruas 120
Russia 120, 160, 161
Ryagan 163

Sabinius 115
Saddle 57, 81
Sajo, Battle of 164, 165
Saladin 135, 136, 137, 138, 141, 143
Saracens 25, 26, 129, 137, 143
  cavalry 77
Sargon 54
Sarissa 36
Saxe 25
Schools of war 31
  Asiatic 6
  see also Armored cavalry, School of;
    Shock infantry, School of; Missile
    war of motion, School of
Scimitars 137
Scipio 89
Scythians 224
  cavalry 78
  stirrup 80
Security 30
Self bows 17
  composite bow construction
  type and modifications 17
  see also Longbow
Selim 216
Seljuk Turks 130
Seminole War 213
Severus 109
Sharps, Christian 14
Shields, Roman 98
Shiloh, Battle of 214
Shock (psychological) 23
Shock infantry 6, 7
  Byzantine 129
  Roman 90
Shock infantry, School of 32
Sicily 113
Siege engines 142
Silesians 163
Silk armor 26
Silk Road 110
Sioux 190
Situation
  Genghis Khan 43

Smith, Sir John 23
Social and class implications of horses viii, 144, 182, 205, 208, 212
Social weaknesses of armored cavalry 40
South American Indians: *see* American Indians—South
South Pacific Islands 18
  bows 226
Spanish Square 217
Spartacus 113
Spartans 71
  equipment 35
  phalanx 34
  soldiers 35
Spears
  Macedonian 72
  Persian 62
  Roman legion 87
  sarissa 36
Speed
  Genghis Khan 48
Slings 13, 33, 34, 72, 98, 107
Statianus 108
Stave composite bow 18
Stirrup 80, 218
Stone Age, Late 15
Stone Age, Middle (Mesolithic) 13, 15
Stragetos 35
String pullers 19
Strings
  composite bows 19, 220
  crossbow 199
  longbow 169
Subotai 48, 150, 156, 159
Sumerians 53, 54
Sun Tzu xi, 6, 10, 42
Supplies 38
Surenas 101, 103
Surprise 30
Surround: *see* Tulughma
Swords

Crusades 141
Persian 62
Roman legion 96
Swordsmen
  Crusades 142
  Europe 122
  Roman 123
Syntagma 36
Syria 100, 107, 109

Tactics, The 131
Tactics vii, viii, 8, 10
  American Indians 186
  Assyrians 55
  bow impact 193
  Crecy 173 fol
  English 15th c. 180 fol.
  European psychology 208
  Genghis Khan 6, 43
  infantry, heavy 33
  infantry-archers 205
  modern war 211
  Mongol 150 fol
  Persians 61, 69, 70
  Saladin 137
  United States 187, 212
  West 211
Tarpan 222
  see also Horse
Tartars 4, 148, 223
  cavalry 77
Taxis 35
Teamwork 30
Teheran, Battle at 160
Templars 163
Temujin: *see* Genghis Khan
Terek-Davan 157
Terror
  Mongols 153
Testudo 108
Teutons 113
Theodosius 120
Thutmose III 224
Tiberias 137

Ticinus 89
Timus 166
Toledo steel 96
Tours, Battle of 135
Traces 56
Trajan 109
Trasimeno, Battle of the 14
Trebia 90
Triarii 87, 96
Tribunes 96
Tribute 5
Tricameron 128
Tulughma 55
Turks 5
    composite bow 9
    Crusades 139 fol.
    range 216
    see also Ottoman Empire
Turks, Khwarzian: *see* Khwarzian
    Turks
Turks, Seljuk: *see* Seljuk Turks
Tutenkhamen tomb 217, 224

Uldin 121
Uniforms 58
Union Army 214
United States
    American Indians 186
    military tactics 212
    see also American Revolution; Civil
        War

Vandals 128
Varinius 113
Varus 115
Velites 98
Velocity 22
Venditius, Publius 106, 107
Vercengetorix 114
Verriculum 96
Victory, Essentials of
    Genghis Khan 48
Visigoths 116
Vladimir, principality 163
Volga Valley 120

Walled cities 42
Welsh bow 219
World War I 214
World War II 15, 215, 217
    see also Blitzkrieg
Wounds, Arrow 22, 25, 199, 202

Xanthippus 89
Xenephon 81

Yakka Mongols 149
Yeliu Chutsai 42, 48
Yeomen 170, 182
Yew wood 169
Yurts 41

Zama 91